"An essential guide for storytellers eager to harness their voices through personal and imaginative discovery. Shaw approaches the short form landscape with useful tools and a little magic to help writers build narratives sustained by human connection. *The Short* is a must for any creative writer!"
—DANA WASHINGTON-QUEEN, Writer and Director, *Under Bone*

"I have written and made close to 60 films since the first time I picked up a camera. I have rarely experienced such a generous and comprehensive approach to writing, making, and embracing the short film . . . Shaw starts by prioritizing one's own self . . . as the true heart of all remarkable filmmaking."
—JENNIFER REEDER, Writer and Director, *A Million Miles Away*

"Rich in storytelling ideas, Shaw's book doesn't lecture us about rules but reminds us of what all good scripts need—that is, story, story, story. This is a smart book about short films and should be required reading for all filmmakers."
—RAFAEL LIMA, Professor, University of Miami

"This relevant book delves into the 'why' behind filmmaking . . . I love how Shaw highlights lesser-known gems, creating a space for underrepresented voices. This guide doesn't just teach; it empowers and reveals a true love for short films."
—ALYSIA ALLEN, Founder, Mocha Girls Read book club

THE SHORT

WRITING TOOLS
to Free the Imagination

RAE SHAW

MICHAEL WIESE PRODUCTIONS

Published by Michael Wiese Productions
12400 Ventura Blvd. #1111
Studio City, CA 91604
(818) 379-8799, (818) 986-3408 (FAX)
mw@mwp.com
www.mwp.com

Cover design by Johnny Ink
Interior design by William Morosi
Copyediting by Justin Sagalow

Manufactured in the United States of America
Copyright © 2024 by Rae Shaw
First Printing 2024
All rights reserved. No part of this book may be reproduced in any form or by any means without permission in writing from the author, except for the inclusion of brief quotations in a review.

Library of Congress Cataloging-in-Publication Data

Names: Shaw, Rae, author.
Title: The Short : Writing Tools to Free the Imagination / by Rae Shaw.
Description: Studio City : Michael Wiese Productions, 2024.
Identifiers: LCCN 2024023765 | ISBN 9781615933501 (trade paperback)
Subjects: LCSH: Short films–Authorship. | Short films–Production and
  direction. | Digital video.
Classification: LCC PN1996 .S435 2024 | DDC 809.2/3–dc23/eng/20240625
LC record available at https://lccn.loc.gov/2024023765

This book is dedicated to my students from all over the world.

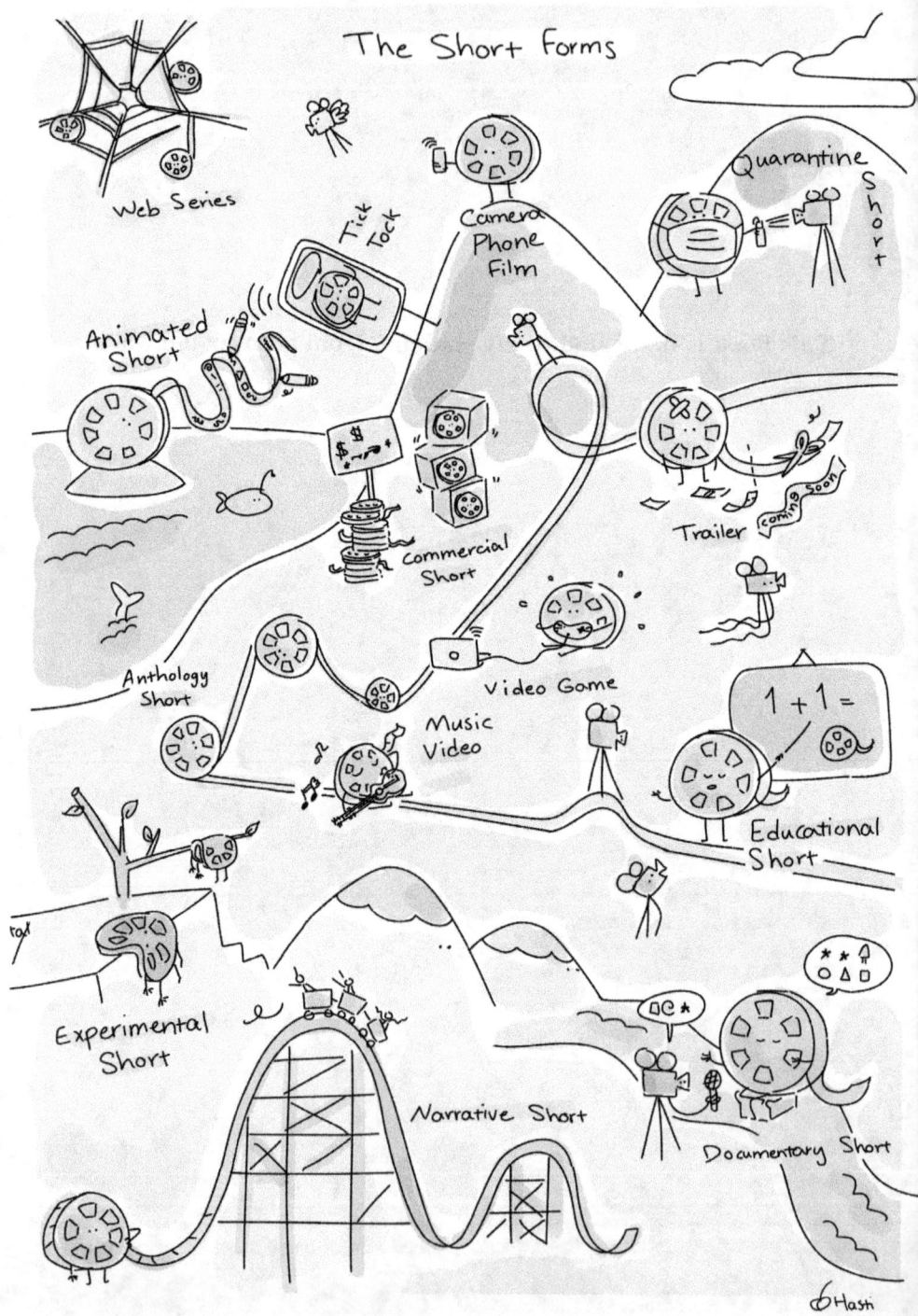

TABLE OF CONTENTS

I. THE SHORT 1

II. IDEAS & PERSONAL INVESTIGATIONS: THE FILMMAKER'S QUEST 12

III. STORYING CHARACTER: EMOTIONAL BUILDING BLOCKS AND ESCAPES 42

IV. SCULPTING A WORLD: WHAT ARE THE RULES OF YOUR WORLD? 76

V. DEVELOPING A SYSTEM: FINDING MEANING IN STRUCTURES 97

VI. TYING THEME & PREMISE: PURPOSE AND INTENTION 136

VII. LANGUAGE AND STYLING: WRITING TO FREE THE IMAGINATION 159

VIII. THE DISCOVERY OF STORY: DRAFTING AND REVISING 190

IX. THE SHORT FORMS:
SHORT LANDSCAPES OF THE STORYTELLER'S IMAGINATION 216
    Narrative Short 217
    Experimental Short 221
    Documentary Short 224
    Animated Short 229
    Web Series 232
    Commercial 236
    Music Video 240
    Educational 243
    Specialty 248
        Trailers vs Proof of Concept 248
        Anthology 252
        New Media 255
        Camera Phone 255
        Quarantine 256
        Video Games 258
        Social Media 261

X.	NOTES ON DIRECTING: THE DIRECTOR'S TOOL	265
XI.	NOTES ON PRODUCING: GUARDIANS OF THE CINEMATIC UNIVERSE	290
XII.	SHORT FILM FILMOGRAPHY	320
XIII.	EPILOGUE	335
	ABOUT THE AUTHOR	338

ACKNOWLEDGMENTS

I'd like to first thank Judith Weston and John Hoskins who have been mentors, friends, colleagues, and family to me on the West Coast. You have weathered my ups and downs in this fickle industry, supported me, and stood by me through thick and thin. You have been a beacon and a constant reminder that love, art, and compassion still exist.

I'd like to thank Michael Wiese and Geraldine Overton for granting me the opportunity to bring this book to fruition—for providing guidance and for believing in me as an author with a unique voice. I am sad that Michael is not here to see this book but glad that it will live on in his honor. I want to thank Ken Lee for facilitating the many steps of this process.

I want to thank my family and especially my mother, Maryann Brown-Martin, and my aunt Pamela Brown who have shared so much in my years as a maker and writer. I would not be where I am today without their sacrifices and vision.

I want to thank my Sunday Matinee crew and my OBS writers group, which disbanded long ago but has continued in new ways to support each other.

I want to thank my interns and assistants; especially Ari Culbertson and DJ Wai Chan who gave more than their time to the making of this book. Your devotion to me and to the book is something I will never forget.

I want to thank Gerald McClanahan, my copyeditor, whom I met through OBS (Organization of Black Screenwriters) when I was only a baby writer. You became my friend and colleague in this crazy industry. Thank you for agreeing to complete this special work with care and kindness.

I also want to thank Pilar Alessandra, who has been such a champion of my work and my writing and who has believed in me and supported me by connecting me to others in the industry every time she had the opportunity to do so. You have always been there to remind me what a wonderful writer I am when I have doubted myself.

I'd like to thank my book readers who all worked within a tight window to accomplish the task of reading and commenting on my book: Ishani Jayamaha, Gina Martin, Peter Klausner, Scott Boswell, and Atim Udoffia.

I want to thank Hasti Jafari Jozani, a future teacher in the making, who accomplished the beautiful illustrations for the book.

I'd like to thank San Francisco State University and the School of Cinema who supported me in the making of this book—and in particular, Kelly Nhu Trinh, who facilitated much of the work. I'd like to thank Jim Delaney, Eric Asetta, Adam Greenfield, and Homa Sarabi-Daunais, who facilitated the making of my short work at Emerson College while I developed this book. I'd also like to thank my colleagues Hassan Ildari and Jenny Lau whose teachings deeply influenced me and encouraged me in the writing of this book.

I want to thank the libraries and schools who allowed me to develop my voice as a teacher, filmmaker, and writer: Erica Cuyugan and the Santa Monica Public Library, Barbara Bozman and the Los Angeles Public Library, Rafael Lima and the University of Miami, Elizabeth Alexander and the University of Chicago, Arthur Helterbran and the New York Film Academy; and Jim Wood, Gail Della Pelle, Hugh Atkins, and Bill Chase at the Tower Hill School.

Finally, I want to acknowledge the many students I've had over the years as a teacher of language, writing, filmmaking, and more. I'm so very grateful to all of you.

THE SHORT

Short

—*A brief story or article*

"If you are free, you need to free somebody else. If you have some power, then your job is to empower somebody else."
—Toni Morrison

I love shorts.

I'd been teaching filmmaking for over a decade and writing for over two, when I began writing this book. I've written short stories, essays, letters, poetry, memoirs, and screenplays. I've written across genres, ranging from young adult coming-of-age short stories, to salsa dancing rom-coms, and finally to dramatic thrillers and horrors. As a writer in the film industry who has fought to break in with scripts that I wanted to write, direct, and produce, I've authored over twenty long-form scripts (treatments, pilots, and features) and received over thirty awards.

There is little that excites me more than writing and directing a short film. However, to be honest, this came to me as a surprise.

While the allure of the feature film or television pilot in the filmmaking industry is urgently real, there remains something so endearingly personal and free about creating short work. My heart is always full when I teach my short script class because I find myself intoxicated by the truly infinite possibilities of the realm.

Unlike the feature film, which is regulated by an already existing system that confines how it is produced, and ultimately distributed, the short form is a blank space. Working on a feature film, we are regulated by human failings of attention and distraction while also dealing with the numerous challenges of an economy-driven system: charming investors and funders to come aboard, negotiating domestic and international distribution, the tentative dance with sales agents and film critics, the constraints of at-risk multiplexes and persevering art houses, the daunting competition of streaming content in the home, a consumerist studio system of market, supply and demand, and an all-too-common Western three-act structure that has been revisited and retold thousands of times.

I'm not arguing against the feature film. There are many elegant reasons to make a feature and to follow a character into a spiraling web of subplots, flaws, and hopes that illustrate the human experience. However, any working screenwriter knows that the first rule of writing a feature screenplay is this: get your reader to keep turning the page. You must keep them turning the page so that a director can keep them bound to their seat for at least a hundred minutes.

The short defies the constraints of time, platform, and genre, challenging many industry standards typically imposed on long-form film. It is certainly not limited by attention spans; if anything, the short leverages its brevity to captivate audiences in ways that long-form film cannot. One might even say that the short form is taking over and forcing the industry to create platforms to serve its many ever-changing forms. With a short, you hold the freedom to create your own structure, find your own pattern, determine your own length, and create your own kind of story.

But these are not the only reasons I love shorts.

The short form is also, in my estimation, the consummate form of expression. It's not just me who thinks this—look at how many auteurs, in their later years, have returned to the short form: Bergman, Kurosawa, Lee, Varda, Saura, and Bigelow, to name just a few. Even among successful filmmakers working today: Ramsey, Waititi, Rees, Bravo, Anderson, and more, there is an embrace of the short form. As I began to research shorts more, I was surprised to learn not only how beloved the form is but also how necessary it has become.

Recognizing that the short form is more than only narrative, documentary, or experimental film, we must acknowledge its expansion over the last few decades to include short documentaries, music videos, commercials, proof of concepts, trailers, web series, TV episodes, experimental shorts, video games, and social media content wherein young people tell entire stories in less than a minute.

The short form has evolved to become both its own form and a respectable space for upholding a career in filmmaking. No longer is the short form considered just a stepping stone to the feature. Look at Spike Jonze, Melina Matsoukas, or Hiro Murai. Their careers have been shaped as much by their short-form work as their feature-length output! And look at what incredible shorts they have made in their process!

Another aspect I love about the short form is that, as a producer-director, you can usually work with a budget that will allow you to have complete control over the outcome. Think this is overrated? Ask any filmmaker who has had their film hijacked by a studio or production company and fought for the director's final cut.

Some directors love the short form so much that they've even opened up production companies for short content—looking at you, Taika Waititi! They use this platform to help other up-and-coming filmmakers by providing greater access to this artisan workspace.

In the past, so much of the Hollywood industry was limited to people of a certain income or background. The internet made filmmaking a free and accessible choice, catalyzing a digital revolution that leveled the playing field. Gone are the days when only the Hollywood elite could engage in the film process. Now, we've entered an era in which cameras are ubiquitous and filmmaking is within reach almost everywhere.

But shorts are not only about control and access. The short form is most urgently about freedom—the backbone of artistry. Having the freedom to share your unaltered vision with the world is nothing short of a miracle. Freedom is the most important value in stirring the imagination of the artist, second only to limits (more on that in the Structure chapter)! While this sounds like a contradiction, I suggest that this dynamic relationship forms the foundation for nurturing the imagination. The tension between the two values of freedom and limits is where, I believe, the imagination lives.

Every time I discover a new filmmaker who finds the courage to write a short in its purest form, in their vision, in their voice, with their potent emotion, I am elated. That is what I wish for you, dear reader; to brave this most enduring experience of telling the story of your heart's innermost desire.

But there are still other reasons to love shorts.

The short, in this global world, is beginning to serve a new purpose. Shorts are becoming a way for filmmakers to connect with each other not only across decades and centuries but also across nations, seas, and continents. Through shorts, filmmakers are finding each other and learning from and sharing each other's traditions, cultures, languages, thoughts, and resources, while also exploring crises and issues. They are advocating for the positive change they desire to see in the world.

So, as we watch the short film lead us into a space of social justice, critical thought, and collective community, one *could* argue that shorts are becoming the new cinema. Shorts are emerging as a space for igniting discussions, taking risks, and challenging ideas. Unlike industry feature films, which often function as commodities, shorts thrive on passion, community, sharing, and the joy of writing.

This is what awaits you, so let's dive in!

YET ANOTHER SCREENWRITING BOOK

There are so many books about filmmaking within the industry, and even more about screenwriting in particular. So, when my mentor, Judith Weston, introduced me to Michael Wiese, I had many ideas I wanted to offer. I'd already written a few manuscripts of my own, but Michael had a particular idea in mind. He really loved that I had made different kinds of shorts.

Interestingly, he found me at a pivotal time in my growth as both a filmmaker and a teacher. When I first spoke to Michael, I was discovering my voice as a professor and as an artist. I was coming a little closer to uncovering the stories I wanted to tell and the vehicles I wanted to use to tell them. At the same time, I was also coming to understand my pedagogy as a teacher and my personal mission in teaching.

I was finding that, after years of learning from older and wiser colleagues and mentors, I, like many in the field, had been looking outside myself and attempting to follow the well-trodden paths of those who came before me. While looking towards role models as a guide is valuable, the biggest lesson I'd learned was that I needed to stop blindly asking what I *should* do and listen to my own heart. Everyone's path is different, and as artists, we need to embrace that. I needed to make films again, but more importantly, I needed to rediscover my filmmaking *voice*.

So, why this book? I believe what's special about it is not only that it's one of the few books focused on short films or that it highlights the many different kinds of short films Michael (in his genius) believed to be possible, but also that it celebrates and emphasizes learning to look within. When I think about my students, I think of a quote from Bela Tarr which proclaims, "I want to see more of you in your stories." More you. I believe that that is the space within which great shorts live. The space where new filmmakers, instead of looking outside, look within.

In this book, I approach filmmaking as a personal and intimate endeavor through readings and exercises that lean into finding more about yourself as a writer and creator. You will also find tools that will ask you to look within yourself to find your story; tools to help you discover and access your deepest loves, fears, disappointments, and triumphs. These will help you look at the ordinary and the mundane, the tiniest and the simplest things that we take for granted and help you use these elements to investigate the richness and uniqueness that lie there. We all have that ability, but somewhere along the way, we've been taught to diminish it, to discard it, to decide that it is not enough when it IS enough. In fact, it is more than enough. New artists must understand that the most important story is their own.

The Joy of Writing

Making is more fun than writing. This is the thought that I sense from many of my students when I meet them in my shorts classes. In my decades of teaching this has been the conundrum I have faced with my students. They are, after all, children of the digital revolution, while I remain a child of the computer revolution.

Growing up, writing, outside of schoolwork, became my primary mode of expression, even more so than talking! Moving around a lot, I didn't have a lot of time to nurture friendships. When dolls and stuffed animals stopped consoling me, my books and writing became my collaborators and conspirators in planning adventures, exploring wishes, and dipping into my dreams.

So, it is not surprising that my students today have made their devices their most devoted confidantes.

Yet writing is a core of not only storytelling, but of communication, exchange, connection, and ultimately, freedom. I believe that writing is still the core of visual storytelling. It's our knowledge of words and language that helps craft the fabric of our visual storytelling. Great filmmakers often take years to develop their visual language, but how can you find your own when you don't have a grasp of language? Writing is the path to freedom of expression and also one of the things in the Western world we take most for granted. People still fight for that freedom somewhere in the world every day.

This book is not only about writing shorts as a fun exercise; which is certainly one way to appreciate this book. Writing shorts is about building a creative practice, extracting culture, building hope, preserving joy, and most of all, expanding the imagination and the possibilities of the world in which we all want to live.

How to Approach This Book

I organized this book with my new filmmakers in mind, focusing on providing them with practical writing tools they can always access. My goal is for students to understand that writing is an ongoing process. In one moment, you may have one idea, and in an instant, that idea can disappear and be replaced with another. With a ritual and a robust toolkit at their disposal, the writer is always prepared.

After this chapter, the book focuses on specific storytelling tools: ideas, characters, world-building, and structural, thematic, and linguistic elements beginning with a revisiting of these concepts from Merriam Webster. These chapters split into two parts: the first part is a narrative about storytelling tools; the second part provides specific and executable tasks to wield these tools, along with examples from existing shorts. Lastly, I provide a set of practice-and-play exercises to help you explore the tools in a creative way.

These practice-and-play exercises were conceived to be somewhat varied to attract students with different learning styles and to draw from ideas expressed within the chapter. They can be used to build a particular idea, if followed in chapter order, or they can be used to revisit or refresh earlier written stories. While many of the exercises are narrative-based, I also sought exercises that could work across various forms, such as documentary, animation, narrative game development, commercials, and more.

In the first section, I'll often reference short films (in a subheader) as examples to illustrate how to use these tools. However, I might use a feature film or television reference if it is a strong and effective example that I feel might be easier to locate. While many commercial and popular feature film and television scripts are accessible, obtaining short film scripts remains somewhat elusive, with a few exceptions. Something I hope to change!

After the tools chapters, you'll find the Draft and Revisions chapter, followed by an introduction to the cosmos of the short form so readers can familiarize themselves with the different short forms that they may encounter, though I'm sure there will be more developments after this book is published, considering how fast the digital world is evolving! I place it here because this chapter will allow you to consider the fluidity of storytelling forms and how one story idea you might have could be developed into many others. This chapter shares examples of each form along with common characteristics, where to find them, how to brainstorm and plan your writing, as well as strategies for working in that particular form.

Beyond the Short Forms chapter, you will find the Notes on Directing and Producing chapters for the writer-director-producer—as these are often the roles the new short artist will juggle in pursuit of their art. These chapters could easily be books of their own, and in many ways, this book is targeted to the new short maker who will take on all of these roles. Knowledge of the entire process can also shape the short in meaningful ways.

However, the new short maker is not the only audience for this book. In fact, I've already heard from many writers perusing my social media channels that the sound bites from this book are great bits of information and inspiration for writers in general.

THE WRITER AND THE SHORT MAKER

It's my hope that this book will serve the short screenwriter and the short maker and also find an audience of other writers and artists as the tools I share and describe are ultimately tools for any artist. That said, these are the ways I feel readers might most benefit from the book:

Finding Your Voice

There is nothing more important in making art, and certainly in making a short film, than finding your personal voice. Discovering, recognizing, and developing your voice is tantamount to establishing a personal style and vision. This is what makes the short film such a unique space. Within this limited time, you get to do anything. And what I encourage is that in that time, you be the most *you*.

Creating Cinema and Content

It doesn't matter if you are looking to create films and content either for the first time or the fiftieth time. Remember all the auteurs mentioned earlier who returned to the short form after their magnificent career-defining features? Whether you want to make a film, a TV series, or a commercial, this book will introduce you to some fundamentals of storytelling.

Moving Past Obstacles

There are times when content creators and artists get stuck, despite their rituals. When this happens, they need to find their voices again. I've attempted to create a mix of "out of the box" and straightforward exercises to get things going for those times when writers feel blocked or stuck in the mundane.

Searching for a Career

This book can expose you to the idea of a career in the short form. When I attended film school, there was an understanding that there were two roads for the filmmaker; the industry or the castle. What I learned is that there are many more roads. There are careers outside of the industry and the academy for short makers and content creators. You don't have to be fully immersed in the industry to make films. Contrary to other beliefs I harbored when I was younger, just because you teach, doesn't mean that you can't also create. In fact, I've found support and joy in teaching that has enabled me to make short films.

Going on Adventures and Explorations

This book can be effective in helping you discern which forms work for you and your purpose. It can also guide you in thinking about how to adapt stories across different forms. I've really admired how the industry can sometimes take an idea and replicate it across various mediums, including games, narratives, TikTok, documentaries, and more.

Touring Places and Immersive Journeys

An impassioned goal I had for this book was to share a truly global and international perspective on shorts. For those who simply love shorts, I hope that this book offers a wonderful world view of them from my perspective. For those who love learning about other cultures, beliefs, issues, and challenges, these shorts are a window and a constant reminder of the vastness of our world.

Making Poetry and Language

When I was freelancing in the industry, I offered a workshop called "Grammarizing Your Script" because I wanted to play with words and language within a script format. As a poet, I was always a lover of words. The more I wrote screenplays, the more I wanted to analyze their structures and break them down into discernible and digestible parts. I did this not only because this could help me write the 'perfectly imperfect' screenplay but also because, quite simply, I love words.

Opening Doors

Finally, I wrote this book because I wanted to create pathways of access and opportunity. I was blessed to have the chance to attend good schools because of the work and efforts of my mother. In these schools I became a thinker, an artist, and a writer. I became someone who wanted to share what I had learned.

Who you are in this world is a very personal thing. Often, it is limited by background, upbringing, class, and many other social and physiological elements of both molecules and mind that I am only beginning to explore and understand. Social constructs of race, gender, orientation, ableism, and more shape not only your identity, but how you get to navigate and perceive the world. Teaching classrooms of students from around the world taught me that, although we are often taught there is only one way, sometimes described as the "right way," that limited approach is a fundamentally wrong approach to any creative endeavor.

There are always many ways and many choices.

This is a core tenet of this book and what I discovered in endeavoring to watch as many shorts from as many countries as possible. This led me to wanting to create the Short Film Filmography that comes at the end of this book and lives in a fuller version online.

The Short Film Filmography

You will find shorts sprinkled throughout the book referencing or illustrating ideas within a section. Each of these shorts can be found in a list, organized by chapter, in the Short Film Filmography at the end of the book.

In this Short Film Filmography, curated with the help and voices of my students, I strove to find shorts from every corner of the world. I also sought to find shorts that may have had less attention, the purpose of which was to create space to uplift less centered communities. Many of these shorts were awarded in film competitions around the world. Others were chosen because they were supported and recognized by social organizations. You'll find some are on platforms that are relatively public, others on subscription-requiring platforms, and some on platforms supported by the filmmakers themselves. For certain shorts, you will be asked to pay to view; others are freely accessible. It's also worth noting that some shorts contain mature subject matter while others are rated G for kids and younger viewers. I am grateful for all of these fantastic hosting spaces and their commitment to enabling makers to tell their stories globally.

You'll find a good number of narrative shorts, followed by experimental and documentary ones. I give examples of all different types of short forms, including commercials, music videos, and more. By far though, the narrative and documentary shorts stand out (I suspect) because many experimental pieces do not appear online in the same way. I hope this curated collection expresses to you the transformative power of the short form and how storytelling is moving and sculpting a better world for all of us.

Finally, I want to share that this curation of shorts is an ongoing project. While the Short Film Filmography will reference shorts highlighted in the book, you can explore a much longer and more globally inclusive selection of shorts on our website, www.theshort.co. I continue to reach out to writers and directors willing to share their shorts and short scripts with new writers of all backgrounds. My hope is that these new writers will learn what storytelling looks like from script to screen through various perspectives around the globe. I invite you to share any of your recognized shorts and short scripts to continue this endeavor. Visit the website above to learn and explore more.

I believe this is the work of the book—to continue this idea that making is never about what's right or wrong. Making shorts is about finding and sharing freedom and joy in the process of discovering you.

IDEAS & PERSONAL INVESTIGATIONS:
THE FILMMAKER'S QUEST

The Idea
—*A well-formulated thought or opinion*

THE FILMMAKER'S QUEST

When I began my career as a filmmaker, I started out with a limited mind set. I was working for an executive who was making reality shows for television. I felt that reality shows weren't really my thing, and I left to go work for a production company that, ironically, really helped me to understand how rigid my thinking was. At this production company, they were making narrative projects, video game projects, and documentaries, in addition to a variety of feature films. They worked across these different mediums, exploring genres such as drama, action, sci-fi, and more. In short, what I learned, but didn't understand until my latter years, is that story is story.

Story Is Story

Robert McKee has a book, which I read early in my career, called *Story* and it opens with a warm anecdote about how his mother told him that she would teach him how to tell a story, and that would guarantee him a job forever. His mother recognized that the world is filled—nay, literally *driven*—by stories. In this highly digital and highly visual age, stories have only become more important to understanding the world and comprehending each other.

Who Gets to Tell a Story?

The beautiful and rare thing about storytelling is that it is likely one of the most equitable processes in our society. Anyone can tell a story. Be it through words, images, gestures, or some other form of communication, stories are limitless and timeless. They are the one standard that allows us all to share the same platform regardless of background, status, or ability. This is not to ignore that some stories get centered more than others. However, never forget that you, as a storyteller, have infinite power to change that. When you become a good storyteller, the world will play at your fingertips.

What Does a Storyteller Look Like?

There are so many grand storytellers out there. I suspect the best of them, we know the least about. Many of them are writers, and for the purposes of this book, we recognize them as actors, directors and producers: artists. But I believe storytelling is much bigger than that. Scientists can be storytellers, along with engineers, physicians, librarians, foresters, and astronauts. Think about storytelling as an approach, not merely a task at hand. Storytelling can be used as a tool in virtually any position to engage, because we are all hard-wired to comprehend stories.

I remember listening to a news article once (yep, a story). It described how some grocery store brands sell their items not through facts, but through story. Picking up my milk carton, I saw it right there: the cows in the pastures were a part of a story. Then I saw it everywhere. Marketers widely understand the advantages of storytelling. So do teachers, inventors, and innovators.

Storytellers are Everywhere.

So where do you begin?

The idea. In the Ideasphere, there exists an infinite number of duplicate, incomplete, and unformed ideas. In this post-modern, post-internet world, where seemingly every story has been told, the industry sends out its media foot soldiers to find that new filmmaker with the next wholly *original* idea. To my students I say, they are searching for *you*, and they are. They are seeking someone to tell that very old story with a fresh take, a new perspective, someone who can breathe fresh air into that next new tentpole film. If you have one great vision for a new idea, chances are you will have more.

The question is 'are you ready for them?'

In an academic setting, finding an idea is an immediate task. In the structured capacity of a classroom, creative writing teachers will often start off with a series of brainstorming exercises. These exercises are always useful, but where they fall short is that these brainstorms are only a beginning. Often, a writer will mistakenly expect that by brainstorming, they've quickly established a solid topic, an idea—when most times the brainstorming alone does not. The exercise has established the *germ* of an idea. Brainstorming is a beginning, and it leads to, but does not replace, the real work that still needs to be done to create the very rare original idea.

There are very few original ideas.

Therefore, I ask my students to come to class with three ideas for us to explore. Many bring rushed thoughts to complete the assignment; some students approach it with thoughtful consideration, others sprinkle wild tosses in the wind. Then there will be the old idea the student has had forever. Sometimes, it's good when a student comes to the table genuinely committed to an idea that they've carried for a while. Other times, an old idea might be confining if they think it is the *only* good idea they have—a limiting notion guided by the fear of exploring or revealing something new. If the idea is not strong enough, it will fall apart, but with my instructions, they'll always have two other options to consider.

IDEAS FALL APART

I watch ideas fall apart when we try to excavate them, when we try to dig a little under the superficial surface of "that sounds cool" or "it's intriguing." As I help new writers develop their ideas through exploratory exercises, it becomes clear that if the idea hasn't come from a grounded place, a place that has meaning for them, it will not be able to endure the gruel of a writer's marathon. A good idea runs a marathon, measured not in steps but in words; nipping, slipping, tucking, and running to arrive at a destination that will end with the thrill of accomplishment.

Many of these potential ideas may have the resilience to blossom into something extraordinary, but new writers will often abandon them or delete them before they even hit the page. After seeing my students' eyes light up after a brainstorming session, I realized that original ideas exist; we just don't share them because we are afraid. Every artist I have met is looking for this little piece of acceptance, to have their ideas embraced, to be hugged in a way that says, "you matter." But this fear cannot and should not overcome the unadulterated truth.

Everyone has the capacity to conceive an original idea simply because we are each a unique system; we are an original.

THE UNIQUE SYSTEM OF THE ORIGINAL

When story ideas fail, it's often because many writers fear that their original selves aren't strong, interesting, or intriguing enough to create a riveting story—whether that story is about them, born from them, or merely interesting to them. But each of us is born unique; there's no copy of you out there. Even twins, triplets, and quadruplets are unique from each other. As individuals, we always have the potential to tell something wholly original.

However, we often get seduced by someone or something we see as better than us. We look at what others are doing, and think, "if I can do it more like that, perhaps that might work." We consider stealing or borrowing other ideas and hope that maybe it will work. Truth be told, artists are always borrowing techniques, strategies, insights, and lessons from other artists, but that is different from borrowing an idea.

How important is the original idea? Ask the U.S. copyright office and its counterparts worldwide who also enforce protections around "the original idea." Committing to this concept of the original idea demands a lot from us as artists. Pulling out an original idea is terrifying. No one wants to be mocked, challenged, or insulted when they propose an original idea. That is why not everyone chooses to be an artist.

Artists are often the best of us. They are courageous in standing up for what they believe and putting it out in the public sphere for others to love, judge, and criticize. They say what no one else wants to say. They bare their souls. They are sensitive and hungry for attention. But artists are also gift givers, profound in their generosity and authenticity, and they largely want to make the world a better place through their art.

So how can you recognize this original idea, this well-formulated thought or opinion? A good, original idea will have legs. It will have vision. A good, well-articulated idea will lead to more thoughtful inquiry and can survive that type of challenge. A good idea is where inventions and experiments are nursed and nurtured. A good idea might be considered the most valuable commodity in the world.

But the most important element to coming up with this idea for your short is that it comes from you. It must spark a seed of passion. It must carry with it a kernel of truth. A good idea for a short, whether for a class or your own purposes, takes patience, rumination, and thorough investigation of yourself and your idea before it can become a good script. So, let's jump in!

PERSONAL INVESTIGATIONS AND DETERMINATIONS

Early in my film industry journey, I recall taking a lot of directing actor classes. The teacher would ask us about our processes. At one point, I told her about the numerous material tasks I would complete when preparing to work with actors. She was shocked, and explained to me that these tasks were not getting to the essence of what I needed to do to properly work with actors. That statement remained with me for years to come as I pondered what it was that I was doing "wrong." Many years later, I came to realize that what she was asking me to do was to investigate a deeper connection between myself and the material. Instead of looking outward, I needed to look inward. That is what personal investigation is all about.

To write a good short, I ask you to start with investigating yourself. This might sound straightforward, but I humbly request and invite you to bear with me.

Why am I Here?

In my youth, I often asked myself this question, and now, I am moved to witness many of the new writers I work with asking it too. I found myself searching for an answer:

You are here because you were put on this earth to contribute something that no one else can. You are important, original, and irreplaceable. No one else anywhere, in any place or time, will ever be like you. Your individual story comes from a place of unique perspective and experience. Your history is based around circumstances or ideas that feel normal and real only to you. Your perspective is born out of a web of environment, circumstance, and histories that have established rules for your conduct, your belief, and your emotional terrain. You are here to become the best you and to share that with the world. I am here to help you.

The Investigative Process

In investigating yourself, consider viewing yourself as an object of the most important study. You are an endless microcosm of connections and complex systems, infinitely curious and intoxicatingly fascinating. When I meet my students, I approach them with this attitude. I wrap myself within the idea that they are all terribly exciting. That is how I want you to think about yourself!

Easy Answers

You may initially think this task is quite easy. But is it? This investigation moves beyond the things you know to be true—that you like strawberries and hate chocolate, that your brother will tell on you every chance he gets. It delves into your inner core: how you feel, what you believe, what is meaningful to you and why. Although these answers might appear irrelevant or superfluous, they are of dire importance.

Determining the Reflection in the Mirror

While I was writing this book, I also developed a short animation project featuring myself as a professor. Collaborating with a former student, I was surprised (and relieved) to see myself through her eyes. The colors, body shape, and height of my puppet revealed her perception of me. More intriguing than the dimensions were the personal accents and adornments she selected for my character after our initial discussions. One thing that came out of these discussions was my bracelet. It was a small ornament that no one really knows about except me and my family. But the story behind this bracelet is that I never take it off. It's an heirloom that I've worn my entire life. It doesn't come off in the shower, at the airport, or when I go to bed; it is a part of my Caribbean heritage. The exercise of creating the film made me think deeper about how I imagine myself, how others see me, and how I want to be seen. So, how do you begin this process?

A Process of Determination

To Imagine:

Sometimes what you imagine can be more important than what you actually see. When we were children, we had endless imagination because we didn't know what was real and what was not. I want you to return to this space of boundlessness. Let go of the obstructions of supposed to, could have, should, can't, no, and impossible. Begin to imagine this subject in your mind as you choose to see it. Your power to imagine is your most powerful tool as an artist and writer.

To Examine:

Approach the actual subject if you can; if you can't, draw it as best you can. Start with the openness of a blank page and expect that you *don't* know everything about the subject even if it seems fairly familiar to you—even if it's yourself! Taking pictures of the subject can be a great first step if you can't revisit the subject often. In this examination, remember not to overlook anything or take anything for granted. Look for facts, both physical and metaphysical, and take notes.

To Inquire:

Begin to ask questions about the curious items of the subject's examination. Don't assume. Beware of questions that analyze and judge like "Why did I think that instead of this?" and instead focus on questions that allow you to jump deeper in: What happened? Why this color? What is this space? Where am I? Avoid dismissing aspects as normal or common; consider every trait a choice.

To Discover:

In searching for discoveries, attempt to come to the subject anew and with a discerning eye. Take note of the things that have surprised you, the things you didn't expect, and the things you had forgotten. Be careful not to criticize or evaluate. Do not try to make sense of what you discover at this stage.

To Report:
Now, report on what you have learned. It is important to write down as much as you can. The recorder or the reporter takes notes. The important thing here is to not carry all of the discoveries in your mind! Why? Because I find that tucking these ideas away can lead to a kind of subconscious editing when you report. This can lead to hiding important information or information that doesn't look relevant at first glance but might become relevant later.

To Review:
Reviewing is the step most often skipped or undervalued. Take a moment to slowly and carefully review all that you have reported. After reading through it, like a detective with a series of clues, connections will naturally begin to surface. Circle the things that resonate with you even if you are not sure exactly why they do.

To Conceive:
At this point I hope that notions are bubbling to the surface. What you come up with at this stage can look many different ways. The idea might feel complete. It might be only the germ of an idea. It might be an idea that makes no sense to you yet. But what you are searching for is the kernel of something that moves you emotionally and yet is immovable from your mind. It has staying power. Write this idea into this template: I want to share ____.

The Excavation Journey

This "process of determination" is meant to help you embark on your journey to freeing your imagination. Like most journeys, your focus will want to be on the steps, the crumbs of surprise and delight you discover along the way, and not the destination. It's very easy for new writers to get ahead of themselves—to get bogged down with getting to the end before even starting. Rushing will cause you to miss important insights, compromise urgent elements, and lose track of the main goal. Use these seven ideas as a template, as different strategies for exploring *you* (or any other subject). If you love them all—go for it! If you only like a few, that works too. I hope at least one or two will inspire every reader.

I call this exercise a process of determination and not investigation because you are doing more than investigating; you are attempting to determine where you will go from this starting point. When you begin this process of determination, these are some of the questions behind the idea. To begin this process, we need a subject. The subject could be anything, a ball, a park, a spirit, a color, or a person. For now, let's start with you.

TOOLS AND TECHNIQUES

In each chapter, I share with you some tools and techniques to guide how to use the practice exercises that follow. With my own students, their questions of 'how do I. . .?' have often confounded me because when I was growing up, no one told me how. I jumped in and created a how. But their questions have helped me to elucidate a process that, even with these directions, still feels quite mystifying to me because we are all so mysterious as artists, as individuals, as human beings!

Consider these seven steps in a process of determination: imagining, examining, inquiring, discovering, reporting, reviewing, and conceiving. Above, I shared a chart for this process of determination, but you may not need it. Perhaps all of these steps might be helpful to you, perhaps only a few. As I tell my new writers, whatever helps you, keep; whatever doesn't, throw away. In the end, I hope this process will help reveal a process of your own.

Quiet, Clear, and Open

Before you visit these tools in each chapter, it is helpful to clear your mind by spilling out all your worries on a piece of paper. I liked to use timed writing exercises with my high school students, but any format or technique will do; whether it is breathing, meditation, lighting a candle, burning incense, or simply staring out a window and observing the world. But you want to take the time to empty your mind of distractions and burdens. I am intensely worry-prone and clearing out the dispensary of my mind's burdens always aids me tremendously.

EMOTIONAL REALITIES AND FERTILE IMAGINATIONS

"Film is a medium of emotions."
—Hassan Ildari

When I teach, I like to begin my first class by telling stories. It's a great warm up exercise for my students and I like to get them comfortable with pitching early on. I ask every student to tell a story and then after everyone has shared, I ask the class what do they remember? Sometimes they remember repeated phrases. Other times they recall specific visuals. But most often, they remember how they felt.

When I try to recall my earliest memories, even when the events are fuzzy, I can always remember how I felt, whether it was deep sadness, disappointment, love, or joy. The same has applied to my students, so it wasn't too surprising when I heard one of my mentors refer to film as a "medium of emotions."

This is important because when I recall films from my youth, if I can remember nothing else, I remember how I felt about them. Perhaps they made me uncomfortable, perhaps they made me swoon. Maybe the film gave me hope. These residual emotions, for many of us, decide whether we will choose to see the movie again.

Films are about experiences.

In the same way that this emotion is something I've experienced, as a writer, I've come to realize that these emotions are not simply *my* experience. Other filmgoers often experience these emotions as well. When I think about what defines a "classic" film, a film that we decide to return to repeatedly, I begin asking the question; what brings you back? I decided that, to a certain extent, what brings you back is the emotion you wish to relive. This starts with the script. But even deeper than that, the story begins with the writer.

Your story always starts with you.

When I first became interested in film, I studied the critical writings of Chicago Reader Film Critic Jonathan Rosenbaum. I didn't know I wanted to be a filmmaker at that time, but what I loved about his writings was that they didn't simply analyze the film. His writings took into account the filmmaker's background, culture, and lived-in experiences which influenced the making of the film. Then, he would discuss the film within *that* context. In doing this, Rosenbaum essentially created a relationship between the film and the maker, allowing you to see what the film represented in the context of their life and the larger world. This came to shape how I would approach teaching filmmaking in my later years.

In my short film classes, I designed an exercise where I would show the film and then analyze articles and interviews from the writer. Through this, I discovered something essential: great films are largely personal.

personal: belonging or relating to a particular person

Whether the story is drawn from personal experience, or the maker has chosen the material, there exists a relationship between these two connected elements, and it is out of this relationship that emotion is born.

I grappled with this idea of emotion in film. Do we feel emotions in telling a story? When do we feel these emotions? Is it possible that we are conveying this feeling in the telling of it... even on paper? Reflecting the childhood storytellers of my youth, the most obvious answer is: absolutely!

"No tears for the writer, no tears for the reader."
—Robert Frost

Thinking about this more, I examined some of my favorite shorts and the interviews that accompanied them. I unearthed an idea that I later saw repeated in a quote. In a film, it is the experience of *feeling* that you are attempting to gift to your audience, and it can only be gifted if it comes from a true and personal space. You cannot gift something that isn't there.

This explained why my confusion would seemingly translate to the page and perplex my reader. I recognized the same effect happening when I reviewed my students' work. A note like "feeling confused here," often prompted them to admit, "Yes, I was confused there." It became apparent that this was a kind of rule: the reader's experience mirrored the emotions of the writer during the process. It also explained why if the writer feels empty in their writing, the reader senses that same emptiness.

Now consider this for a moment. How does film communicate a feeling and what does it take to execute that?

Lynne Ramsay's *Small Deaths*

I often use Lynne Ramsay's *Small Deaths* as an example. The intensity of emotion that is expressed in this anthology of childhood experiences that Ramsay shares with us is tender and moving. When I discuss this film with my students, I point out the challenges that Ramsay faced: holding onto a feeling from her childhood and choosing to convey that sentiment from her heart, mind, and body to the page and all the way through the bodies and machinations of her crew—likely some 20 people. And for that feeling to travel to us, seeing it on the screen. *All these years later!*

It's remarkable, isn't it!?

How do you capture emotion like that and hold it like water so it can be carried through the passage of time and across all of these mediums?

Emotional Potency

It must have something to do with the purity of emotion. The most potent emotions are the most likely to traverse these seas of bodies, span across time, and transcend various mediums. Where you have the least potency is where your film will fail in connecting. Accessing this potency is at the crux of storytelling.

So how do you find this? Like Ramsay, I recommend starting with your childhood.

EARLY RECOLLECTIONS AND FERVENT EXPLORATIONS

THE CHILDHOOD STORIES

Kia Moses and Adrian McDonald's *Flight*

When I work with new writers, I enjoy starting by having them explore childhood memories, a rich and deep reservoir for any new filmmaker. What I love most about this experience is that childhood memories, often devoid of dialogue, provide an excellent opportunity for students to grasp what CalArts professor and film director Alexander Mackendrick referred to as learning "visual language". How do you tell your story through visual imagery? This is the crux of visual storytelling.

I suspect these memories are tied to our understanding of the world before we could read and write. We come to understand the world through our senses. Tying our experiences to sensory perceptions is a way to bring others into our experience, and that's what filmmaking does best—it transports us to other realities beyond our own. This "suspension of belief" allows us to sever our ties to our current world and explore another. A rich storytelling experience can provide so many sensory visual elements that we can summon the rest via our own memories to complete the sensory experience. Even though we might not actually smell the pie in the film, its visual appeal can evoke such a vivid sensory experience that we find ourselves recalling the aroma and taste from another moment in our own lives.

Kia Moses and Adrian McDonald's charming astronaut film, *Flight*, immerses us in the childhood adventures of Kemar, who aspires to reach the moon. He does everything in his power to build a ship to get him there—in between gazing at the stars and wondering what's behind them. The film eloquently transports us back to this space of childhood innocence and wonder.

Our childhoods are unique and timeless spaces, whether filled with joy or dread. I've found that writers can often express themselves more potently when channeling important experiences from their past rather than their present. Sometimes, when we tell stories from our present, we inadvertently encounter a rawness that may hinder or influence our process. We might find ourselves creating protective layers both around ourselves and our story elements. Childhood memories usually tend to be distant enough to not seem emotionally severe, yet close enough for their emotional reserves to appear seemingly endless.

For the childhood story, consider which stories from your childhood standout to you: What is memorable? What is resonant? What is emotional? Exploring this childhood story is a great beginning!

THE FIRST MEMORIES

Maryam Keshavarz's *The Day I Died*

Begin by identifying which memories stand out to you the most. It can take a moment to pull these out of the ether, especially with older memories, but I'm always surprised at just how much I can pry out when I am patient, quiet, and open. If you need a prompt to get your creative juices flowing, here are a few:

What are some of our chief disappointments, deepest fears, or our fondest longings? I have also found powerful insights when exploring the moments where I felt the most loved, safe, and cherished. Maryam Keshavarz's *The Day I Died* explores the relationship between three young children floating through the summers of youth. The way Keshavarz weaves a tale around first disappointment is delicately nurtured and considered.

Here are some examples of other early memories that typically make for good fodder. I've used 'first' here, but I use that term loosely. If a memory stands out to you as significant, we will refer to it as a 'first.' This exercise also works with 'last' memories.

First Punishment
First Kiss
First Fear
First Love
First Hurt
First Injury
First Joy
First Remorse
First Forgiveness
First Disappointment
First Betrayal
First Loss
First Triumph

Even though these occurrences in a movie may feel small alongside the grand events of explosions, crime heists, and superheroes, these personal dramas are momentous in our lives. They are also universal shared experiences that significantly color how we see and move through the world.

Thinking in Color

Cid's *Colors*

As a young high school teacher, I drew many of my writing exercises from a book called *The Practice of Poetry*.

Many of these exercises were simple timed writing exercises that I used in my classes. Two of my favorites had to do with the relationship to color and mood or emotion. One of them, by Rita Dove, asked you to write about your grandmother's kitchen. What I love about this exercise is trying to recall long-forgotten details from my childhood.

In my earliest recollections, I couldn't often remember words, but I could draw from sensory experiences to remember my feelings: gold meant summers sucking honeysuckles in the sun; baby blue was smelling clean air under clear blue skies with cottony clouds; pink made me think of ice cream, carnivals, and cotton candy.

When I picked a specific place, I marveled at how colors defined my childhood and conveyed the emotions I felt. This reflection led me to develop an exercise exploring the inverse. Take up a color wheel or even a tray of crayons or colored pencils and think about where that color takes you.

Cid's *Colors* is an animated film with a rather simple narrative. What really makes this short stand out is its animation style and use of colors in a medium that truly feels like a cross between the real world, a photography negative, and an animated comic book. The colors blur the lines of reality in a visceral way; prompting us to question what is and isn't real.

Here are some colors to get you started:

Black
Brown
White
Grey
Red

Yellow
Gold
Blue
Purple
Green
Indigo
Magenta
Orange

Another vehicle for accessing early recollections is examining dreams.

RESERVOIRS OF THE SUBCONSCIOUS

Nightmares, Dreams, and Dreaming

Tim Burton's *Vincent*

Have you ever had a dream that haunted you?

As a child, I had a recurring nightmare. It began in my home, where my family and I were trying to escape from a coven of monstrous creatures. I was tasked with saving both my parents, despite being seven years old. I was able to save my mother but failed in saving my father. This dream followed me all through my adolescence and into young adulthood. As a college student, I finally wrote a story about it, helping me discover that the dream was about my parents' separation—something for which I felt responsible for many years.

Dreams have always been considered a tunnel into the subconscious, and certainly, many feature films have drawn rich content from this idea. From Wes Craven's *Nightmare on Elm Street* to Joseph Ruben's *Dreamscape* to Tim Burton's *Nightmare Before Christmas*, plenty of filmmakers have explored the intriguing realm of dreams. A lot of Burton's popular work was explored in his early short, *Vincent*. In this short, you can see early models for *Nightmare Before Christmas*, *Beetlejuice*, and even *Edward Scissorhands*. Interestingly, the titular Vincent is Vincent Price, who narrates the poetry for the film, and eventually, also worked with Burton on a few feature films. This leads me to wonder if working with Vincent Price was a dream that came true for Burton?

It's no accident that Freud learned a lot about people through their dreams, this cauldron of subconscious repression and desire. While I've never come to think of my dreams as anything literal, their ability to reflect our state of mind, anxieties, and desires has been commonly documented. Dreams certainly come up in my classes more often than not.

I also think there is something to be said for daydreaming. Growing up in an immigrant family where work ethic was always stressed, I came to find that precious elusive moments where I could take the time to dream, envision, and allow room to do nothing at all really opened up creative possibilities for me. Whether it's dreaming about the future, new worlds, or other realities, dreams also allow the landscape of ideas to widen for the new artist.

At the very least, the exercise of dreaming can help us find a new approach, perspective, or idea that shakes us out of repetition and generality.

WISHING, LONGING, PINING

Nuotama Frances Bodomo's *Boneshaker*

There is something truly powerful about longing. Wishes, when filled with emotion, can become more real than reality. Longing can give rise to dreams, stir emotions, and spur action, even under the worst of conditions. Sometimes, we find that our minds are filled with our deepest desires—those things we desired but we never believed we could attain.

Many shorts have burst forth from these potent yearnings.

In Nuotama Frances Bodomo's *Boneshaker*, we watch the protagonist grapple with a yearning for acceptance, a place to call home, and a sense of belonging as she navigates the desires of her family and their vision for her future. Sometimes our deepest yearnings can manifest as daydreams, visions, or even ideas we capture in our work. If we are a photographer, it may be the scenes we capture. If we are a quilter, it may be represented in the symbols and colors we embed in the quilt. If we are a woodworker, it may be carved into the curves of a handmade desk for a daughter we wish we had. I've often found writers will write their deepest desires into their stories in an emotionally resonant way, perhaps without even realizing it.

Yearnings are as powerful as any memory and any dream. At times they can even cause us to unconsciously reshape our realities.

This is not to say that the writer is always conscious of what they may be writing. Much of this occurs in our subconscious. We create things without always knowing why we are drawn to them and why they make us feel a certain way—whether these feelings are good or bad. As writers, what we seek is *access* to these emotions.

We may yearn for things that can be either beneficial or detrimental. As creatures of habit, sometimes maintaining our rituals is easier than instituting change.

Throughout my youth, I desperately wanted a sibling. I wanted to know that I wasn't alone in the world, and I thought that having a sibling would be one way to accomplish this. I was often filled with deep longing for this sibling that my mother told me could've come before me. That longing became the basis for one of my most awarded screenplays.

Many of our wishes are often concealed deep within our subconscious. Delving deeper into what these objects represent to you can bring you closer to examining your deepest wounds and the flaws that have surfaced as a result.

Consider the wishes you've had at different points in your life. What did you wish for when you were a child? How about as a teen? When you were an adult? What about now? How do you see these wishes being connected? How have these wishes changed?

Superstitions, Values, and Beliefs

Alex Westfall's *Rose of Manila*

In my family, flies are seen as the filthiest creatures on earth. As someone who regularly watches horror films, I can think of a few things more abhorrent than a fly. However, when a fly shows up in the house, everything stops. Life ceases to move forward until the fly is captured, killed, or removed. I've watched family members balance on unsafe chairs, tables, and boxes to access the furthest, highest, unlikeliest corner to make sure that the fly is addressed. As a child, I witnessed this behavior, but didn't understand it. By observing my family's behavior, I was taught that this fly could cause the downfall of us all. Superstitions make for great excavations because they are belief systems that often stretch our current reality. They reveal a lot about our background and upbringing, reflecting what we believe.

IDEAS & PERSONAL INVESTIGATIONS

Alex Westfall's *Rose of Manila* speculates on the formative years of Imelda Marcos, the former First Lady of the Philippines and wife to the controversial president Ferdinand Marcos, in an experimental hybrid documentary. Blending an imagined youth with actual footage of the subject as an adult, this film provides an innovative way to deliver and reveal the values of a reimagined Imelda as a young woman.

What do you believe?

Belief systems have to do with our values. These are shaped as we grow into adults and sometimes, they change. We learn and evaluate our belief systems as we grow into adulthood and then again as we enter different phases of our adulthood: parenthood, middle age, caretaking, and the golden years. Our belief systems tend to shift as new experiences cause us to rethink what we have been told (by family), learned (through community), and witnessed in our environment (by society).

We are not always aware of how much our belief systems are engaged in every decision that we make. What we believe manifests in even the simplest of choices, from what we order at a restaurant, to how we park our car. Does how you park the car reflect your values of attentiveness or aloofness, consideration or selfishness, sloppiness or perfectionism? Do you leave room for others to get out of their space, or do you crowd into the space and assume other drivers will work it out? Consider all of the beliefs that are reflected in this small task. This becomes even more apparent when we create art. We are putting on display our belief systems for all to see.

How can you find your belief system or values? A good place to start is identifying challenges in your life. Where do you find arguments and disagreements arising? With whom? Why? Disagreements occur when someone's strong belief system contradicts someone else's. This conflict is something you will come to know very well in the screenwriting world.

Drama is born from strong internal conflicts.

Reflecting on our belief systems can be a great exercise for preparing to write. What things do you believe in? What don't you believe in? Attempting to write a sketch that is based in something that you don't believe can be a wonderful exploratory exercise.

LANDSCAPES, SPACES, AND UNIVERSES OF THE MIND AND BODY

Pastimes, Hobbies, and Passions

When I meet my students for the first time, I like to start with some introductions. As a part of introducing themselves, I ask my students to tell me about a hobby or pastime that is important to them——but it cannot be film. I add that caveat to the question because, in a film class for film majors, that is an obvious choice, and it is a commonality we already know we all share. I am looking for what makes us different because film, like most art forms, is constructed through our personal experiences. The distinction between these personal experiences is what makes each film unique.

What can you do well that no one else knows about?

I once had a teacher who told us "make the film that no one else can make." What this teacher was saying was to draw from an experience that is so individual to your own lens, to your own life experience, that no one could replicate it. One effective way to achieve this is by focusing on the things you love and excel at and casting a fresh perspective on them. These are your gifts. We all have gifts that make us human and distinguish us from others. However, I find that many of us tend to dismiss our gifts as too common, too boring. But alas, the combination of you is complex, dimensional, and indefatigable! It's important to invite the mundane into our scrutiny. What seems ordinary to us is often extraordinary to someone else.

Martin Scorsese's *The Big Shave*

In terms of film topics, I find that paradoxically, the more mundane something is, the more interesting it can become as a subject! Building a bike, brushing your teeth, and yes, shaving in the bathroom mirror could make amazing short films for the right director. Check out Martin Scorsese's bloody good short, *The Big Shave*!

Sitting in my dentist's office, I watched as my dentist sculpted the structure for a temporary bridge for my mouth. When I mentioned to him that it was some bit of craftsmanship, he denied it. Yet, of all the dentists I had seen, I'd never seen one pour his concentration into such an object with such meditative attention. My mind was popping with all sorts of narratives and storylines as I observed him with my mouth hanging open. It was a much-needed distraction!

Those skills and talents that you disregard the most are often perfect subjects for a short film.

On the other hand, there are deeply fervent passions that we recognize as such. The activities that we cannot live without can also make for a grand resource for writing. The weirder, the better. Whether it is knitting political socks, collecting worms, or painting with aromatherapies, we all have activities that we're drawn to that invigorate us, activate us and incite us to action. Passions are experiences filled with zest and fervor and have the capacity to emotionally endure in a film.

DATES, TIMELINES, AND MUSCLE MEMORY

Andrew Ahn's *Dol*

I had been living in California for most of my adult life, when I returned to the northeast coast one winter. One of the buried experiences that washed over me was cold toes. I slowly remembered, in a bit of a fog, that the East Coast winters of my childhood were filled with days of toes that could never get warm, no matter how many socks I wore. Squishing my toes together, scrounging for warmth, the memories seeped into my consciousness. Living in warmer climates, I'd forgotten this. But this muscle memory awakened so many other memories of what it meant to live in a seasonal city.

Do something you haven't done but used to do.

When we take the time to look back at our lives, we often find moments that we treasure, along with moments we wish had never happened. Sometimes these associations are through memories, other times through dates, and sometimes, they are through muscle memories.

Anniversaries, birthdays, and holidays are dates to which we ascribe specific attention. But there are other dates that will have resonance for us: the date of a wedding, a bad storm, some terrible event. Some of us may create a lot of fanfare over these dates. For others, the date will pass with barely any recognition. Often, these dates are filled with ritual. These rituals can also hold meaning for us.

In Andrew Ahn's *Dol*, Ahn explores the relationship between a gay Korean man and his family around the traditional event of his nephew's first birthday party. Filled with cultural ritual and nuanced detail, Ahn's tentative and emotional piece conveys the weight of an important moment that the character Nick yearns for but experiences as an outsider.

Singling out these days is simply a way of saying something special happened on this day. These are days that we associate with special feelings. Searching the timeline of our memories can reveal a story that is perhaps waiting to be released.

Timelines tell stories.

As someone who has always been infatuated with graphs, stats, and figures, I have a deep appreciation for timelines. Timelines can tell us a lot about who we are and where we are in our lives. If you were to create your own timeline, where would you put the turning points?

It's also fun to create timelines based around themes. Maybe it's the family reunion timeline (family drama), the new boyfriend/girlfriend timeline (rom com), or the 'how many times have I moved' timeline (coming of age)? These timelines all tell different stories about you! Looking back at your own timeline, what stories do you see?

Locations, Totems, and Talismans

Ephraim Asili's *Kindah*

One of the scripts I wrote was based around the home of one of my grandparents. It was a home that scared me as a child. It was a dark place with high dusty ceilings, long emaciated hallways, and treacherous dark corners. At night, there never seemed to be enough light. There was also a creepy cat who liked to growl and follow me around. This was the perfect setting for a film about a girl who was running from a scary villain. I could certainly make up a place, but why make up a place when this one is already endowed with such personal emotion for me?

Memorable places can harbor deeply minable material.

Places or objects that have specific meaning for you are great jumping off spaces—particularly if the emotions are potent. Does a home, a park, or a lake carry emotional memories for you? In film, you are constantly constructing new worlds with new rules. A location that you know well, but that no one has seen, can become a strong touchstone for a new story.

What is your relationship to that place? We tend to think of relationships only as existing between people but, certainly, relationships exist between pets, places, and even inanimate objects. The relationship forms based on the value we assign it. We can, and actors expertly do, create relationships with people, places, and things all the time.

Can you think of a favorite item that has meaning for you?

Objects you share a personal connection with offer excellent story opportunities. These don't have to be dolls or pets, they can be mundane objects like pens, glasses, or towels. Taking mundane objects and creating entire stories around them is an exciting way to find an original or new perspective.

Family totems can also serve as wonderful inspiration. Objects that have reverential resonance for a family or community, especially if it is historical, exist as story caverns. Objects with historical relevance can help create narrative grounding in the story. In their investigations, writers love jumping down historical rabbit holes that reveal new topics and storylines. While often linked to the spiritual realm, totems don't always have to be supernatural—although that's how we typically see them. What objects are the pride and joy of your family or community? What keepsakes do they keep hidden away or protected? Even a family bowl could become a totem in the right writer's hands if there's an intriguing story there.

Ephraim Asili's powerful *Kindah* references several totems in the film: drums, water, and houses. But it is the title that Asili uses to direct our attention to the Kindah. The Kindah tree is a large ancient mango tree that is said to have united the Maroons against the British in their fight for autonomy in the 1700s. Today, this tree is still standing.

You will also find many films that are replete with charms, lockets, and medallions. These are all objects that have become talismans that a writer can assign for a character to carry. After my grandmother passed away, I wondered if any pieces from her large jewelry collection held any special meaning for her. I wished I had asked. I wanted to know. Speculating can also be a good jumping off place.

Can you think of an item that held meaning for you? Consider a favorite piece of jewelry or equipment, or a place you like to visit for solace or leisure, or an item that holds familial significance.

CUTTING AND PASTING THE IMAGINATION: MAKING THE OLD NEW

The Mosaic and Inspired Media

For new writers, looking within is a necessary place to start. However, if you have already learned how to look within, do not overlook looking *without*. Doing so doesn't mean that your story does not still come from you. What you like, what you are drawn to, what calls you—these are all still based on who you are as an individual.

So, things that catch your interest and pique questions are also luxurious writing fields to explore. Sometimes, you can find that in other media. I like to ask my new writers to come up with one idea that is inspired by other media.

Newspapers
News reports
Magazine articles
Poems
Music and Songs
Nursery Rhymes, Fables & Fairy Tales
Short Stories
Books & Novels
Other Films
Paintings
Television Shows
Comics & Graphic Novels
Video Games
Social Media
Amusement Parks

Then there is media that you might forget you could use!

Diana Cam Van Nguyen's *Love, Dad*

The delightful and poignant mosaic of textures and mediums, pictures, letters, and animation in Diana Cam Van Nguyen's *Love, Dad* make for a simultaneously revelatory and agonizing film. Van Ngyuen places herself at the center of a refreshingly honest documentary that asks questions about the father she remembers and why he left.

The things that you are attracted to are not accidental. What clothes you decide to wear and what food you decide to put into your body are choices that are reflective of who you are and what you believe. These all contribute to who you are today.

In this way, you can use other sources of media as tools for inspiration and investigate why they've inspired you. You will want to go through the same process to determine what it is that has drawn you to it.

One thing to note is that inspired media is different from copied media. In an inspired story, the writer takes liberties with elements of a true story and uses those elements to go in a new direction. However, taking a story and retelling true events is very different from finding inspiration in an existing story, and requires more legal investigation and permission that revolves around questions and status of private and/or public domain. If any real people are referenced, exercising caution is a good rule of thumb. Putting yourself in their shoes is a useful approach for considering if any libel or slander may be involved.

INSPIRATIONS, DEVOTIONS, AND LOVE

Firas Khoury's *Maradona's Legs*

Firas Khoury's charming and teasing *Maradona's Legs* centers on two brothers and their pursuit of the one last soccer card that will complete their beloved soccer magazine collection and win them a prize. Their journey takes us on an Alice in Wonderland-like adventure, introducing us to a lovely collection of memorable characters and scenes of glorious places that illustrate the boys' devotion to their sport and their hero.

Jacob Lawrence and Gwendolyn Knight Lawrence. Frida Kahlo and Diego Rivera. Georgia O'Keefe and Alfred Stieglitz. Precious little is more powerful than the act of making art for or from the love of someone. Whether it is romantic, familial, or platonic, love is an enduring and unconquerable inspiration for artists. It's the one emotion that overrides everything; whether it comes wrapped in joy, anguish, or sorrow. The recesses of love can seem infinite, and its artistic expression has the capacity to transcend mediums, moving mountains and valleys.

IF ALL ELSE FAILS

The What If

Maribel Vasquez's *Entre Mamushkas*

The "What If" is a very simple, economical brainstorming tool for when you begin to feel stuck. You begin with something ordinary, and you start to play a game of wonder with yourself.

I might recall something that happened to me long ago, but when I begin to reach into my imagination through this tool of the "what if," I can explore other possible scenarios. "What if" I didn't go to school that day? "What if" my dog ran away? "What if" my father had never left? The emphasis departs from the reality of what happened and pursues a new, imagined reality.

Maribel Vasquez's dreamy, fantastical *Entre Mamushkas* applies the very simple premise of a "what if" to nesting dolls without arms by making a doll with arms. Her arms also come to metaphorically represent her desire to become more than a mother, to be different, to fly.

These are great jumping off points for a story that may feel old and overused, but has potential for interesting reexamination under a new light. You can use "what if" to stay grounded in a current reality while considering new or alternative storylines, or you can use it to abandon your current reality completely in favor of a new one. For example, "what if" gravity didn't exist? "What if" no one had vocal cords? "What if" water was the most prized resource? The "what ifs" in sci-fi, fantasy, and speculative fiction are limitless. Even in high drama, the "what if" will stimulate new directions and possibilities.

Opposites, Contrasts, and Contradictions

Nikyatu Jusu's *Suicide by Sunlight*

When advising my students on their stories, I employ various tools and exercises to adopt their perspective and enter their heart's mind, attempting to eliminate my biases in the process. While I do so to ensure that my feedback is helpful and productive, I occasionally encounter instances where it only succeeds in discouraging them. In such cases, I tell them to do the exact opposite of what I've said—discard everything and explore a contrasting direction. I've witnessed remarkable breakthroughs emerge as a result of this approach. Far from a new idea, iterations of this advice, such as the "opposites tool" in Judith Weston's 25th Anniversary *Directing Actors*, have been used by many artists and teachers. Its effectiveness lies in breaking away from preconceived notions and exploring unfamiliar territories.

Opposites and contrasting ideas can lead to exciting contradictions—a very human aspect of life. Take Steven Spielberg's *Jaws*, for instance; which features a sheriff who lives in a seaside town but is terrified of water. In a similar vein, Nikyatu Jusu's *Suicide by Sunlight* opens with a vampire whom we learn is a nurse and mother—caring, compassionate, and beloved by her patients, all of which challenge the conventions of vampirism. This contradiction offers immediate intrigue. Contradictions in thoughts or beliefs add emotional color to stories. Finding contradictions hidden in our hypocrisy, feeling differently about something when it doesn't apply to us, can also be a powerful storytelling tool.

Your Best Guess

When faced with these questions, students often say, "I don't know," to which I reply, "OK, but what's your best guess?" This liberates them from the pressure of being right or wrong. Conjecture in creativity can be a very powerful tool, as a best guess doesn't carry the weight of an assertion, claim, or an intended fact. Sometimes, we need permission to express our thoughts, even if they may be incorrect or unpopular. In these situations, "your best guess" is a fantastic tool that opens the horizon of what may be possible.

The other thing I love about "your best guess" is that sometimes it aligns with your intuition—and, many times, it turns out to be correct! A friend once shared a fascinating story. She crafted a script based purely on her imagination, only to discover through research that the ideas were all true! The place she had envisioned actually existed. What does this reveal about the untapped knowledge within our intuitions and subconscious? I suggest paying attention to our innermost thoughts and perhaps not taking them for granted.

CONCEPTION: THE ORIGINAL IDEA

Shola Amoo's *Dear Mr. Shakespeare*

We are all diamonds in the rough when we start out, yet to find form—this only comes with time. I encourage you to think about your idea this way. It may not seem like much initially, but consider it like a snowflake: irreplaceable, delicate, and ethereal. As it takes on additional layers, it will grow into something amazingly robust and beautiful.

Shola Amoo's *Dear Mr. Shakespeare* takes a simple approach to questioning Othello, simultaneously provoking, challenging, and urging us to examine race in this classical Western treasure.

So, once you've done all this work, how do you recognize the original idea? It's simple, and once you find it, it will be clear, even if you can't yet articulate it as a story. However, this idea will have meaning to you. It will be personal to you. It will be irreplaceable, like you.

PRACTICE AND PLAY

1. Write a one-page story from your childhood. Write the lesson you took away from it. Then, write a one-page script based on a scene from this memory with no dialogue in standard screenwriting format.

2. Write your three favorite colors and choose one. Draw anything you can remember from your life that represents that color to you. Don't worry about how it looks or how good the drawing is. Just fill the entire page. Then pick one of the objects and tell a story about the color's relationship to the object. What matters is capturing what the color means to you.

3. Write an emotional logline using these three templates below: I want to share ___ [a feeling], I want to share a story about ___ [a character and a feeling], I want to share a story about ___ [a character] who seeks to feel ___ [a feeling] and discovers ___ [a different feeling].

4. Research fables or folktales from your family's ethnic or cultural background. Find a fable that has a lesson that you disagree with in some way. Conceive a retelling of this story from a new modern perspective aligned with your own beliefs.

5. Approach a family member and ask them about a family object that has been passed down through generations. These sometimes surprisingly ordinary objects are examples of totems. Write about this object as if it were a person. What story does this totem reveal about your family history?

6. Consider a superstition within your family and conceive an idea imagining the worst possible outcome if this superstition came true. Explore how your family would react. (This is a version of a "what if.")

7. Make a personal story timeline across 1, 5, or 15 years. Draw the line and on it, add notches on the timeline for turning points in your life around either: love, family, home, career, or identity—choose only one. Examine the big turning points and write a half page around one of the bigger notches.

8. Make a personal wish for something that has deep meaning for you. Write a one-page story about your life as if you already had it, lost it, and found it again.

9. Think of a favorite hobby or quirk. Write a one-page summary of a story if that hobby or quirk somehow led you to a location you've wanted to explore.

10. Draw a scene from a recurring dream you've had. Try to remember spaces, objects, and colors. Pay attention to shadow and light. Conceive an idea around you (or the character in the dream) moving toward or away from the light or shadow and why.

11. Take out or look up a favorite game from your younger self. "What if" you lived in this game and couldn't find your way out. What would you do? Write that as three paragraphs.

12. Find a favorite isolated spot in your home or neighborhood. Using a camera, make an inquiry of this subject by taking ten pictures of it from different angles and perspectives. What details captured in these images prompt questions that you wish to explore further? Write ten exploratory questions about this space to which you don't automatically know the answer.

STORYING CHARACTER:
EMOTIONAL BUILDING BLOCKS AND ESCAPES

The Character
—One of the persons of a drama or novel

WHAT'S YOUR STORY?

The main character in your story is guided by principles, perspectives, and attitudes. This character will make decisions, take action, and move towards a variety of goals every second of every minute. They will make mistakes, experience disappointment, and wrestle with challenges. They will encounter love, triumph, and admiration at different turns and fear, anger, and failure at others. This character might tend to resist change, as many of us do, but in some circumstances will be forced to make uncomfortable decisions that may make their lives better or worse. At the very least, it will alter their life in some big or small way. This is life. Every character lives at the center of their own story.

You are the main character in your story.

As human beings, we are truly complex and, in some ways, perhaps unexplainable. There's a lot that goes into what makes us who we are. To try to translate this to the page is no simple task, and yet, we find artists of all backgrounds and crafts who choose to put some version of themselves out into the world. I loved how, in Amanda Palmer's memoir, *The Art of Asking*, she simplified the process of the artist down to three simple actions: think, make, share. Artists love to share themselves, and more so, they love to share their discoveries. Have you considered that, like any character you may create, you are a discovery?

Who Are You Really?

So, what makes you, you? Some might seek answers through science; others through spirituality, and some through deep introspection. Are you the sum of your feelings, appearance, or thoughts and actions? These questions start to deconstruct the myriad aspects that distinguish who we are. However, the conundrum we face as writers is how to express a fully developed character on the page. For new writers, it is easy to get swept up in the process of building characters through lists: lists of this and that, of physical and mental traits, of favorite objects and colors, of hobbies and pastimes. This is not wrong, but it is incomplete. Often, in this list-making reverie, characteristics are attributed within a vacuum. Being cheerful, sardonic, or selfish means very little on the page when we do not get to witness these traits in action. We must not forget that like real humans, story characters are organisms—"complex structures of *interdependent* and subordinate elements whose relations and properties are largely determined by their function in the whole." Like human beings, characters are constructed through relationships.

THE RELATIONSHIPS OF CHARACTERS

We have never been alone; we exist within systems that precede our arrival. This phenomenon occurs on a cellular level within our physical body and resonates throughout the larger world via society, community, and government. In our writing, this system is called a story, and it encompasses the events and relationships that help develop characters over time. Your characters' relationships shape them as they grow and develop. We observe this in our own ability to adapt, evolve, and change. The interactions we have with other organisms sculpt how we think, what we know, and ultimately, what we do. However, these relationships only begin to scratch the surface of what it means to create a character. Although it might not seem apparent at first, we also have relationships with other organized systems. We have relationships with things.

Thinking Out of the Box

In my classes, one of my favorite projects to assign is the "no-dialogue script." I've been filled with wonder when I watch the requirements of the assignment take root. Many are frustrated by the challenge. Some take it in stride. Others try to find a way around it by using text messages and long letters. A small handful of students will choose to think out of the box, telling unexpected and marvelous stories by exploring unspoken relationships with inanimate objects or places.

We all have relationships with objects, though they might not be immediately apparent. Whether it's a favorite dress, a lucky basketball, or a prized boat or car, we establish connections with inanimate items. When we apply care and attention to these objects, we decide how we want to relate to them. Some of us extend these relationships to technology by speaking to our computers, phones, or GPS devices. Now, technology validates our need for connection by responding in turn. Hi Siri and Alexa!

We also have relationships with less obvious things, like places. If you attend church religiously, have a ritual to go swimming in Lake Erie, or keep up your child's bedroom long after they've moved away from home, you have a special relationship with a place. You associate certain meanings, resonance, and feelings with this space. This is how you've connected to it. These connections create stories.

Creating Connection

Is this novel? Not at all. For artists, constructing connections to people, places, and things is often inherent to the craft. Actors often form connections to props with personal meaning to the character. Painters require favorite brushes, select canvases, and particular mediums to execute their expression. Film director Guillermo Del Toro often builds his sets in spaces that are geographically and historically significant to the story[1]; linking the story to its setting. Characters frequently have relationships to clothing, dolls, or even robots. Some people believe that inanimate objects harbor

---

[1] Pans Labyrinth, a film set during the year 1944, five years after the end of the Spanish Civil War filmed some of its locations in the city of Belchite, where there are ruins from the actual Spanish Civil War.

spirits based on certain events associated with them. Whether true or just superstition, their resulting behavior around these objects creates a relationship and reveals a story.

The Systems of Story

As children, we are taught many things about stories. Yet, the most significant part of the storytelling process is not learned via instruction, but rather, through intuition. That part is the connection. By simply telling a story or sharing a film, we are spontaneously generating connection—something we all seek. This is what these aforementioned systems of life have taught us. As characters in our own stories, we continue to form pathways between the new and the old. We constantly build connections between what we have, what we don't have, and what we want. We are building a system of our own personal story, and that system is defined through relationships.

RELATIONSHIPS MAKE STORIES

You cannot have drama, conflict, or resolution without relationships. The fundamental piece of every story is the tapestry of relationships it unveils, setting in motion the journey that unfolds. Whether in film, fiction, or fable, as the writer, you bring together a network of interactions to reveal some portion of a character's history, illuminating the character's evolution through experiences, conflicts, and resolutions. As characters in our own stories, we continuously seek ways to relate to other people, places, and things, along with experiences, thoughts, and realities. These relationships remind us that we are alive. They remind us of how we came to be and how to understand our place in the larger world. So, when you start to break down how to construct a character, you want to begin by considering that character's relationship to many of these entities. One way to go about this is by doing what I call "storying character."

STORYING CHARACTER

I had a college roommate who became an enduring friend. Despite our different backgrounds and appearances, we grew very close, often playing games that, in this era, might be labeled as cosplay. In our cosplay, she was the villain, and I, the hero—the irony lying in her smaller stature. No one would ever believe her capable of any villainy. During these sessions, she would toss me around with her eyes, flinging me about the room and enacting all sorts of treachery that none of our friends could witness, and I could never prove. One day, she bought me a children's book as a gift, as we both loved children's stories. Inside, she wrote, "from your evil roommate." When I received this book, I stashed it in our room, declaring that I finally had proof of her wickedness. Soon after, she hijacked the book and scribbled hearts over her confession, foiling my clever plot. To this day, I still have that book.

What have you learned about my roommate?

In the telling of this story, you've learned a lot about her. She was creative, silly, fun, youthful, cunning, generous, and caring. You've also discovered her love for children's stories. She was smart, intelligent, resourceful, and lived in a community where she was loved, surrounded by friends. You know her general age and her general size. You know that she was decisive, active, and thoughtful in her choices. Through this anecdote, you gained insights into our relationship, our connection to the book, and our shared personal history. This is "storying character."

In revisiting this story, the question arises: How could I build a story from objects, places, or personality descriptions? I could start with the children's book and construct a story around it or any associated memories. I could start with life in a college dorm, and search for a specific experience there. If I described the character as mischievous, I would want to find and erect a story that allows us to see how the character is mischievous through an example, and not just an explanation. The same principle applies to playful, imaginative, and silly characteristics.

Understanding a character goes beyond viewing them as a list of traits and attributes. While many different character-building templates exist (explored below), the issue lies in how to *apply* the list. We are not lists, but constellations of relationships. For every attribute you assign a character, there should be some kind of story—some basis, some grounding—for it to exist. The list is useless in isolation; it must be organized into some sort of body that consists of cause, effect or action, and reaction. Lists do not make characters feel real—stories about characters do.

A character is a part of a system, encompassing who they are in the context of their background, history, environment, ability, perspective, physiology, desires, flaws, psychology, and so much more. Build this system in a consistent way, transforms this character from a mere construct into an individual with decisions, determination, and dimension. When the system works, the items on the list feel connected, and we start to release our doubts about whether this person could actually exist. We accept that the character feels real.

WRITING EMOTION FOR VISUAL PERFORMANCE

Novice script writers often come to a screenplay with a background in fiction or short stories, which is helpful in many ways. While fiction incorporates many storytelling fundamentals, it also allows greater flexibility for the story to unfold in the reader's mind. When we write fiction, we have a license to tell the story in various ways, using techniques like diaries, journals, omniscient or third-person narration, or inner monologues. In fiction, conveying a character's thoughts, providing insights, and explanations are permissible. However, in a script, many of these tools are unavailable because it must show, not tell, how a character feels.

A script is written to be performed.

In many ways, the script acts as an intermediary step in completing the film because we aim for the reader to envision the story, anticipating its ascension to the screen. When I meet with my students, we discuss how they can construct characters on the page through relationships and behavior.

Show and Tell

One of the most important aspects of constructing a character in a screenplay is understanding that characters on the page are recognized through drama, struggle, and effort. Conflict is created through what appears on the screen—what we "show" the audience. This is behavior.

When I was young, I knew a couple who were initially close friends. One day, the boy asked the girl out on a date, and they began dating. After dating for a while, they shared confessions about their very first date. The boy told the girl that he thought it was going very badly. He only realized the date had gone well after she hugged him. The hug was very long, and she didn't let go. That marked the beginning of them falling in love.

I find that what many new writers often struggle with most is creating stories through behavior instead of just "telling" us. Behavior is how we express feelings in our daily lives. Someone holding a door open for us, someone spending their last dollar on their child's holiday gift, someone gifting a friend a ticket for a long-needed vacation—these actions tell us how a person feels, not through what they say, but what they do.

Actions mean more than words

In a screenplay, as often in life, actions can speak more than words. Many of us have heard the term "lip service," when someone tells you they support you, but there is little evidence of any real action behind it. Many of us are guilty of lip service from time to time—when we intend to do something, but we haven't done it. . . yet. The lack of action speaks volumes, even more so in a film.

Our conduct towards a person can suggest a lot as well. Have you ever watched a person walk away from you while you were speaking? Little things can matter. A friend of mine shared with me how much the little things would matter to her in a relationship—whether someone pours her water before their own, offers to share food on their plate, or attends a party separately or as a couple. There are stories behind these behaviors that we absolutely want to investigate to learn more! Applying conduct can tell us not only about a character but also how one character might feel toward another. We can learn about attitudes, viewpoints, and values through how a character conducts themselves in different situations.

Gestures, quirks, and habits are also wonderful behaviors to consider for your character. A gesture or a look can convey more, as a replacement for a repetitive or obvious line of dialogue. When we want to convey that someone is nervous, we can instead think of the idiosyncratic behavior that will show us their nervousness—whether it's drinking huge gulps of alcohol, sewing yarn for jump ropes, or tearing a piece of paper to shreds. We all have these distinct behaviors that help us to get through both difficult and fun times.

Consider how to make that shift. Instead of telling us how a character feels in a scene, show us. For instance, instead of stating that they feel angry, do they hit the table? If they are sad, do they curl up into a ball in bed? If they are happy, do they jump up and down for joy? These are cliché examples not attached to any specific character, but they can help you transition from telling to showing.

Reflecting on what a character can do to express their feelings marks a significant shift from thinking in terms of fiction to screenplays. The best screenwriters achieve this effortlessly with two tools: a rich and vibrant vocabulary of verbs (which we will discuss in the Language chapter), and an active, motivated process that makes your character feel specific, consistent, and distinct.

TOOLS & TECHNIQUES: WHAT MAKES A CHARACTER FEEL REAL?

Some of the immediate issues that arise when sketching out a character often revolve around establishing the character's believability on paper. When watching a movie, we often take for granted how difficult this process is. How do we execute the creation of a person on the page who then is brought to life by an actor? Great actors make it look easy, and some infuse much of themselves to inhabit the character. However, with less experienced actors, we may detect inconsistencies that make us doubt who this character is. We may not immediately diagnose it as a character fault, but it contributes to the whole experience of the movie. In both cases, the actor is dependent on the script, and the essence of the character must be well expressed on these pages. This is where the writer's job becomes urgent.

Authentically capturing the essence of a human being on paper is a marvel. I slowly get a sense of my characters when I can distinguish what I, as the writer, want them to do from what they would actually do. You begin to get a sense of them in their own right. Other readers of the work will help you see this as well if they tell you things like, "I don't believe the character would do that," or if they laugh at a part that isn't meant to be funny. In one of my student assignments, someone wrote that hearing that a character should be like a real person was a revelation. This is precisely what you aim to do in writing a character.

This process takes time to develop. Spending only a few hours on developing a character may result in your character seeming incomplete or indistinct. This is why many writers invest a significant amount of time with their characters, either on the page or in their minds. If it's a real person, that may happen in deep research, or it could happen in books, if the character was created there, before being transferred to the screen. One writer I asked told me he thinks about characters everywhere he goes; they just accompany him. I could relate to that because sometimes I have characters who haunt me in my dreams. If developing a character in this way feels elusive, here is a different tact: avoiding pitfalls. Commonly, character issues revolve around three areas: distinction, consistency, and specificity.

THE CHARACTER'S REALITY RULES

Maria Brendle's *Ala Kachuu—Take and Run*

Characters that feel real are those we perceive as distinct, consistent, and specific in their behaviors and actions. We can consider these actions and behaviors as rules that we set. Breaking a character rule risks pulling the reader or viewer out of the reality we've built the character, disrupting their suspension of belief. Use these rules not as rigid directives but as guideposts for establishing a solid foundation for your character and assessing how "real" they feel.

Take a trait and make it a reality for your character. Let's use the trait of *persistence* from the main character in Maria Brendle's *Take and Run*.

Sezim is distinctively persistent.

Distinct

A character distinct in both appearance and action stands apart from other characters.

This distinction on the screen is easy to identify because we see a person's face and body. However, the writer must evidence this distinction by embodying the character on the page; names, physical description, and costuming help. Distinction can also be communicated through dialogue. Nevertheless, character recognition primarily hinges on actions. This means that the character is not doing what everyone else is doing; the character should not mimic common or general behaviors. If this happens, the reader will start to question the reality of the character. When your story begins, you must establish who this character is by defining the differences among the characters.

In *Take and Run*, we meet nineteen-year-old Sezim, her sister, her parents, the members of her village. In an effective opening scene that could easily be brushed off as irrelevant, Brendle shows us that Sezim can run. It is also quickly established that Sezim wants to go to school despite her parents' hesitations and objections. What her parents desire is for her to marry and live a similar life to theirs in their village. If we want to describe Sezim as persistent, we must incorporate that into behavior. We see that Sezim is persistent in the way that she argues with her mother about school, talks with her friends about school, and takes a test and follows up about school. We know this persistence is unique to her because we don't see any other characters doing this.

Human beings rarely do anything precisely the same way as any other person; therefore, mimicking someone intrigues us. Despite our similarities and commonalities, none of us are identical. Our voices, fingerprints, and DNA define us, just as your characters' will define them.

Sezim is consistently persistent.

Consistent

A character who feels consistent is one whose actions and behaviors align with the information provided.

If a character is angry, we expect their actions to differ from when they are happy. Their actions need to make sense to us, although the character can still do things that contradict or surprise us, as long as they are consistent with the established information. For example, if a character is initially afraid to speak up, we can believe they will speak out later in the story if certain events prompt their transformation; this is called an arc. While growth for the character is important, it must align with the reality of behaviors you've provided.

As we follow Sezim, we see that she is consistent in her pursuit of her dream of going to school, even in the face of obstacles. Even when she is captured and forced to marry a young man from her village, Sezim continues to pursue her desire. Furthermore, Brendle establishes that Sezim deeply loves her younger sister, leading her to protect her sibling while persisting in her goal. Sezim's persistence remains evident throughout, reflecting her character from the beginning.

Sezim is specifically persistent.
Specific

Specific refers to a character who does things that are related to a particular person, situation, or circumstance.

Another way to think of specific, and how it is different from how I am describing distinct, is that it means the character feels grounded in a specific reality. To go one step further, it may mean that a character expresses happiness not only through smiling or laughing, which are generic behaviors of happiness, but by taking 3 scoops of frozen yogurt when we know they normally only eat one. That makes this occurrence of happiness specific to them. When we get a sense that a character is acting in a way that doesn't appear specific to them, we begin to question if they are real enough for us to keep following.

Finally, we get to see that Sezim is specific in how she demonstrates persistence. This is about considering the character's background and where the film takes place. How do we see Sezim specifically pursue her goal of going to school within the world that has been presented to us? We watch Sezim use the tools that Brendle has established in the film: that she can drive a car, that she can run away, that she approaches friends who want to help her.

In this film, we see a good example of strong writing that pays off through the character details that it establishes at the beginning of the story. The title, in this case, is a great example of setting up the story before we even watch one second of the film.

The Character Star Map

Jia Zhangke's *Cry Me A River*

One of my favorite character development tools is the "character star map." As mentioned above, a character can be developed through relationships and behavior. Realizing that, you can surround your character with a supporting cast that will help to establish the character's value and belief systems. Think about whom we will meet in the short: the parent, the lover, the nemesis, or the best friend. Like a star, your character is a part of an existing system in the universe of your story. Observing your character's interactions with others is a valuable method for character development, particularly if the characters hold opposing beliefs and you craft scenarios where those beliefs will be challenged.

Jia Zhangke's *Cry Me A River* introduces us to an ensemble cast of old school friends who return to honor their retiring teacher. What's effective about the short is that we learn about the characters and their beliefs and desires through their behaviors and conversational histories, but all in indirect ways. A scene when we watch two characters engage over the washing of hair is an intimate moment that speaks volumes about their personalities and past relationship. Zhangke also delivers information through rich dialogue that always reveals, but never explains. Zhangke's film serves as a great candidate for a star map. By choosing one of these characters, you can start to examine their relationship to their peers and to their teacher.

THE TRIANGLE OF CHARACTER BONE STRUCTURE

Cauleen Smith's *The Changing Same*

Earlier, I shared some common methodologies for developing characters. Searching online for character bios, templates, or construction methods will yield a plethora of specific strategies. Some writers like to create charts and diagrams; others apply interviewing techniques and experiential sketches, such as "here's a scenario; what would your character do?" In most cases, you will find laundry list prompts of character descriptions (as mentioned above). None of these are wrong or right, as long as they help you develop a character that feels real. You should seek whatever form helps you, as a writer, develop your character enough to feel like a human being on the page.

As a teacher of screenwriting, I like to use Lajos Egri's character bone structure from *The Art of Dramatic Writing* due to its approach to character dimensionality. Egri examines character through three categories: physicality, sociology, and psychology. However, there are other character templates that expand upon this concept by incorporating additional columns, such as growth, traits, or communication. Some templates further break down Egri's structure into more digestible sections, including physiology, demographics, physical appearance, and history. Whichever method you choose, I find this exercise effective only when done thoughtfully and in ways that allow these categories to interconnect and influence each other.

What I really love about Egri's bone structure is its foundation in social and natural sciences. It acknowledges the influence of both an individual's physical attributes (nature) and their environment (nurture) on the development of their psychology—how they think. This concept resonates with my background in developmental psychology, which I studied before embarking on a career in storytelling.

Ahead of its time, Cauleen Smith's science fiction noir *The Changing Same* offers immediate context for the characters we meet in the film: two aliens, one of whom desperately wants to go home, while both are stranded on our planet. Smith expertly uses a radio transmission to deliver the *psychology* of the male character, including his fears, wants, needs, and desires over a black screen prologue. We learn about the other alien through her conversations with her AI, which shares information about their mission, Earth, and the human "incubators." The devices that occupy the aliens' skin and body further contribute to the development of their *physiology*. The location the characters inhabit, along with how they relate to each other, provide us with insight into their current environment. We also learn about them through their skills and occupations—their *sociology*.

It's also important to note that you will likely not use MOST of what you write in a bone structure to discover these things about your character. The writing process is iterative and not cumulative. It's not about how much you write, it's about moving deeper into the process of a character or story as you continue writing. I was always told by my teachers that 90% of what you write will never make it into a screenplay. But the 10% that does is gold! More on this in the Revision chapter!

These prompts, while not unique, will encourage you to find the detailed and specific aspects of your character's life, granting you access to the richest parts of your character's existence. Even if you are working with a real-life character, the bone structure can aid you in fleshing out narratives around them. While many of these questions feel obvious, I want to highlight a few that I think are very telling.

Determining Defects, Heredity, and Posture

Defects
Adolf El Assal's *Full Memory*

Defects, whether physical or mental, hold a fascinating level of specificity, not because *you* think they are defects, but because your character does. What distinguishes a defect from a birthmark? Consider the birthmarks of different relatives: one has a mole, another has some discoloration, and yet another has a tuft of red hair. From your character's perspective, are these traits that make them pretty or ugly? Does the character believe that they help or hurt them? Is the classification of "defect" assigned by the character or others? When there exists contrast in perception, the narrative becomes immensely compelling. Imagine a story where a character comes to realize that the very mole they despised is what initially captivated their lover.

Adolf El Assal's *Full Memory* takes an intriguing approach to scars from both a physical and mental perspective. We follow Zaid, a young man, as he awaits the arrival of his visiting brother. Playing with a looping structure narrative to build tension and anticipation, we watch Zaid's memory slowly reveal more and more contextual information that recalls a dark truth about his brother.

Some writers might approach this situation in a concrete way, searching for a literal physical impairment, deformity, or disability. While this tactic is valid, I've observed students leap to assigning impairments without reflecting on the sensitivity of that choice. It's crucial to deeply consider any disability, taking into account the values of the specific community it represents. Simply endowing characters with random impairments or traits is not only disrespectful but also socially irresponsible, and will lead to gaps in the credibility of the character. If you lack comprehension of what it's like to be blind, can you truly replicate it in a story? However, through personal experience, research, and personal investment within that community, you can still learn a great deal. Remember, it always takes more time and personal investment to authentically tell stories that differ from your own.

Heredity
Emir Kusturica's *Guernica*

Emir Kusturica's early short, *Guernica*, solemnly examines heredity through its reflection on a family during the Holocaust. In this short, a professor's son questions the relevance of noses, exploring heredity and its meaning as the family struggles to explain to their young son a situation they don't fully comprehend yet. The film is striking in how it considers inheritance as both a physical trait and an idea.

Inheritances, whether they be physical, mental, psychological, or even metaphysical can be things we embrace or run away from. We consider our genes, DNA, and cell formatting, but what about our habits, mannerisms, and colloquialisms? Heredity doesn't need to be limiting, nor should it be seen as good or bad, except through the character's eyes. Inheritances have influence and tell us more about the character. What story could you come up with about a trichotillomania disorder that has traveled through four generations?

Posture
David Constantin's *Made in Mauritius*

In David Constantin's simple but humorous *Made in Mauritius*, two endearing and quirky characters, retired farmer Bissoon and shopkeeper Ah-Yan, take different stances on the advantages of advancing technology. This becomes evident when Bissoon's older radio model breaks down, prompting him to search for a battery to keep it going. What stands out to me while watching the two characters interact is the distinction in their postures. It is not their age difference but rather their respective postures, along with how the camera captures them, that tells us who is going to win the conversation.

I grew up with a tall friend whose posture often made her appear shorter than she actually was. Eventually, I realized that when she felt less confident, she hunched her shoulders and appeared shorter, but when she felt cheerful, she suddenly became taller. Her posture was a reflection of her self-confidence and self-esteem.

Posture is one example of how body language can define a character. Consider posture in different situations: are arms open or closed, legs crossed or relaxed, turned toward or away from the person speaking? Watching how people carry themselves when they walk into a room can say so much about their character, upbringing, and approach to the world.

Whether shoulders are held back, hunched forward, or lopsided can provide valuable insights into a character. How might a story illustrate the perceptions of others toward this character's posture? And what potential impact could those perceptions have?

POKE AT THE POLITICAL

Cheryl Dunye's *Janine*

My students often think of politics the way it is defined in Western governments, but politics are largely based around individual community. Depending on the character, this will manifest differently. Instead of approaching politics from your own standpoint, try to step back and visit politics from your character's point of view. Consider characters that might be a towel, a cat, or a tree.

One of my favorite answers to this challenge involved a student who understood that politics are defined by who we are, when we are, and where we are. She answered this question for her character, a child, by considering what government might look like to a child. Her decisions were made according to the center of her universe—her teddy bear.

Cheryl Dunye's *Janine* is a deeply personal and profoundly honest retelling of her high school relationship with another young girl, Janine. This short is notable for exploring how a young teen navigates their own sexuality amidst the influence of familial and peer expectations. Politics are never easy but they are present in almost every social group. Especially in high school.

Choose the politics that exist for your character.

Politics are situational and societal; they revolve around time periods, movements, and governments. For an eight-year-old, politics might revolve around who gets to the top of the monkey bars; for an animated cactus, it might be the different political factions in a desert; for a teen, school functions as a government, with different social cliques as political parties. Even opting to stay out of a group's decision can be a political statement, but you should know why your character is making that choice. Does this character reject conformity? Are they an individualist?

Explore your character's politics and determine where they stand—perhaps it's in the middle! Then, create an event or circumstance that challenges your character's political stance and makes them shift from one side to another.

Motivating Movement, and Forwarding Action

Terence Nance's *You and I and You*

Most of us are caught in soap opera stories of our day-to-day lives: commuting to work, exchanging sentences with friends and colleagues, making dinner, etc. . . . This routine reflects the monotony of everyday American working life. It can be boring and listless. However, stories cannot afford to be boring, or viewers will check out. Therefore, films often eschew mundane moments in favor of action. One way that they do this is by creating forced movement for the character.

Occasionally, a student will write a character that is *static*. They do not "move forward" in the story. An old screenwriting teacher used to say that often. As a student, I didn't really understand what that meant. He was saying that the character is inactive.

An inactive character is a character that is passive and *reactive*. They are not making choices or decisions that are forwarding the plot. An inactive character will commonly appear emotional but not actionable. We will understand how they feel through description instead of movement.

This character is stuck.

We have all been stuck at times. Stuck between a rock and hard place—faced with two horribly awful decisions, unable to choice. In life, we may avoid making these decisions for a very long time. In a short film, we truncate the inactivity that exists in real life to get to the highest points of drama. In a short, the character must move in one direction or another—they cannot stay still. We make the character move by creating situations that push them forward. One way to do this is by creating motivation.

Motivations can be depicted many ways. A character might be driven by love, hurt, fear, pride, or loyalty, to name a few. Characters are often stirred by both tragedy, reflected in the abundance of films about death and dying, and love, evident in the prevalence of dramas about intimate relationships. Manipulating your character through scenarios of loss is another common tool to creating actionable character.

Dance film, an experimental genre of filmmaking that has emerged as its own category in recent decades, is a great format for considering movement and motivation. The family we meet in Terence Nance's *You and I and You* wander through a sinister wonderland, followed by mystical figures that summon, and eventually take, the child of the couple to another place. Their movement, guided solely by music, serves as a powerful reminder that observing how people move is a great way to understand character. Through the pursuit of the mystical creatures and the couple's attempts to evade them, we emotionally grasp the desires, feelings, and priorities of the characters.

Characters are moved by their circumstances only after we understand who the character is. We must discover what they fear, value, desire, and cannot afford to lose. If you don't know the answers to these questions, then you cannot motivate them. When a character feels stuck in your story, ask; what is their motivation? If they have none, it's your task to create one. Several tools can be used to create motivation. One of them is stakes.

THE SLIDING SCALE OF STAKES

Janicza Bravo's *Pauline Alone*

A stake is a cost. It is something your character has the potential to lose. We all have things that are more and less important to us. Understanding how to leverage stakes within a story is an important tool for managing character motivations.

Janicza Bravo's *Pauline Alone* is striking for its depiction of a character for whom the stakes of being alone are so high that she breaks rules of conduct and ignore social cues, often at her own peril. She is a memorable character because the character's fear of being alone is so urgent that she behaves in ways we don't expect—like chasing strangers simply to form a connection.

Another way we can play with stakes is by building them around objects that we characterize. We can look at elements of access, resources, and circumstance to develop relationship to an object. Let's say that your character has a pen.

Who cares about a pen?

Right now, a stock market broker making hundreds of thousands of dollars a year will not care about a ten-cent pen. It has little value to her because she earns much more than the monetary value of that pen. When considering its loss, it carries a small stake. But stakes can be adjusted through changing value. Value can be determined in a number of ways: in its relationship to others, to itself, and to the character.

The pen means nothing as a "pen." But what if I say the pen is the last of its kind? It can never be replicated or replaced, the materials that were used to make it are gone. I have affected the availability of access to another pen exactly like this one. Suddenly the value of this pen has been altered because of its relationship to other pens.

This pen is rare.

If I say this pen is made of gold and diamonds, I have altered the value of the pen by defining the precious materials that were used to construct the pen. I have determined the resources needed to make this pen—making it more valuable.

This pen is precious.

If I say this pen was given to me by my grandmother on the day she passed away and she told me it was the pen that she used when she wrote her Pulitzer Prize-winning poem, I have further altered the pen's value through its relationship to someone I care about. In this case, I have affected the circumstances surrounding the pen.

This pen is meaningful.

By changing the value of the pen, I have established the description, history, and background of the pen, and in turn, created a relationship that increases the stakes around the pen. When the stakes were low, the value of the pen was also low. However, as I increased the value of the pen, the stakes increased as well. We can now imagine that if this pen could potentially be taken or lost, this would cause the character to act.

I have characterized the pen.

Notice how, by changing the stakes, we have also given the pen more *life*. Although it is not living, we have begun to consider it like a character by assigning traits to it. This is important because it illustrates how animation works. We animate objects to create characters we know and love—by bringing them to life.

THE HIDDEN PLACES OF THE SUBCONSCIOUS

Bend or Break Morality?

Jennifer Phang's *Advantageous*

Every character has morals. They have standards they live by, like rules and laws, but morals are more important, because morals are deeply personal. More than directives like "wear your seat belt," morals establish what the character feels is right and wrong. Many characters will break rules. However, few characters break their moral code without significant ramifications and/or consequences.

The most difficult aspect of creating action around a moral code is establishing that code. Writers can present a moral code through behavior, which is more impactful than simply telling us through dialogue. Stakes are set around the moral, so bending or breaking it becomes something difficult or tense for the character. Stakes, rules, and values can create this moral tension. So can emotional wounds.

When a movie establishes that a character never kills dogs and then puts that character in a situation where they are pushed to kill a dog, we witness this moral tension. We also see it when we see characters in situations where they must choose between their values and death. Morality is something we are taught by society and by our families. It shapes what we accept and what we reject about ourselves and others.

After Jennifer Phang establishes a mother's morals in the science fiction fantasy *Advantageous*, she challenges this character by placing her in a position where she must choose between surrendering her visual self and providing for her daughter. We, along with the mother, are anguished in making this decision. We feel the great weight that is upon her. We feel empathy for her.

How Naked is Your Sex?

Jennifer Reeder's *A Million Miles Away*

Sex. Gender. Sexuality. These elements all establish your character's relationship to intimacy, pleasure, their body, and how they move through the world. Shorts can often be sexy while remaining sexless. Jennifer Reeder's *A Million Miles Away*, about a substitute teacher and her students, focuses on female sexuality in a novel way.

A character's sexual identity is an integral part of their humanity and relationship to adulthood. How a character has dealt with their body, such as sharing it or hiding it, means a lot. It's important to understand that sexuality is, in many ways, about vulnerability. As the writer, you want to have an understanding of these relationships.

Certainly, sexual identity can deal with intercourse. However, gratuitous sex scenes are not the answer. You can approach sexual identity in more creative ways than simply showing sexual activity. Keep in mind that we want to learn something about the character. A character that overindulges in sex, has no clue about their own sexuality, or pretends sex doesn't exist are all traits that say something about the character, but none of these require an NC-17 rated scene.

Try not to reduce your character's sexuality to whether they have sex. Instead, consider how their sexuality expresses itself in their everyday behaviors. How is it reflective of their morals and/or values? How is sex used in a character's life? Is it used at work? Is it simply for pleasure? Does it elicit shame or joy? Examine your character's connection to these elements as a way to reveal the nakedness of a character's soul.

RIPPING OFF THE BAND-AID: THE WOUND STORY

Spencer Susser's *Save Ralph*

Wounds are another great tool for developing character. We think of a wound as a kind of physical injury inflicted upon a person, a painful laceration, cut, or blow. Consider mental or emotional wounds. Emotional wounds are often used in feature films, television, and short content to provide background for the character's choices.

In a short film, we sometimes learn of a wound immediately. Other times, it is slowly revealed to us. Wounds never fully heal, especially deep ones. They leave scars that you will never forget. I found this to be an exciting metaphor for character development.

Spencer Susser's stop motion mockumentary commercial, made for the American Humane Society, takes us directly into the life of a rabbit who participates in horrifying animal tests for cosmetics. The physically wounded Ralph the Rabbit introduces us to his world, revealing deep emotional wounds. He bleakly recounts the harrowing stories about his parents and children that have resulted in his defeatist mentality. He has abandoned all hope of escaping his destiny of being a test subject. It is the wry satire that makes this commercial effective.

A character who may have been hurt in the past can be driven by situations to confront this wound. Consider abandonment. Every time your character confronts abandonment, they must choose to revisit or avoid it, creating movement in the process. This might appear as the character running away from any deep relationship because they believe that any long-term relationship might lead to them being hurt. Conversely, the character might be drawn to characters who are constantly leaving. They seek out abandonment because, although it is painful, it is familiar.

In life, we have many wounds. However, in a short film, we would typically only focus on one. I find this idea of the wound especially helpful when considering a series. A series asks you to think about your character over the long term. Like real people, they can grow and change or *arc* over time. In real life, it takes time to move past our wounds, wounds which actually never really go away. As scars, however, we can learn to manage them. That is a part of being human.

FEARS, FLAWS, AND FAILINGS

THE FIGHT WITH FEAR

David Sandberg's *Lights Out*

David Sandberg's proof of concept horror short (it's less than three minutes) introduces us to a woman who is haunted by a shadow in a doorway—a shadow that can only be seen only when the lights are out. Tight and clear in its focus, the short resurrects a fear of the dark that many of us have experienced at some point in our lives. *Lights Out* serves as a wonderful illustration of how fear can shape a story.

Fear is one of the most powerful tools for character building. It is consistently a strong motivator. Just watch any horror film and you'll witness that with glaring clarity. These films are filled with the kind of life and death chase that fuels the action, suspense, and thriller genres. This is fear that comes from external dangers. Stakes are high, and that breeds intense responses.

However, in dramas and comedies, we also will ask our characters to confront the internalized fears that will rise to the surface in tense situations. Those fears create conflict.

In everyday scenarios, we face fears of being disliked, rejected, or excluded. Fears that we may not be able to pay bills, protect loved ones, or find safety. Sometimes these fears are presented through coping mechanisms that make the fear present, but not immediately apparent. Other times, the fears are urgent and intense. Then there are those deep-seated fears that we carry for years: that we will never amount to anything, that we will never be loved, that we will never be enough. These are the fears that are created by our deepest wounds, and that you will uncover in a strong bone structure. These fears will motivate your character and drive the story.

What is your character's deepest fear?

Fears, like all elements of character, will shift with age, status, relationships, and personal growth. In our younger years, we may fear simply for ourselves. But as we grow into adulthood, our fears will grow beyond ourselves. We start to fear for those around us. When you surround a character with family, friends, and colleagues, you stretch the potential for more fear, responsibility, love, and concern. This will heighten the risk. The more you care, the greater potential there is for fear. This is why character relationships are so important.

Once you identify the fear for your character, you can use their fear, along with something they love, to create conflict, contention, and action. You can build a character who is ready to fight. Films are not often filled with characters who run away or simply do nothing (unless that is the beginning of a great arc!). Films are filled with characters who are compelled to act. Whether they win or lose, their struggle with fear is resonant, visceral, and familiar. We rarely forget our own fears, and in a short, this is what we can ask our characters to face.

In a short film, we often work with large emotional strokes when confronting external and internal fears, so that, with high enough stakes, a character may be moved to overcome them. This does not explain where fears originate. If you look deeply enough, you will find that external and internal fears (in your bone structures) are often linked to each other, and sometimes, to flaws and mistakes.

Goading Flaws

Charles Burnett's *The Horse*

The dexterity of Charles Burnett's direction is demonstrated in his early short, *The Horse*, where the flaws he reveals are not those of the main character, a young boy, but those of the supporting cast. A group of city men huddle on a porch in the middle of nowhere, afraid to undertake a task that they want the main character's father to accomplish. The grown men sit around all day, waiting for this boy's father to finish this terrible job. This ends up being the central drama of this short film that examines race, privilege, and class.

Writers love discovering flaws in characters because they lead to mistakes, and grand mistakes create drama.

It's important to learn your character's flaws, as they open up new realms of possibility for creating conflict, drama, and tension; the elements that make a story move. A flaw is a character trait that we view as a fault or as a weakness of character. The main issue you will encounter with flaws is their tendency to be too commonplace. Generic flaws might be chewing too loud, sobbing too much, or shaking a leg out of nervousness. These are flaws we have seen used in the past. They are flaws because they deviate from societal standards of acceptable behavior.

The best flaws are character flaws. These are specific flaws that are rooted in the particular construction of a character. The young student who can't stop whispering answers to the test out loud. The winning athlete who can't stop bragging about herself. The cat lover who can't stop collecting cats after his entire home is overrun, and even as he faces eviction because of them.

In these examples, flaws have not been deemed flaws all by themselves. They are traits that have transformed into flaws because they create problems for the character. We understand that a student whispering answers for a test out loud might create a problematic situation because we understand the social norm in school is to not share answers.

Because we know this background information, we can recognize that this trait is not helpful to the character, and we can reflect on the potential conflicts and drama that may result. A simple solution for the character would be to stop whispering, but when this trait is a flaw, that makes it difficult for them to do.

Some traits have both positive and negative connotations. While in one instance, the trait is a blessing, in another, it may be a curse. What's the difference between being confident and egotistical? A collector versus a hoarder? Being stubborn as opposed to being persistent? A good flaw will be recognizable within the context of the character and situation. Like many traits, perspective can affect how we view the positive and negative connotations of that trait. A flaw only really becomes a flaw when it is something that creates downfall for the character. Sometimes flaws can lead to mistakes.

MAKING GRAND MISTAKES

Jack Niedenthal and Suzanne Chutaro's *Zori*

One of the most important things that my directing teacher Judith Weston taught me is that, in the creative world, mistakes are where magical things can happen. While a "grand" mistake seems like an oxymoron, bad things for your character often lead to great story developments.

When mistakes happen in our lives, we tend to regard them, and ourselves, badly. Society looks down on these mistakes, especially if they cause injury or worse. Yet, even small mistakes have taken on this negative connotation, even when the results are not as deleterious. We've been taught that, when we make a mistake, we "should" have acted differently.

This is one way to look at mistakes. But here is another; life is full of mistakes. Mistakes help us learn about life. Sometimes, mistakes even make us better people.

The sweet and simple *Zori*, directed by Jack Niedenthal and Suzanne Chutaro, follows a young boy who is asked to complete his chores before going on an ice cream run. However, when his mother realizes that he has lost his sandal, called a *zori*, his mother chastises him, telling him he cannot return home until he finds it. While completing his chores, he learns a lesson that makes us, and his mother, smile.

In our short films, mistakes can help a character grow. Sometimes, I find that new writers will want to protect their characters from mistakes by having them make only good decisions. This results in boring, and more importantly, unrealistic characters. We all have failings and missed opportunities, and we've all done something we regret.

Allow your character to fail.

Sometimes writers only create small mistakes. This is also not enough, unless the small mistake snowballs into something larger. In a short film, we are compressing life to the most impactful moments, so mistakes don't have a lot of time to occur. Grand mistakes have big consequences *and* opportunities for big rewards. This is when we grow. Make that mistake count, and you will find an active character behind it.

PROPERTIES OF THE MIND AND BODY

Skills, Gifts, and Triumphs

Kathrin Steinbacher's *In Her Boots*
Skills and gifts are sometimes overlooked in the construction of character traits because many Western stories are fixated on the idea of struggle—conflict, conflict, and more conflict! Sometimes we get weighed down by thinking of traits and situations as obstacles, and we may forget how these attributes can also be advantages. It's a great reminder that characters, like us, have many dimensions.

In Kathrin Steinbacher's *In Her Boots,* we are taken on an animated odyssey of a grandmother who loves to hike. We learn so much about this character through her affection for her boots and the places they have traveled together.

We all have gifts!

At the end of each chapter in Pilar Alessandra's *Coffee Break Screenwriter,* she provides a series of exercises called Take Tens. One of my favorite Take Tens (found in the Character chapter) shows how to take a character's flaw and turn it into a skill! This is a great exercise because it points out how traits, attributes, and characteristics are not innately positive or negative. They become that way through how we use them!

In this superhero-filled era of moviemaking, we've gotten used to thinking about gifts as being "super," far-reaching, and rare. However, we all have gifts that we share in our relationships, gifts like kindness, love, and forgiveness. There are also gifts that are skills, exemplified by grandmothers who knit blankets, mechanics who fix cars, or doctors who save lives. These are skills: learned activities that can reveal to us not only who the character is, but what cards they have to play when the circumstances turn sour.

Playing the Skill Card

In a short, skills hold particular significance due to the limited timeframe. To portray a character confronting and resolving challenges within a condensed period, we frequently turn to the character and inquire, "What can she do?" Revisit that bone structure to look at opportunities where your character can show off their talents and their resources.

When the character faces their obstacles, particularly the most difficult one, having these skill cards to play becomes crucial to story development. Why? Simply put, because we need a narrative that showcases the potential for a character to triumph. These are stories about hope, and hope plays a huge role in our society. Hope is about feeling that we have the choice, opportunity, and ability to change a situation.

Many stories in the industry delve into societal issues that feel or appear hopeless, in an attempt to rally our action and attention. The short is a place for narratives that open our eyes and allow us to see the world's concerns. The commercial industry still largely focuses on escapism, which is rooted in hope. Many audiences are drawn to stories about hope: hope that the underdog will win, that justice will be served, or that the hurt will be healed. Whether these stories are true, they are the stories we want to believe. Endowing your character with a skill to affect these changes allows you to make room for this possibility, because it creates tension and suspense.

So, what kind of skills or gifts can you use? Some can be learned activities, while others can be traits or characteristics that the character knows how to wield, whether it be making someone feel important or sacrificing something for the greater good. These are gifts, and your character needs these to survive, just like a real person.

SCEPTERS AND SWORDS, DRESSES AND HATS

Agnes Varda's *Les 3 Boutons*

Another really great way to build character is through their relationship with props. Sure, some superheroes make it look easy by wielding any tools at their disposal. But for great characters, their tools are more than just a function, Spiderman and his webbing, Wonder Woman and her lasso, or

Shuri and her vibranium gauntlets. They reveal things about the character, Spiderman is a scientist, Wonder Woman stands for truth and justice, Shuri is an engineer.

This can also apply to characters in more realistic shorts where real-life people wield tools in their everyday life: the writer's pen, the garbage man's truck, or the crossing guard's sign. These can become intriguing tools when you don't allow them to become generic. When they become valuable, their loss can elicit action. In the same way, costumes and wardrobe also make wonderful dimension-building elements. The dress in Agnes Varda's *Les 3 Boutons* serves multiple purposes, telling us about the young woman who wears it and the principles she embraces every time a button falls.

Dialogue, Accent, and Idioms

Michael Keegan-Key and Jordan Peele's
Top Ten Key and Peele Sketches

Students often ask me about dialogue. I love to send them to some of the best television writers out there on the longest running shows (like the X-Files). Great dialogue will do three things for characters: it will reveal new information, convey intention, and distinguish who is speaking through their specific words, rhythm, and idiomatic language.

Short films, sparkling with brevity and reliant on cinematic language, tend to eschew the lengthy dialogue sequences common in feature films or TV episodes. However, comedic shorts often blend visual and verbal techniques to achieve a mix of absurdity and humor. Analyzing Key and Peele's top sketches can absolutely offer valuable insights.

When actors Jordan Peele (now a renowned director and producer) and Michael Keegan-Key step into character roles, they skillfully utilize not only costuming, hair, and makeup to establish distinctions between their characters but also linguistic differences. Pay attention to sentence length and structure, elevated or slang vocabulary, regional or class-related colloquialisms, and most importantly, intention.

These artists excel at examining intention, pacing, and word choice. Crucially, they understand how to engage in winning and losing. Intention is about the subtext, and great actors know how to apply subtext to the most mundane lines. Great writing allows them to deliver that subtext in an impactful manner.

Bryian Keith Montgomery's *Chickens*

At the other end of the spectrum is Bryian Keith Montgomery's *Chickens*, a social horror film that explores issues of law enforcement, justice, and race in the US. The film opens on two cops who have just shot a man in a diner, as the victim's friends scramble to figure out why the cops haven't reported it and won't allow anyone to leave. The language between the cops is heightened and exaggerated, and it becomes easily clear who is who. One of the cops launches into a vicious monologue that is hard to forget.

The cops' dialogue is easily distinguishable from that of the patrons because of word choice, sentence length, and intention. This is also a function of a power dynamic. While the two cops are portrayed as distinct from each other, this power dynamic helps to separate their dialogue from the patrons'. In this situation, the cops speak more; their intention is to protect themselves, and they employ derogatory and vulgar language to this end. The patrons speak less and cautiously; their goal is to leave the situation unharmed.

So, how do you bring this kind of detail to your characters? By listening. The best dialogue exercises are the simplest. Observe, record, and study how people talk in real life. What are the differences in intention, in rhythm, in pacing, and in word choice? Study the people close to you, strangers on the train or bus, and kids in the neighborhood. Listen actively and you will learn a lot.

In my early years, I wrote several stories based in other languages. I spent hours studying and practicing the rhythms of their foreign speech out loud so I could replicate it on the page in English. This taught me how to utilize accents, idioms, colloquialisms, and slang—all in service of articulating myself like a local. When I first arrived in Boston, I called the street Massachusetts Ave. and I was quickly corrected, "It's Mass Ave." These are things that can only be learned by being a part of the community.

When considering the use of accented or dialect language in scripts, there is debate over whether to write dialogue with the level of inflection seen in works by Alice Walker or Zora Neale Hurston. Executives reading your work may become frustrated if they struggle to decipher the words, but knowing your audience will always be paramount. So keep it simple and concise and know the purpose behind this choice. Writing shorts is about striking the right balance, providing just enough detail without overwhelming the reader.

THE TROUBLE WITH CHARACTER: THE TRIPLE D'S

Earlier in the chapter, I discussed how consistency, distinction, and specificity aid in building a believable character. Here, I want to directly address some of the issues that arise with characters who may feel flat or stagnant as the story progresses. In these situations, character issues usually deal with the concerns of decisions, determination, and dimension.

Decisions
Yasmine Chouikh's *El Bab*

Characters must make decisions. In real life, we make decisions constantly, but usually, they are low stakes. We may also put off making larger decisions for a little while, possibly forever. However, in a short, we focus on immediacy by removing some of the less significant decisions and concentrating on making every decision count. We expect characters to make decisions that are significant or emotional for them, whether they are good or bad. We seek decisions that have consequences and provoke action. In a short, a character who fails to make decisions can lead to your story's downfall—unless this indecision is intentional and excessive.

In Yasmine Chouikh's *El Bab*, we watch a young girl, Samia, repeatedly choose to bask in the soft magical light that comes through her window. Despite being constantly summoned by members of her family to attend to chores around the home, her decision to keep returning to the light, despite these responsibilities, acts as a commentary on choice and freedom.

Determination
Tourmaline and Sasha Wortzel's *Happy Birthday Marsha*

Determination is the process through which a character seeks to achieve something difficult. In real life, our determinations shift and change with age, understanding, and knowledge, from the minute to the expansive, whether it's figuring out how to get to the nearest bathroom during a road trip or finding a lost love from college. We are always seeking people, places, and things for various reasons. Similarly, your character, when the story begins, seeks something, and that pursuit forms the journey of your film.

In Tourmaline and Sasha Wortzel's documentary *Happy Birthday Marsha*, we follow Marsha P. Johnson through archival footage and re-enactments as she struggles to celebrate her birthday in the way she envisions. Her perseverance and persistence are demonstrated through how she gets navigates the many obstacles she faces along the way—all leading up to the Stonewall uprising.

If you're unsure of your character's goal, your logline can help clarify what they've determined in their brief on-screen existence. Much of it may feel mundane and ordinary, and may not, at first glance, appear to be good film material. You must remember that the pursuit of a goal or an objective delineates the borders of your story; it forms the opening and the closing, especially in Western storytelling. This pursuit carves out the space of your story. This works not only for traditional genre fare but also for comedies and dramas when we ask, "What does the character want internally and externally?" Without a clear pursuit, the boundaries of the story may be called into question.

Dimension
Dania Bdeir's *Warsha*

When we meet a character, but only see one side of them, we deem them flat or one-dimensional. Dimension refers to the elements or factors making up a complete personality or entity. This limitation is often evident when a female character's storyline revolves solely around her involvement with a male love interest, neglecting to explore any other facets of her life. This is an issue addressed by the Bechdel test, which questions the portrayal of female characters in media.

Dania Bdeir's *Warsha* takes us on a delightful and unexpected journey with a harangued worker. Initially, we know very little about him, but when he accepts the chance to operate a towering crane in the sky, he dreams a most fantastical and unexpected dream, revealing much about his character without uttering a word.

Admittedly, we don't get to see as many sides of a character in a short as we would in a feature. Features are populated by subplots that help to show all the different ways we can get know a character; especially through their relationships. Nevertheless, in a strong short, we still want to understand that the character has a diversity of traits and qualities, some of which may surprise us. As with *Warsha*, this can be done in small ways through reveals. Just as we lead multifaceted lives with the potential for new experiences each day, we should anticipate the same complexity in our characters.

Don't Short Your Character!

I've noticed that new writers will sometimes underestimate the level of commitment and depth required for character development when crafting a short film. They presume creating a character in a short is somehow easier than developing a character in a feature-length screenplay. But that isn't the case at all!

In fact, in some ways, writing a short is harder than writing a feature, because you have to create a fully fleshed out character with elements that must be tightly selected, succinct, and focused. Even in a short your character deserves a full life! It's essential to create fully realized characters with rich backgrounds and motivations. Each character should feel alive and engaging, whether they're the protagonist, a friend, or a foe. We seek characters who enrapture us with journeys we want to follow, whether it's for minutes or for hours.

Another pitfall is when characters are introduced solely to serve the needs of another character, resulting in what are essentially throwaway characters. These characters may appear flat, underdeveloped, or contradictory. In short, they are incomplete in both their development and their ability to feel real.

In the film world, a strong actor might fill in some of these missing spots, making the character feel more real. However, on the page, you are confined to the reader's perspective. The reader might automatically fill in some spots if some basic components feel familiar to them, but if they don't, the story will just appear lacking. An incomplete character can lead to a story that is flat, confusing, or too boring to hold attention. I encourage you to engage with your characters as much as you would a close friend—this will take you very far.

The Secret about Character: All About Me

Ngozi Onwurah's *Coffee Colored Children*

As I mentioned earlier, many writers, as well as actors, imbue their characters with aspects of themselves. Therefore, writing characters is about knowing and embracing both the best and worst parts of yourself. We are all a conglomeration of traits: kindness, absentmindedness, or selfishness. As storytellers, we can examine these traits and shape how they are represented. For example, paying for someone's dinner could be perceived as an act of kindness, but with a little context, it could be portrayed as manipulative. As writers, we have the power to present any trait as either a skill or an obstacle.

Ngozi Onwurah's autobiographically-influenced *Coffee Colored Children* depicts two siblings dance, play, and attempt to erase their identity with paint in one of the most anguished scenes I've ever seen in a short. Informed by the director's personal experiences, this film meditates on themes of race, identity, and acceptance between a brother and sister, offering an emotionally devastating yet urgent viewing experience.

When writing a character, try to think about each character as a piece of yourself, just in a different reality. Is this character a version of you that didn't have a parent, a home, or financial security? Is that villain really a villain? Or are they just misunderstood? Do they think differently? Did they have a harder life?

Allow the reader to know more about you through the characters you create.

PRACTICE AND PLAY

1. Create a bone structure for your real or fictional character according to Lajos Egri. Look at a section of the bone structure (you can find it online): psychology, sociology, or physiology and choose three elements from one of the sections. Create a story around it. Do this for each of the three elements.
2. Write ten character-reality rules for your character. Think about behaviors, moral codes, and fears.
3. Identify one of your character's flaws and gifts. Do they mirror each other? Create a three-section chart for your character from beginning to end and demonstrate how the flaw becomes a gift or the gift becomes a flaw.
4. Draw or sketch your character, paying attention to costuming, and explain how each wardrobe piece adds a new dimension to the character.
5. Characters are so often different versions of ourselves or people we know. Compose a character bone structure based on yourself.

Breakdown the physicality, sociology, and psychology, being as honest with yourself as possible. Where do you see overlap with your character and where can you stretch the character to be more ____ than you?

6. Make a list of ten current songs that your character would listen to and try to have the songs reflect ten different feelings/shades of your character. Which song do they listen to when they are feeling a certain way?

7. Write a 1-2 page prose wound story for your character and explain how this wound guides their decisions.

8. Create a relationship character star map by drawing a six-pointed star—two intersecting triangles should do the trick! In the middle of the star, put your character's name and their motivating theme. Then, in each point, add a character and describe their relationship in one word.

9. Imagine your main character in a game. What are the decisions that the character must make to make it to the end? What are the obstacles and what are the levels? At what level do they receive rewards or skills?

10. Take an ordinary prop that your character might use and create stakes around it so that object becomes precious. Using pics or animation, create a picture of the character using the prop and use three words to describe what this prop means to the character.

11. Make a list of 5-10 moral codes that your character would not break. Take three of them and write what the character would do instead if forced to confront them.

12. Research a real person speaking who is from the town of your character. Use a film, a commercial, or educational video. Study their dialogue. Identify the colloquialisms or idiomatic language in their speech. How can you incorporate this authentic language in your character's speech or environment?

SCULPTING A WORLD:
WHAT ARE THE RULES OF YOUR WORLD?

The World
—The sphere or scene of one's life and action

THE WORLD OF YOUR STORY

Creating a sculpture is an intensive endeavor. It involves enshrining a vision from virtually nothing—a process not unlike the Big Bang birthing an entire universe. This mindset should guide your approach to storytelling.

Constructing a world can be the most difficult element in constructing a screenplay. This is why so many science fiction films are based on books and novels, where other writers have already invested countless hours in developing intricate worlds. However, regardless of genre, every storytelling endeavor demands this level of commitment. This realization often surprises new writers.

Unfortunately, world-building is often overlooked in short screenplays. Among new screenwriters, there's a common misconception that world-building is only the domain of science fiction and fantasy writers. This can lead to insufficiently detailed worlds.

Remember, you are building a world from scratch. This world has crevices, scars, and imperfections. Most of all, this world is influenced by *you*.

WHAT IS THE WORLD?

In storytelling, the world we create encompasses both place and time, which form the setting. This task is monumental, as it offers a glimpse into our personal world. The world we live in shapes the ones we create.

The Place

When discussing setting, we draw from spaces we've visited, seen, or learned about. Beyond considering *where* the script occurs, we must also consider the *environment*, encompassing landscapes, geography, and astronomy. This involves determining the population density (urban, suburban, rural) and the societal structure (city, town, village). Consider the type of dwelling. Is it a bedroom, a hovel, or a cave? The Place reflects not only the location's physical organization but also its laws, ordinances, and policies. Do not neglect the social customs, traditions, and rituals that shape its inhabitants. Additionally, we must determine their resources, ceremonies, food, religion, transportation, education, and currency.

The Time

The world also encompasses time, making it crucial to determine the timeframe of the film. We reference time based on our personal relationship to it. Reflect on when the story unfolds—whether it's B.C., A.D., 1745, or 2045. Consider the passage of time within the film itself. Does it span a month, a day, a week, a lifetime, or multiple lifetimes? Is it set after life ends or before life begins? Will there be flashforwards or flashbacks? Think about the seasons and weather. Is it daytime, nighttime, or in a realm where traditional time doesn't exist? Define the rules of time. Is it about visions, memories, or another reality? How will the passage of time be indicated in the film? Consider all these factors when beginning this process.

But wait, we're not done! There's one more thing.

There's *you*.

You are the center of your world, and in your story, you are the sun—even if you are not the main character.

Although the earth revolves around the sun in this universe, we don't often think about our relationship to it unless we are astrologers or astronomers. The sun is a part of a system that we have an awareness of, even if we don't fully understand its impact on us. Sometimes, that impact may seem very direct, such as when we get sunburned or suffer from a light-induced migraine. Other times, it may feel subtle, like when we open our blinds or don sunglasses.

In this same way, you shape the world of the story, as it is born from an ecliptic set of circumstances and situations known only to you. No one else, not even your parents or your life partner, will ever know everything that you have experienced and endured.

This uniqueness is the gift you bring to your world. It's a reflection of your perspective, point of view, and vision. It's crucial to realize that your view will consciously *and* subconsciously permeate the world you create.

Throughout the writing process, we call on both our subconscious and conscious selves to sculpt these ideas, making them clearer, more digestible, and more recognizable. By doing so, we strengthen the impact of theme and emotion in our work, enabling us to convey our feelings more easily to the viewer.

However, to achieve this, you must first reflect on your own unique world, understanding how it is distinct from anyone else's.

WHAT IS YOUR WORLD?

This question may initially seem silly. Aren't we all living on Earth? Don't we all share the same air? We all see trees, shop at grocery stores, and work on computers. . .or do we?

Some parts of the world, due to excessive heat or cold, lack a climate that permits tree growth. Some countries have better air quality than others. There are even counties within the US that have significant air quality concerns. Some nations don't have grocery stores but instead, have outdoor bazaars. Not everyone has a computer, and those who do may not have a MAC or PC.

> *To comprehend the distinctiveness of your own world,*
> *you must first look beyond the world that you see.*

To approach how to examine your world, you must consider a world outside of yourself. You must consider that some people have things that you have and other people have things that you don't. Embrace the understanding that everyone's reality is unique.

> *Your story begins with you.*

This includes your comprehension of, and perspective on, the world. They will always be as unique as your fingerprints and DNA.

Your perspective of the world is shaped by an infinite array of experiences, your sociology, and anatomical connections, your physicality. Both have affected what you think, how you behave, and what you believe, all of which are your psychology. While your perspective has the potential to change, or *arc*, we start with where you are right now. Now, consider how many others are in their own worlds at this very moment!

An experimental film from the 1980s featured vignettes of events happening simultaneously around the world. This provocative experiment sought to highlight the vastness of the world, our relative insignificance within it, and the boundlessness of time by capturing glimpses of one specific minute from countries around the world. It encouraged us to look beyond ourselves, a crucial step in world-building, as no one knows your world better than you.

WHAT IS NORMAL?

In my classroom, I often have students who will try to fit their world-building into one word: "normal." Sometimes, this manifests as "today's" world, "present-day," or the "everyday" world. This 1980s experimental film shed light on the limitations of this notion of "normal" in a truly special way.

> *Normal is only normal to you.*

Normal varies from person to person. For example, normal to you might be turning off all of the heat at night and keeping warm with blankets, a scenario I encountered during my first sleepover at a friend's house. Normal to you might be watching a soccer game on a gigantic screen rigged to a skyscraper in the middle of the street, as I witnessed during my first trip to South Korea. Normal to you might be trashing a four-floor, six-bedroom mansion and getting grounded for the weekend, an experience of one of my high school classmates.

These things were all new and different from the world I knew growing up. They reflected traditions, customs, race, and class, although I didn't know it at the time. They made me realize that the world was a much bigger place than I had imagined, full of other people with lives different from mine. As a young person, I became curious about the lives of others, which helped me grow as a writer. It taught me how our lives appear different through various lenses.

LENSES, PERSPECTIVE, AND POINT OF VIEW

Did you know that horses have one of the largest eyes of any land mammal? Imagine seeing the world through a horse's blinders, with a girdle which prevents you from turning your head left, right, or even back. These limitations shape the horse's *point of view*, or position, from which they consider and evaluate the world around them.

Horses also have a different depth of field than humans, so their *lens* of focus is distinctly different from their rider's. A horse's depth of field is smaller than that of humans, allowing us to focus more, and further, than a horse can. So, through the lens of a horse, the world will often look less varied or clear, making differences less recognizable. Interestingly, domestic horses tend to be near-sighted, while wild horses are generally more far-sighted. Can you guess how the environment has influenced this gene evolution?

Similarly, our worldview, or perspective, is directly impacted not only by the environment but also by the experiences that occur within that environment. Adaptation for survival is a well-known skill of organisms. We've learned that our environment shapes the development of our physiology in ways that scientists continue to explore. So, our view is certainly influenced by what we understand to be "normal" in our everyday circumstances.

WHAT DO WE SEE AND WHAT DO WE KNOW?

You perceive life through a single perspective of how the world works. Director Akira Kurosawa's *Rashomon* is a remarkable film and one of the earliest forms of an anthology short. The film tells a story from three different perspectives: those of a thief, a wife, and a woodsman. Kurosawa does this to pose questions about perspective, truth, and the uniqueness of individual experiences.

Each character's experience and *point of view* is informed by their background and upbringing. A thief might see a forest as a suitable place to stage a robbery, while a woodsman might see it as a familiar workplace. Conversely, a woman traveling alone might see the forest as unsafe and fear for her safety—in the film, she testifies that she is raped. Each person's background and experience shapes how they approach the forest and anticipate the events that unfold.

In this way, world-building is not an isolated endeavor, but rather a system of relationships. Understanding the relationship between character and world is essential for accurately depicting how your character will inhabit the story. Our identity is as dependent on elements of our character as it is on the environment in which we were raised. This environment is carved from the reality introduced to us through its boundaries, standards, and rules.

SOCIETIES, STANDARDS, AND RULES

While society might dictate what is considered "normal," our interpretation and application of these standards is affected by time, age, and community. As we age, our worldview expands to encompass familiar spaces and trusted individuals, along with the principles and lessons we are taught to accept and follow. These are "unspoken rules," established by parents, extended family, peers, schools, and our community.

Parents and extended family establish what rules we follow as children: what time we go to bed, what punishment looks like, how much money translates into a healthy bank account. Through puberty, we start to rely on our peers and re-establish rules based on acceptance and social hierarchies. Schools and community groups like churches, art organizations, and sports clubs teach us still more: we may learn that prayer can change things, that school is a space that teaches some histories and not others, or that cheating is not a fair way to win.

As adults, we discover different sets of rules in our workplaces and homes, and response to these rules often comes from our upbringing. How much these rules matter will be determined by how we were taught to prioritize social acceptance or disruption—did I grow up in a household where questioning was encouraged or where questioning was criticized? Regardless of how we react, we come to understand these rules as normal to our world.

Tools and Techniques: Rules of the World

Kate Messner's *How To Build a Fictional World*

I love using Kate Messner's Ted Talk animation short in my classes to describe world-building. It's a wonderful tool for getting students to ponder how to build a world. Messner stirs up marvelous ideas about how to approach world-building, providing some areas to focus on, including social customs, currency, government, law enforcement, and transportation. Many of my students stumble over this part of short story creation. They often think "it's today's world," without considering that "today's world" can look different not only based on where you are but also how your socioeconomic status, race, and gender impact your interactions with the world.

What is a Rule in your story?

When I moved to Southern California from the humid eastern shores of the Atlantic, I slowly discovered that even though the Pacific Ocean was only a few miles away, I was living in a desert. Countless news articles regarding water shortages prompted me to re-evaluate how long my showers could be, if I should turn off the water when I brushed my teeth, and why I should never leave a faucet dripping.

SCULPTING A WORLD

Rule: In this world, it rarely rains.

Living in Miami had been a lush and humid experience for me, where rain, even if intermittent, was a constant. However, in Southern California, rain was a gift to some, and a plague to others. The rain meant different things to different people. A rule must begin to explain what rain means to the characters in the world you are creating.

Rule from the surfer perspective:
In this world, when it rains, the water sends trash and pollutants from the gutters into the waves.

Rule from the homeowner perspective:
In this world, when it rains, it means my home built on a hill may be in danger of sliding.

Rule from the librarian perspective:
In this world, when it rains, homeless people come inside to shelter within the library.

A rule in your story functions like a law, dictating how this world operates. Our world is full of them. Some are societal customs: shaking hands, kissing, or hugging when you meet someone. Others are scientific principles: gravity keeps us grounded or Ohm's law powers our electrical devices. Likewise, there are rules at work, rules at home, rules at the park, and rules at school. We live in a world full of rules.

Your job is to discover the rules that define your character's normal and then illustrate them.

We don't know what normal is in your story, so you must establish it on the very first page. "Normal" will always begin with your perspective.

At the beginning of any story, the reader is trying to get a sense of the world and its relationship to the character. To do that, you must begin to set rules, but where do you start? Or rather, when?

Clocking the When

Wanuri Kahiu's *Pumzi*

Time is a wonderful place to begin. Time is even more important than location. If we are telling a story in Washington DC, that city will look different depending on when we tell it. Wanuri Kahiu's short film, *Pumzi*, tells a futuristic story about a world that lacks water. When does the story begin in the timeline of this world as we know it?

In *Pumzi*, Kahiu opens with a title card that sets the time 35 years after World War III: The Water War. In establishing time, she expertly establishes story, highlighting the scarcity of water as a central theme. Even with a title card, the film goes on to reiterate the value of water through a series of images. The images, including skeletons, news articles, and the desert, reinforce the concept of a world deprived of water. Kahiu not only establishes the time period but also vividly portrays its characteristics and challenges.

Rule: In this world's time period water is the most important resource.

Time is a very broad concept. It's helpful to break down some different ways to think about time in your script.

When considering time, think about:

The Calendar
The Year
The Day
The Time Period or Era
The Length of Days/Nights
The Season
The Time of Day/Night
The Organization of Time
The Representation of Time
The Resource or Value of Time
The Relationship between Past, Present, and Future
The Length of Time of your Story as represented by Pages.
The Length of Time that transpires in your Story.
The Length of Time felt by your Character in the Story.

One of the unique tools of filmmaking is its potential to play with time. You can stretch it, shrink it, and jump around it.

Mapping the Where

Thanasis Neofotistos's *Patision Avenue*

It is necessary that the audience comprehends where they are at the start of a film. As a filmmaker, you are tasked with bringing your audience to a new place and providing them with a unique experience. While building a world from your memories and experiences is a start, digging a little deeper may be more fruitful. If you are depicting a location you've never visited, research through archives, photographs, and articles is a minimum requirement. Researching people, communities, culture, and more will become a part of your rule-building.

Eventually, you will need to craft an immersive experience of being in this place, whether through your imagination, connecting with others, or studying others' experiences. This is what travel books and videos are marketing—the place and the *experience* of being there. It is not sufficient to merely state the location; we must also feel it.

I imagine that Thanasis Neofotistos must have plotted different maps to guide the wonderful actress in his remarkable short, *Patision Avenue*. In this high-concept film, we follow a young mother as she navigates the bustling streets of Greece. We follow behind her, never seeing her face. What sets this short film apart is the immersive way we experience the character's journey, passing streets, people, places, and communities as she talks on the phone. As the narrative of her phone call intertwines with the narrative of what's happening around her, we watch the character's world erupt into chaos and violence, culminating in an intriguing double climax.

> *Rule: In this world, Patision Avenue is a street of community, culture, and violence.*

Building a world always starts with determining the emotion you want to evoke about a place. Once you know this feeling, you can then identify the images and elements that will effectively convey it.

When thinking about the where, here are some things to consider:

The Primary Location
The Organization of the Location: city, town, province
The Population: urban, suburban, rural

The Landscape and Topography
The Geography
The Rules of Space
The Neighborhood
The Educational Institutions
The Places of Worship
The Workspace
The Community Haunts
The Cultural Centers
The Law Enforcement
The Home

While you may not use all of these spaces in your short, the awareness and knowledge of how these spaces relate to your character and story is still relevant.

The Macro and Micro Rules of Your Character's World

Stefani Saintonge's *Seventh Grade*

I've had the blessing (or curse) of moving a lot both as a child and as an adult. Over time, I've learned how to evaluate a potential home in a variety of ways. So, my best friend has become mapping software. Once the software finds the location, it offers me several views: a street view, a topographical view, and a traffic view. Each of these views gives me a lot of information about the experience of driving, walking, and living in this area.

If I want to get an experience of the community from the street view, I can turn and see what's on the street, what's across the street, and what's around the corner. But sometimes, I want a larger view of the world. When that happens, I zoom out and explore the neighborhood. Is it close to a school, market, or train? Is it near water, making it vulnerable to flooding, or is it high up off the ground? The goal here is to capture a 360-degree view of this world.

In your short, you must communicate your character's full view of their normal world.

When starting to think about some of these rules for your world, it's helpful to think about the map. You want to be prepared to help readers zoom in and out of the character's world. To aid in this, I teach my students about micro and macro rules. Micro rules are concerned with details that will be directly relevant to the story—rules that we might recognize. In Stefani Saintonge's *Seventh Grade*, a micro rule might be:

> *In this world, parents are not around because they work hard.*

Stefani Saintonge's *Seventh Grade* tells the story of a young girl struggling with her sexuality. It primarily takes place in two locations: her home and school. This is a rule that establishes that, although we see Patrisse at home, her parents will not appear in the film. (One character says: "Mom is sleeping.") We have some understanding that her parents exist because she has a home, responsibilities, and a sibling, but they don't show up as an engaging presence within the film.

However, a macro rule in this case might be:

> *In the 1980's, many middle-income parents worked long hours, leaving their children to occupy themselves at home.*

MACRO RULE

We could expand upon "why" the parents are not present, including issues of economics, events, etc., to deepen this rule. This information doesn't appear in the film, although it does impact the character's world. Having this time to herself certainly equips the character with more time for imagination, rumination, and exploration. It provides her with the time to play with her dolls, which helps us to learn about the character.

Other macro rules might be:

> *In this world, New York suburbs children take school buses to school.*
> *In this world, teens text and share videos with cell phones.*
> *In this world, older sisters take care of younger sisters because parents work long hours.*

MICRO RULE

A micro rule brings us deeper into the story, allowing us to examine the world from a closer perspective, revealing details, elements of the world, and issues of conflict between characters. Micro rules can share story.

Strong and specific rules can become a kind of outline for the story. Specific rules can open up more of the story in an intriguing way, drawing us in. Other rules that are established with Seventh Grade are:

In this world, talking about female sexuality among girls is common.
In this world, young, sexually active female teens are ostracized,
even though male teens are not.
In this world, boys pester girls with little accountability.

These rules lay the groundwork for the conflicts the characters will encounter and the challenges they must overcome, thereby contributing to the narrative's structure.

Here are some rules to start with, many of which are taken from Kate Messner's video. You will see some of these overlap with elements from the When and Where above:

Medicine
Social Customs
Transportation
Law Enforcement
Government
Time
Resources
Currency
Education
Weather
Work
Technology
Clothing

GIRDLES, TECHNOLOGY, AND TIME

Keisha Rae Witherspoon's *T*

Did you know that girdles were a status symbol for both men and women in the early 1900s? They were used to carry all sorts of things, from money to knives, and eventually evolved into important status symbols, embroidered with gold and silver. In the 21st century, girdles and corsets have evolved. An exhibit of corsets at the Oakland Museum demonstrated how a garment once worn to shape, sculpt, and even constrict the human body largely reflected shifts in the women's movement.

Costumes play a crucial role in identifying both time and place, serving as visual markers of social status and wealth throughout history. They also serve a dual purpose by conveying character traits and emotions.

In Keisha Rae Witherspoon's experimental documentary *T*, meeting Dimples is a profoundly emotional experience. Through her costumes and jewelry, we come to understand Dimples, her courage and grief. We also come to know her deceased son, whose memory she honors through her home—which she has transformed into a shrine to him. These images not only convey the time period but also offer profound insights into Dimples' character and her relationship with her son. Costumes constructed from unorthodox materials, such as the silver fringes of potato chip bags, imbue the short with layers of meaning.

Cristian Mungiu's *Zapping*

More than anything else, we rely on technology to identify time. There are so many devices we can use to help us understand the *When* of your movie: communication devices, household items, and writing utensils. Endowing seemingly mundane items with a bit of specificity is a subtle but effective building block for world-building. Even the materials that are used to construct things reveal insights into advancements and levels of industrialization.

Cristian Mungiu's *Zapping* is filled with technology, from guns to television, clocks, and more. It is, however, the remote control that takes center stage and places us in the early 2000s.

Eating utensils are another tool we can use to reflect time:

> *A fork made from bone suggests a prehistoric era.*
> *A fork made of reeds suggests a pre-modern era.*
> *A fork made of silver suggests a classic era.*
> *A fork made of plastic suggests a post-modern era.*
> *A fork made of Jupiter's minerals suggests a future era.*

James Cameron's *Xenogenesis*

The history of weapons serves as a marker of time. Torches, spears, and bows certainly suggest something different than flamethrowers or ray guns. The evolution of firearms, from the fire lance established in 13th-century China to the machine guns and tasers of today, spans centuries. I love James Cameron's early short film, *Xenogenesis* (1978), particularly for its futuristic ray gun fight sequence, which intriguingly foreshadows his later work in the *Terminator* and *Alien* franchises that he seemed destined to make.

Lisa Harewood's *Auntie*

Telephones serve as excellent indicators of a specific time period. Growing up, the kitchen telephone that hung on the wall with the stretching, coiling cord symbolized the 1980s. My grandmother's rotary dial phone that sat outside her bedroom, one of only two phones in the house, evoked the 1950s and 1960s. The advent of early cell phones definitively put us in a more modern era, while camera phones place us near the turn of the century.

The cordless phone that Auntie answers in Lisa Harewood's *Auntie* effectively situates us in the early 2000s. Beyond providing a temporal reference, this scene also contributes to world-building by revealing crucial information about the characters and their circumstances. It tells us that the daughter's mother is in the U.K., and Auntie has been caring for her until her mother is ready to send for her. This is a specific custom related to the cultural Caribbean setting depicted in the film.

Though writing tools have evolved over the years, some, charmingly, have stayed pretty much the same, like the pencil! However, the ink pen has experienced a remarkable evolution. Like the keyboard's progression from manual typewriters to electric typewriters to computer keyboards, ink pens boast an equally fascinating and extensive history dating back to the ancient Egyptians.

BEDROOMS, TRAFFIC, AND FORAGING

Matthew Cherry's *Hair Love*

In Matthew Cherry's heartwarming *Hair Love*, we learn about Zuri through her bedroom, which is decorated with pictures, hair products, and other accessories, before we even meet her. We even see a "Z" for her name (though it's never spoken aloud, we see it when she uses her computer). Character bedrooms offer profound insights, not only into the characters themselves but also the time period. Home design serves as a remarkable tool to define both character and era. Kitchens, living rooms, and dining rooms tend to reflect the era during which families move in, as they tend to decorate heavily upon arrival. Subsequent changes are rarer, due to time and financial constraints. Consequently, these spaces seem to be suspended in the time they were first decorated. Household items, from lamps to kitchenware to appliances, become a marker for that time.

Traffic can reveal a lot about civilization and its norms. In a present-day world, traffic can provide a sense of the city. Is the traffic on small roads, sky routes, or six-lane freeways? Do we see cars, hover vehicles, or horse-drawn carriages? Are people using trains, buses, air tunnels, or dirt paths? Transportation methods play a significant role in depicting how individuals commute to work, travel back home, or seek recreational activities, offering rich visual cues that convey a wealth of information.

The way food is foraged, whether from grocery stores, farms, or scientifically-delivered rations, sets the tone for the time period. Foraging will also ask us to consider what resources are required for existence. Is it water, meat, and vegetables? Is it oil, some other known energy source, or is it some square of engineered ingredients that act as a substitute for poultry, like in *The Matrix*?

Timelessness, Infinity, and Space

Barry Jenkin's *Re-Migration*

Sometimes, writers intentionally conceal the precise time period of a story to evoke a sense of possibility. This ambiguity can provide a mood of hope, suggesting that the story could occur at any time in the future or past. This can imbue the story with a feeling of chance, which may even have some effect on the story's resolution.

Barry Jenkin's *Re-Migration* opens in a field that could be almost any time or place on post-ice age Earth. Only upon seeing the characters, their clothing, and the furniture in their homes do we get a sense of time period. Roads without signs, open fields in the wild, and blank rooms all give us the feeling of not knowing.

CONNECTING TOOLS

The World & The Bone Structure

Julie Dash's *Illusions*

Julie Dash's *Illusions* would feel like a much different film if it didn't take place on the studio lot. By following this Black female studio executive and watching how she navigates race, gender, and power in a racialized environment, we learn about her struggle to create change. The high and shadowy concrete walls of the studio spaces convey a lot about the character's struggle to be recognized in this setting. Dash's title works precisely to set the stage for a short about a character trying to make her way through the Hollywood filmmaking industry.

When preparing to write a story about a character, you must decide where it will take place. You can identify this space in your character bone structure. The sociology and psychology sections are invaluable for setting the stage for where and how your character identifies comfort and terror. Understanding their flaws, fear, and inhibitions, as well as their attitudes toward life, obsessions, and intimacy will tell us a lot.

While, at first, it may seem arbitrary deciding where to locate your character, it's anything but. As products of our upbringing, culture has shaped us, motivating us to either move toward or away from our experiences. These factors play a crucial role in determining where your characters' stories unfold. These elements are deeply intertwined; we are shaped by both nature and nurture, each exerting a significant influence.

Furthermore, if your story treats a place as a central character, it can profoundly shape the narrative arc. Introducing characters to a space can transform it, much like a pond drying up due to pollution or a scorched forest rejuvenated by the return of its inhabitants. Characters and places influence each other in a dynamic interplay of storytelling.

Places Have Stories

Shabier Lee Kirchner's *Dadli*

Shabier Lee Kirchner's personal exploration in *Dadli* follows a child, Tiquan, along with other residents of Antigua, but it's not the people who tell the story. The experience of the place is deeply felt, yet only partially expressed through the human characters we meet. Shot with care and affection, the film plays as a testament to a community, a place, an essence of Antigua that feels both personal and ethereal at the same time.

Places make wonderful characters. Sometimes we can forget that. Just imagine taking a home, a school, or some other space that your character occupies from your bone structure, and instead of focusing on a person, focusing on the place instead. What if, instead of writing a character going into different spaces, different characters went into this one space? Consider how this space might change to reflect the different people, their moods, and their desires. How could this space take on human characteristics to tell its story?

THE WORLD: GENERAL AND BROAD, SPECIFIC AND DISTINCT

Samira Saraya's *Polygraph*

Kitchens are also a popular space in short films. The kitchen inhabited by characters Orr and Yasmine in Samira Saraya's *Polygraph* feels specific to these two characters. The appliances in Yasmine's kitchen reflect her role as a nurse, her preference for fresh vegetables, and her nurturing nature, as she enjoys cooking for Orr and her family. Blue tiles in the kitchen reiterate her presence and calm. Coffee pots make sense for late nights, and a hand juicer tells us that she is health-conscious. The repeated presence of red among some of these items could suggest to us that something is about to explode.

Can you see how these details give us more information about Yasmine and the story? The terms "specific" and "distinct," like "general" and "broad," get used when discussing character but can also apply when discussing world-building.

When I discuss world-building in my classes, I start first with spaces and situations that are familiar to all of us in that room. I begin with the classroom and student life to provide an example of how to talk about the world, since we commonly start with the idea that this is our "normal" world.

I talk about us in the room and things that might be common to our experiences, things like films, wireless internet connections, computers, cell phones, the campus, or the city. Then I look out the window and gaze at some of the people on the street below. These are strangers of various ages, heights, sizes, gender identities, abilities, and sexualities. They may be multiracial, or multiethnic, or come from various socioeconomic backgrounds. Then I ask, "Do you think that *that* person's experience and lifestyle is the same as yours?"

I also remind my students that, right now in this classroom, we know a few things about each other. Some things we assume, some things we guess, some things we know, or think we know based on our understanding of our brief interactions within the classroom. But aren't we other people outside of the classroom? Spaces can also bring out different characteristics. This is who I am in a classroom, but who am I on a mountain top, in a club, or at a beach? How much more can we discover?

COMPASSIONATE WRITING IN TODAY'S WORLD

Noora Niasari's *The Phoenix*

Many of the students I have worked with are sophisticated and knowledgeable about the world. However, many are not, and have not been exposed to experiences outside of their own. They know the world only through what they see in the microcosm of the digital spaces they frequent. While technological advances have aided us in connecting with those around the world, it has also simultaneously siloed us into very narrow perceptions of the world in which we live. This first-world experience can make us feel very powerful and important, sometimes causing us to forget that there are worlds outside of our own—worlds with those who have less and worlds with those who lead different lifestyles.

Even though I have access to a computer, I acknowledge that many others do not. Even though I have a home to live in, I recognize that others do not. Although I climb out of bed every morning and walk to work, I know that others cannot. Watching Noora Niasari's *The Phoenix* was a refreshing experience. This film portrays an exiled Iranian acting teacher who brings the magical joy of performance to young asylum seekers in an Australian detention center, all of whom face the threat of deportation to their home countries. This tender short demonstrates the need for compassion—something I'd like to see more of in today's world.

If you haven't been exposed to people, communities, or places different from your own, it may be difficult to remember that your normal is specific to you. Understanding this is crucial for writing your character, as this realization leads to compassion, which is essential for creating a strong story.

Compassionate writing allows every character to have space in your story; for them to be judged as neither wrong nor right, but as fully dimensional people who have the choice to do good or bad things. People are not caricatures or stereotypes; they are individuals who love, bleed, and make mistakes, just as your characters should. However, grasping this concept can be difficult without experiencing someone else's perspective or spending time with individuals from diverse backgrounds and different identities. Being mindful of our own privileges and distinctions allows us to become not only stronger writers but responsible ones too.

PRACTICE AND PLAY

1. After watching Kate Messner's Ted Talk, write fifteen rules of your character's world. Include macro rules and micro rules that may or may not appear directly in the story. Include some basics of time, place, technology, government, currency, transportation, culture, and customs.
2. Write a scene where your character tries to convince another character to go on a date with them to a space that you think is absolutely ridiculous for the conversation—like a date in a laundry room.
3. Draw the space the character feels is most terrifying. Then mirror that space and draw it again but change it to be comforting. Consider colors, textures, and shapes of this space as well as items within the space.
4. Take the villain or antagonist in your story and write a scene about them as a young child in their bedroom. Remember that villains don't start out that way. What can you include in this room that tells the story of how the villainous character became who they are today?
5. Identify one of your main character's favorite environments. This can be a public, private, or imagined space. Then interview this space in relation to the character. What story do they tell?
6. Write a scene paragraph that establishes the world at the beginning of your story and another one at the end. Reflect on the arc of the world and how it has shifted or changed to reflect the personal growth of the character.

7. Remember that worlds can be characters too. Find an interesting historical space in your real life and look up its history. How has its function evolved over time? How could this location take on human aspects to become more of a character and attack and then comfort your character?

8. Write a scene where your character tries to desperately reach their loved one through a form of technology. Demonstrate shifts in time periods by varying the tools of technology. Write four periods as four scenes.

9. Write three scenes for your character where they are searching for a treasured item in three different spaces. Consider how the character's behavior shifts depending on their relationship to the space.

10. Build a maze using ordinary household objects like playing cards, pencils, glasses, or Legos, and make them extraordinary for your character. Write an experimental scene where your character gets lost in this maze and must find their way out. What are the rules that they will learn along the way?

11. Place your character on a set or against a backdrop for an interview that documents a lot about the character without saying a word. Examine five elements in this setting. What do they communicate about the character and your story?

12. Consider the world of your character when they are a child, an adult, or a ghost. Draw this world at these different stages of their life and populate each drawing with tools or props that are meaningful to the character.

DEVELOPING A SYSTEM:
FINDING MEANING IN STRUCTURES

Structure
—*Something arranged in a definite pattern of organization*

FINDING MEANING IN STRUCTURES

As human beings, we constantly build, organize, and arrange various structures, including physical objects, relationships, time, and spaces. For many, structures form a core foundation, shaping our thoughts, beliefs, and actions, and offering comfort through the security and predictability they provide. They help us build families, homes, and schedules, dictating when we eat, where we play, or how we work.

However, sometimes we find structure to be too intense or too monotonous. When schedules constrain rather than assist us, we yearn for freedom, novelty, and unpredictability. While we appreciate the confidence of knowing a plane's arrival time, there's an undeniable thrill in the possibility of it arriving early, granting us unexpected freedom, or arriving late, disrupting our plans.

This tension in our relationship with structure arises from change, reflecting our evolution from childhood to adulthood.

Everyone's relationship to structure is deeply personal, stemming from our genetics, upbringing, character, and environment. Just as our physical and biological structures define us, so do our social, technological, and cultural structures. Structures serve as tools for achieving our goals, whether it's prolonging life or simply sustaining it. Through specific systems like media, both through content and form, structures share vital information about cultural norms and background.

Therefore, rather than learning about structure to tell a story, try investigating your story to find the most fitting structure.

How Structured Is Your Life?

Structure is deeply personal and individual. Observe your surroundings and note the structures that matter to you. Are they the intricate systems within computers, the orderly arrangement of pages in books, or the sturdy wooden frames of chairs? Each item's arrangement tells a story!

Consider the structure of time: the hours of the day, the routines of your week, the endings of months, or the last days of years. Where are the peaks and valleys of your day, and what moments bring you stress or relaxation? A cousin of mine who dabbles in numerology always sees nines everywhere. What numbers have meaning to you?

Structures extend to the traditions and customs of our society. They dictate when a kiss is more appropriate than a hug or when a phone call is more acceptable than a text. The words we speak and the cadence behind them, like the jaunt of words on paper, are lines, verses, and unrecognized sestinas.

Our lives are three-act structures as often as they are one-act ones, or even four, twelve, fifty-two, a hundred, or three hundred and sixty-five acts. It all depends on the story you're telling and how you want to tell it. Remember, we create structures to serve our needs. As a storyteller, the structures you employ should deepen the purpose and meaning of your story.

Finding Purpose, Finding Structure

Finding a structure for your film is akin to finding a purpose in life. The questions I've asked about living a meaningful life have astounded me by how frequently they're echoed by my students: Who am I? Why am I here? What am I supposed to do? Storytelling is one of civilization's earliest pastimes. Consider how it has addressed deeper questions of survival, protection, and safety. Historically, storytellers spun tales not only for amusement but also to establish justice, preserve culture, and shape morality. Many stories translate as cautionary tales or lessons. This is how we think of mythology, fables, and fairy tales: as lessons that teach us how to live good, long, and productive lives that extend our footprint in this world.

Even though the world has changed and evolved since these earliest narratives, the questions of purpose and intention remain. We still look to information, content, and stories (however they are delivered) to guide us not only on how we live, but also why we live. Artists today still grapple with these questions, and it is through their work that they answer them.

In this way, you should think of your film as an extension of who you are as an artist. Whatever your path, you've come into existence to leave an imprint on the world. How memorable this imprint is has much to do with what you have to say (premise), how you say it (structure), and why you're saying it (purpose). We all come into the world for a moment, contribute something, and hopefully leave something behind. This is an excellent way to think of your short film. But sometimes, navigating these paths of premise, structure, and purpose can be challenging. During these times, you want to create a space for a new system to take form.

System

—a regularly interacting or interdependent group of items forming a unified whole

Processes, Boundaries and Systems

Just as we live in a world of rules and characters, we also live in a world of systems. There are systems in motion all around us, from our bodies to our communities, from streams to rivers to oceans. We are always one part of a whole. What makes systems fascinating is that we don't begin as integral components; rather, we evolve and develop alongside them. Our miraculous journey through life, marked by growth, mistakes, and challenges, shapes these systems as much as they shape us. Indeed, we are inseparable from the systems, and chaos, that surround us.

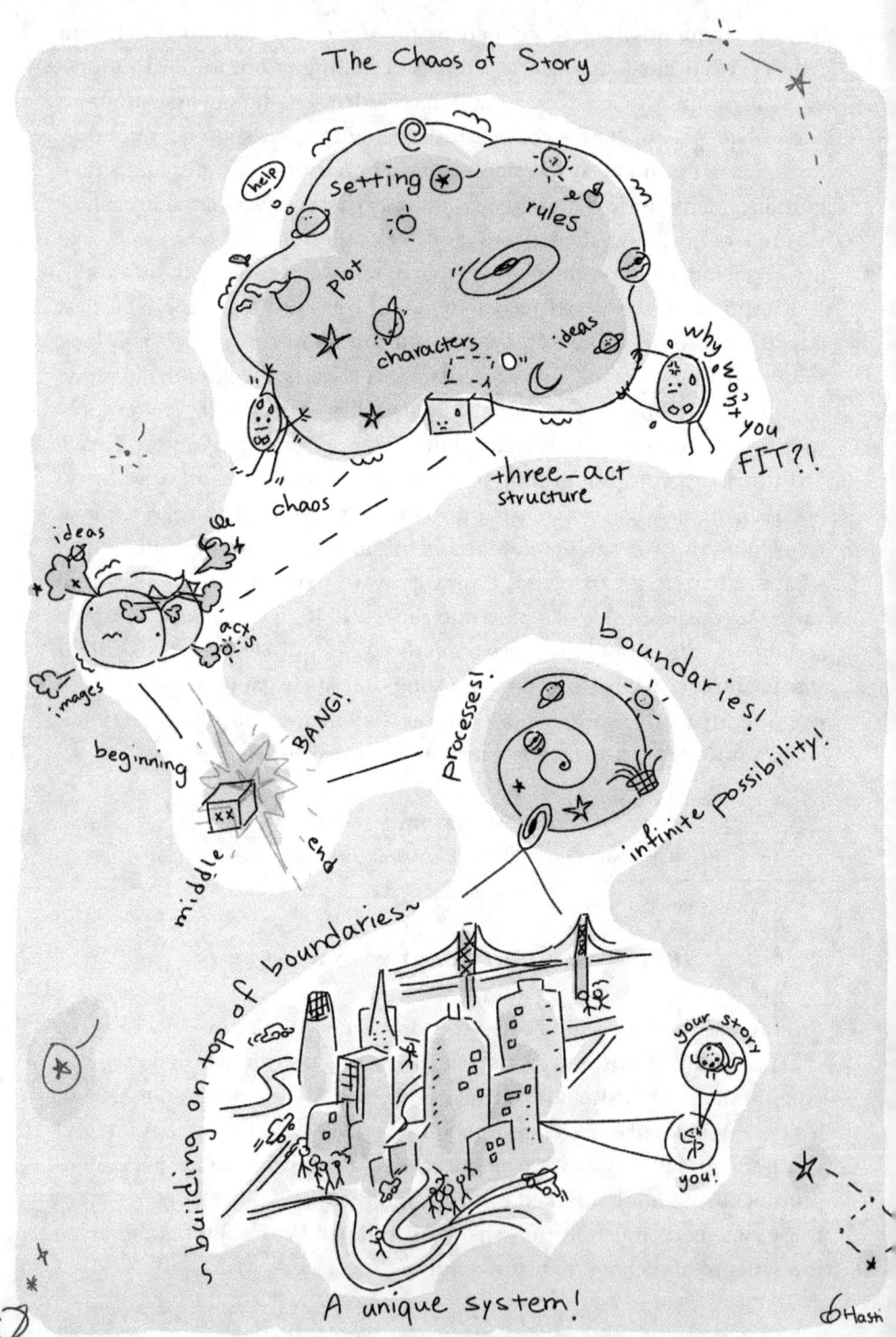

DEVELOPING A SYSTEM

Chaos is equally as important as structure.

My first job out of school was recruiting for college admissions. Later, I did college counseling work, helping students write personal essays, first through organizations that hired me and then independently. I had one student who was particularly eco-conscious. When we worked on her essays, she would pull out a sheet of paper that was almost black with ink from notes, doodles, and scratches. She declared that we needed to preserve paper by using every single white centimeter of the paper sheet. That is where she wrote her notes. Upon and around this messy black hole is where she wrote kickass essays—that messy piece of paper helped her identify her writing process.

There are times we simply do not know how to start or what to do. And that is all right. Not knowing allows us to find unexpected answers. The times when I have struggled the most to fit story into a box have turned out to be some of the most difficult stories to write. However, the stories that came to me openly, sometimes in a rush, other times slowly, turned out to be the most impactful. I've endured some of the most turbulent moments in my life by surrendering, and that has always yielded something with promise. Surrender feels like something to avoid in a society that constantly urges us to know more and do better, but surrender is simply a type of openness. It's where chaos starts to become order. Then order starts to become process. And process leads to structure.

Process

—a series of actions or operations conducing to an end

When working with my students in a world that demands immediacy, I find that the idea of process has been warped and truncated. I suspect we've lost sight of the understanding that process is a cycle of developing systems, and not simply following predefined steps. We don't develop a process by copying or imitating, but rather by adapting, attempting, failing, and then starting again. Most importantly, we develop processes through our values and kinship to the world. Yet, these values and systems always change; sometimes over days, sometimes over years. The writing process I had when I was in my twenties is a far cry from the one I employ now. You may discover that the same process will not work for every short. Just as our work varies, so might the process needed to create it because we, as artists, are always evolving. This evolution of process will lead you to your structure.

Let the structure find you.

We must resist the notion that structure is a template and embrace the idea that structure is an evolution. I've made several shorts, and none of them are the same in story, concept, or structure. Their processes also differ. One came to fruition over a year's time, another over the course of four years, and one took merely a couple of months. Some stories hibernate in my consciousness for years, while others are awakened by relationships, demands, and changes in both the world and my own life. Each short has its own challenges and successes, which contributed to my knowledge and growth for subsequent projects. Yet, it's difficult amidst all the information around us. It's often scary trying to find where and how to start when there appear to be so many already existing processes in motion! The prospect of starting anew can be terrifying, which is why we set boundaries.

Boundary
—something that indicates or fixes a limit or extent

Boundaries exist to help us shape material, information, and ideas into something more digestible and manageable. Boundaries can be "start and stop," "full and empty," or simply walls and ceilings! For writers, templates make for easy and quick boundaries, but they may not be the right boundaries for your project. What I see happen often when I'm teaching three-act structure to my students is that, if their story doesn't fit into the structure, they spend too much time trying to force it into this pre-existing framework instead of allowing the story to develop organically. However, when exposed to many different structures, they can find similarities and differences, and explore choices, options, and possibilities, instead of being confined to a single solution.

How do you find these boundaries? Boundaries are about examining the shifts within your story. They aren't always just walls; look for places of change in your story, often inspired by limits! Where are the changes in emotion, location, or time? In my latest film, I examined the number of days I put in the film and then questioned whether it was arbitrary.

Boundaries might manifest through song or music, or through day or night. A boundary often suggests a pattern, and a pattern is a structure.

It's terribly important to avoid relying on a single structure as a solution. This can lead to a fear of experimenting, making mistakes, or starting over. It can prevent the potential for innovation and discovery. My most prolific students are the ones who can completely let go and start anew—those who are thrilled and excited by the potential of many ideas, instead of only one. When considering our planet, bodies, and minds, we must remember that something can come of nothing—even something that results in many systems and possibilities. Within that realm of infinite possibilities, a story can emerge that is as unique as you are.

We are a unique system.

I ask my students to start by looking into the chaos of their ideas, characters, and rules, building and writing something simple. I ask them to write a treatment, only I don't call it a treatment to avoid intimidating them. Sometimes I'll call it a summary, or I'll say, "Just write your story as prose and we'll start there." This way story will find itself. In a system, you can't pretend; there are too many parts and mechanisms that need to fit for it to execute properly. Chaos can save us by leading us to process, which ultimately leads to truth, and ultimately, to finding new structures. This is where I often find the very best stories. However, the one boundary I will set is that there must be a beginning, a middle, and an end.

MAKING THE LIFE OF THE STORY

BEGINNINGS, MIDDLES, AND ENDINGS

Now that I have introduced the idea of unique structure, let's look at what we can learn from one of the most established structures in our life cycles. Living organisms have this basic structure in common: they have a beginning, a middle, and an end. Whether we are discussing the eight-to-ten-day life cycle of the mosquito or the four-stage growth cycle of bacteria, we are born, we live, we depart. What makes life interesting is how we embark on these different stages of our life. Our lives are interesting not only because of who we are but also because of what we *do*.

There's a great montage in the animated Pixar feature film, *UP*, that works as its own short. It shows, through several short scenes, the lifetime of the main character, hitting all the great events in this character's life. We see him propose to his loved one, get a job, and have children. Watching this montage, we fall in love with the character. It shows us an entire life in mere moments. We feel we know him. In a short film, we strive for exactly this—the experience of another life.

To get this peek into a new and different world, even for a brief period of time, is a treasured opportunity. When we get weighed down by the stress, banality, and complacency of our own lives, films, like other storytelling forms, offer a refreshing escape. Each of these moments is comprised of smaller moments, within which we witness a beginning, a middle, and an end, along with the events that unfold in between, for a character, a place, or an object. These basic components are recognized as the traditional three-act structure of Western feature films; which we will explore as one way to organize your short. So, let's start at the beginning.

BEGINNINGS: INTRODUCTIONS, EXPOSITION, AND SETUP

INTRODUCTIONS

Lance Acord's *The Force* for Volkswagen

The first thing you should know is that when someone presses play to watch your movie, they want to fall in love with it! Beginnings are all about introductions. In a short, it is crucial to find quick, impactful, and immediate ways to introduce your character, world, and story. Lance Acord's *The Force* (a Volkswagen commercial) introduces the story concept in the first eight seconds of this one-minute advertisement. The music establishes the Star Wars connection, the costume establishes the character, and then the setting, a modern home, tells us. . .this is different.

A child-sized Darth Vader motions at an exercise machine, expecting a "ta-da." We know what that means and we know what to expect. The commercial uses one of the most popular franchises in film history to provide this information. But *every* short film should find economical ways to accomplish context, connection, and anticipation.

When a story begins, we want to absorb foundational pieces of information: the who (a child), the when (modern-day), the where (a middle-class home), and the what (the VW vehicle). In goal-oriented stories that dominate Western storytelling, we want to know the characters, their setting, and their mission. As the writer, it's your responsibility to visually demonstrate and communicate these answers within the story, however, this is not where structure ends.

Structurally, whatever you introduce in these opening pages must align with the reader's expectations for the rest of the story. You are establishing the organization of the story, which encompasses the pacing (rhythm and timing), style (talky or cinematic), narrative approach (the flow of story elements), and the organization (shaping patterns of information).

The organization of your film is akin to building a body, consisting of both skeleton and flesh. What you build must be stable and consistent from these opening pages. It's like a house of cards that can come crashing down with the slightest quiver. If you've ever been pulled out of a film, it's likely because something inconsistent has occurred, disrupting the "suspension of belief" required for drama and performance.

The Intricate Care of Introductions

Your introductions require intricate care. Your care must be woven into the earliest moments of your story. Beginnings, like endings, are a special part of your film. Introductions are magical; they're the moment when anything is possible because we are starting from ground zero with that black screen. Whether this story occurs in a world that mirrors or starkly contrasts from our current life, the beginning is where all these elements get established. In a film, we always start with an invitation from a blank page when a writer asks us to take part in this experience. You, as the writer, are always starting this new canvas for the reader and the viewer.

Yet, strong beginnings can be elusive! Sometimes, it's hard to discern exactly where the story begins in the timeline of your character's journey. New writers often start too early, or may occasionally start too late. Too early and the reader grows impatient waiting for the story to start. Too late and the reader gets frustrated by not knowing enough to commit. The timing of all this is intuitive, but it can be dissected by examining the exposition and noting the information needed to complete the setup.

Lastly, introductions are emotional. When you think about firsts in your life, consider how they've moved you. Remember the exercises about firsts from the ideas chapter? Firsts can be momentous, even if they are ordinary. Even in the most action-packed script, emotions are crucial to the story because they're how the audience connects to it. Emotions are universal; they don't need to be explained; they're felt. In your introduction, never underestimate the presence of feeling. Your emotion is the key to developing this connection. If you feel nothing, how can you expect your reader to feel anything?

Exposition

David Lowery's *Pioneer*

Exposition is often a bad word in the screenwriting world, but every story needs some context to get the action rolling. Exposition is the information we need to receive so that when the plot starts to move, we know enough to care about the characters and their predicaments and want to see what happens next. Sometimes, exposition is necessary, and often, it is superfluous. In narrative films and documentaries, some exposition is a requirement. We tend to see less of it in experimental films that seek more active audience engagement.

In a short film, you want to reduce the amount of superfluous exposition. The main exposition should be relevant, direct, and affecting. Superfluous details, such as excessive descriptions of a character's clothing that do not move the plot, can detract from the narrative impact. Impactful exposition would be detailing a character's faulty relationship with their mother, leading to the character running away. Over-reliance on exposition can unbalance the weight of other narrative elements; then exposition becomes a problem.

Recognizing unnecessary exposition is key; when there are pages of excessive dialogue with little conflict and too much explanation, it can raise red flags. Some directors are experienced in conveying important exposition through visuals, or by subtly integrating it with footage to keep your attention. David Lowery's early film, *Pioneer*, is a good example of a short that is primarily dialogue-based. However, this is appropriate for a film that focuses on the technique of storytelling while carving tension and drama through its articulate visuals and writing.

Your exposition will paint the broad strokes and detailed background information we need to establish the foundation of your story. These details might show us the character's upbringing, era, occupation, or living circumstances. Exposition can reveal class, status, value systems, and history of relationships. Lowery's *Pioneer* elegantly provides minimalist details that highlight the story elements. The subtle tag on the father's uniform indicates his working-class status and strong work ethic, which are further reinforced throughout the storytelling. This short's strength lies in its indirect approach, conveying the story through clothing, dialogue, setting, pictures, and technology.

THE SETUP

The full setup of the story will include introductions to the character and world. There will be some exposition, but the most important aspect of the setup is understanding the situations, issues, and conflicts of the story that will propel the plot forward. Meg LeFauve, the writer for Pixar's *Inside Out*, calls the setup the "story engine," while my former writing professor in film school called it the Quest. Despite the many names for this, the most essential thing you need to know is that without a good setup, the story won't take off. It won't take us to the next chapter. Movement is fundamental to the story, whether it's about turning the page, the frame, or the next act. We need the reader to make the choice to stay involved in each moment of the story.

However, this doesn't mean that we need to know the ending of the story, or even every twist and turn. The setup establishes the playing field, the game's boundaries. We also will have twists and turns, because, like a train leaving a station, we do have an idea about the destination, but the ride itself is the fun part, and it's why we've decided to board this "story" train.

The setup, especially in a short, will need to include stakes, costs, and motivations. Stakes are not only related to the characters but also to the situational story. Knowing that a character might die, and that they have children, a partner, or a dependent younger sister, quickly establishes the stakes of what they have to lose. In long form, we have more time to set up these things, but a short moves quickly, and we want to absorb this information early on.

Patterns are also vital to the setup. Story structure relies on establishing patterns in the beginning so that, when they happen later, we're not thrown out of our suspension of belief. If this is a story about memories, flashbacks may need to be established. If this is a story where we jump to different points of view, that needs to be established. If we are going to switch back and forth between different realities, that also needs to be established. The setup must outline the path we will take so that the reader does not leave before the story begins.

As for how much setup is necessary, it depends on the story and the writer's ability to provide just enough information to keep the reader turning the page. If the reader gets too much, they will move ahead of the story and grow bored. If they have too little, they might become frustrated and decide to read (or watch) something else.

Find balance in the writing process.

In some cases, you can deliver less setup if you provide other engagement tactics. High tension, intense emotion, and extreme action can make us hang on until later to get more information. If the anticipation is high enough, we will wait. Just think of those long lines concertgoers wait in when they want to see their favorite bands perform. They predict it's going to be a good experience based on earlier information.

Finally, a good setup needs to make the reader turn the page. Within these first few pages, the reader is subconsciously making the most important decisions—when and if to put the script down. This is where you are ultimately tested as a screenwriter. If the setup has not been strongly established, there will be a lack of motivation to delve deeper into the story. For any given script, your simple objective is to make the reader turn the page. . . all the way to the end.

MIDDLES: BODIES, CLIMAXES, AND STORYLINES

THE BODY

Mohamed Echkouna's *Trail of Hope*

The middle, or body, of the film, is where most tasks, actions, and developments take place. Like the human torso, it is where the heart is also located. Think of that heart as the location of the climax—the most significant organ in the story but also the most protected. The biggest challenge here for the new writer is to stay focused on what the heart of your short is. Shorts are about thinning the fat and really delving into the meat of a story. You can't "start to go" there. You must *go* there. This can be challenging because the body is often where the writer first figures out the story they want to tell, and most writers don't discover the heart of their story until they are in the middle of writing it!

As an art form, writing is like dyeing fabric. You don't really know what the end result is going to look like until you get there. You may experiment with various elements: colors, dyes, and fabrics. You may try multiple techniques: ombre, tie-dye, marbling, shibori, or batik. Even how you organize the order and length of the immersion is a question and a choice! Also, like dyeing, you see different things depending on whether you are up close or far away. You must be able to look close enough to see the tiny veins of subplots winding along, but also pull out far enough so that you can see how the arteries connect to move the plot forward.

Most importantly, the body is where we get to fall in love with your film! In Mohamed Echkouna's *Trail of Hope*, we learn to care for a taxi driver as he searches for the student passenger who left her notebook with him. Watching him unravel the mystery of his passenger through his exchanges with her family is really where we learn about him, them, her, and the transformation that is about to take place. This is also the space where we get to see the rules of the world come to life; how the character's behaviors define them and how the themes of the film are expanded upon. The body is where we really get to know your characters, their situations, and their backgrounds. This is where we learn that they are human and that they are real.

The Climax

Ryan Coogler's *Locks*

The build to a climax or crisis defines the middle of the story. The climax is the conflict-driven peak of the film with the highest emotional intensity and, in a goal-oriented structure, the place where the character makes the most difficult or most impactful decision. In feature films, this is where the big fight takes place, where the Western shootout occurs, or where the scorned lover makes the decision to walk away. In a short, these events revolve around similar moments, but without the budget of the larger film. We can still see high stakes, confrontations, and big decisions, but there is an opportunity to see them in more novel and original ways.

You want to think about the climax as a major space of change in the story. This climactic event must shift the scales for the character in the narrative. The character cannot be the same after the climax. The same goes for the world. The climax, as this significant turning point, dictates where these changes occur.

The climax presents a unique challenge as it functions as a pivotal event, which must act in tandem with the turning points of the inciting incident and resolution (turning points are discussed more below). This crucial moment of change in the story must resonate with the themes introduced in the beginning. For instance, if the initial conflict revolves around a parent-child conflict, the climax will highlight the specific issues that have instigated the conflict, so we can see if the characters have earned the right to resolution, for better or worse. Often, new writers will create a conflict that deviates from the original issue, leaving the viewer confused or unsatisfied; or they create a conflict that resolves with only the slightest of struggles thereby diminishing the impact. The climax should not be just *any* high peak, it must be *the* highest emotional peak for this particular story and character.

Ryan Coogler's *Locks* is notable for reaching its dramatic yet emotional climax in a barbershop. Watching Dante reflect on the significance of his locks, both for him and for the various other characters in the film, creates tension. We empathize with him, only to discover that Dante's dreadlocks have an entirely different relevance.

The placement of the climax varies across story structures, sometimes positioned in the middle or towards the end. Rarely does it occur at the story's outset, unless it is used as a teaser. The traditional climax for modern American films usually comes very close to the end of the story, in a truncated third act. Perhaps this is a digital evolutionary change from earlier American films that carried extended third acts. Short films often adhere to this condensed format as well. However, the climax never appears before the middle of the story because the preceding narrative sets up the conflicts, stakes, and character complexities. This is so when we do reach the climax, we have a full understanding of everything that is at stake. This allows us to invest fully and emotionally; it's in this intense moment when we hold our breath. Conversely, if the climax comes too early, the reader becomes impatient with the end.

THE STORYLINES

Park Chan-wook's *Simpan*

The body is also where storylines get developed. Now, in a short, we often don't have time for several storylines, so it will often stick to one main plot with very few, if any, subplots. A wonderful and tight ten-minute short should really focus on the main plot, but we can have a sense of what other subplots could be.

Longer short films will tend to have other storylines presented in creative ways. Park Chan-wook's early short work, *Simpan*, introduces the storyline of an earthquake, conveyed through a news report, before we enter the main plot of the story. It's an important piece of exposition that helps set up the main storyline, which takes place in a morgue and gives us the relationship to one of the central characters.

Other shorts might allow the storyline to be interwoven into the story. Some of these other storylines may be relegated to a half page, or even just one page, in a short film. Plotlines are often braided into the main plot through the stories of other characters, locations, or alternative approaches to the themes in the story.

CLOSINGS: ENDINGS, RESOLUTIONS, AND CONCLUSIONS

ENDINGS

Kareem Mortimer's *Passage*

Beginnings tend to be rosy times for many writers, filled with hope and infinite potential. Conversely, the middle often finds writers traversing a tundra of storylines. Grappling with logistical challenges and overwhelmed with the task of making sense of it all. However, endings are all about discoveries. In a short film, I would argue that the end holds even greater significance than it does in longer formats. Shifts are monumental in short films. That doesn't mean artificially-created explosions, but rather emotional and thematic spectacles. You want these discoveries to resonate, signifying more than only a character reaching a destination; it's about them arriving at that destination after enduring everything they've faced.

Endings can be exhilarating simply because they mark the conclusion of the journey. Getting to an ending often feels like an exhale, or, sadly, a sigh. It can feel like finishing a race before we even know whether we've won, where we're just grateful to have made it to the end. It's at this moment that we pause to reflect on the journey: what we've gained or lost along the way, and why we embarked on the journey in the first place. Sometimes, we discover the journey is what we thought but not at all what we expected. Interestingly, great endings are all about new beginnings.

Resolution

The ending is also important for its capacity to wrap up the various story elements you introduced in the beginning. This may come in the form of different storylines attached to various locations, people, or themes. You must ensure that there are no loose threads that could unravel the entire story. For the short, this may not seem necessary, but consumers of today are quite sophisticated and quick to detect inconsistencies or unresolved storylines. They are also quick to recognize an ending that comes without the corresponding cost, an unearned resolution. Whether consciously or subconsciously, viewers may be prompted to switch channels when they encounter an unsatisfying conclusion or unaddressed plotline.

This is why many films and shows set in the American West remain beloved. They are traditionally straightforward films that deliver problems, conflict, and resolution in a clear and dramatic way. For instance, the twenty-season series *Gunsmoke* still lives on streaming platforms and cable stations thanks to watchers like my family who still love the idea that justice is always served.

Conclusions

Finally, readers want a sense of closure. They want to feel that, after they have waded through the waters and come onto the shore, there has been something gained; new knowledge, some accomplishment, or maybe just a realization. Conclusions are about doors closing, boats docking, lights going out at the end of a performance. It is the satisfying end to a long and engaging journey filled with attempts, trials, and lessons learned.

In Kareem Mortimer's *Passages*, Anna reaches the shores of a new country. After witnessing her struggles and seeing what she has lost, we are devastated and conflicted about feeling any sense of triumph in her journey. As viewers, we need a release from the unwavering tension built throughout the film.

A conclusion should guide your reader down from the emotional peak of the climax and usher them into a new state that makes them feel that they have completed the end of a cycle, experience, or adventure. Readers need that release after the height of the story so that they have a bridge back to their normal lives. Without that bridge, an unsatisfying ending, or even a cliffhanger, will deprive them of the comfort they need to go into their next experience.

THE DIVERSITY OF STRUCTURE

Now that you've defined the boundaries of your story, the next crucial step is determining how its elements will coexist within the story. This is structure. Structure, fundamentally, is about shaping change, whether it is a change toward resolution, achievement, or the attainment of knowledge. The changes within the story create the structure, not the other way around. Whether these changes manifest in shifts in character, setting, or theme, you, as the storyteller, dictate what your film will revolve around. Your task is to decide how to depict the evolution of this change—be it centered on a person, an object, an idea, or an issue. The structure serves to facilitate transformation, not dictate it. That being said, transformation looks different based on culture and upbringing. This is where diversity comes in.

Diversity's relationship to narrative structure has been explored by writers such as bell hooks, James Baldwin, and Joseph Campbell. While Joseph Campbell's popular *Hero with a Thousand Faces* emphasizes the similarities between structures, short films have charmingly highlighted differences and distinctions between structures. Studying shorts has helped me recognize how influential and under-recognized cultural influences are to our storytelling. Short films have become a platform for showcasing the diversity of narrative structures worldwide. Cultures across continents are reimagining traditional storytelling traditions and finding new ways to capture them in this new era of media.

In addition to traditional Western paradigms (Cowgill, Vogler, Seger, and more...), I've encountered non-conflict-centered Eastern Kishōtenketsu and oral Native American styles, as well as storytelling structures from Latin America, South Asia, and Africa, many of which are characterized by lyricism and spoken verse. Exploring cultural histories is a wonderful way to understand your personal storytelling voice, as you may discover that cultural influences have a more profound impact on your narrative style than you may realize.

A 2023 article, "Investigating Storytelling Differences Between Western and Eastern Computer Animation," offers a comparative analysis of storytelling structures in Japanese and American cultures by examining animation. The authors conclude that storytelling structures are deeply influenced by culture and origin, highlighting the application of cultural value systems in character, theme, and plot development. Not every character undergoes transformation, not every film is about plot, and not every story begins with a hero.

Recognizing that our ideas of storytelling will always be shaped and limited by our cultural frameworks is useful for understanding that these limits seed our ability to innovate and change. Within each culture, systems of story have been shaped not only by the storyteller and their intentions but also by the tools of this culture's time, technology, and language.

Just as a good game of cup and string telephone will never end with the same words it began with, due to the influence of the players, their backgrounds, and their tools, what we hear and comprehend is inevitably guided by the contextual information we already know. This underscores the concepts discussed in the world-building chapter—that our individual perspectives invariably inform how we tell stories, both consciously and unconsciously. Because of this storytelling operates as a fluid and ever-evolving system, that is subject to questions of time and knowledge, purpose and intent.

INNOVATIONS IN FORMATS AND VOICE

Agnes Varda's *Les 3 Boutons*

Unlike features, short formats constantly adapt to align with the preferences of both consumers and creators, unsurprisingly leading to a revolution in storytelling forms. Shorts demonstrate how to inspire innovation in longer formats because they thrive on experimentation and exploration, particularly in areas such as character development, perspective, and story construction. It is in these cases that the function of the story will dictate the structure.

Agnes Varda's narrative commercial for Italian high fashion designer Miu Miu, *Tres Buton*, inserts feminist discourse within the narrative of dress buttons, to redefine perceptions of the company brand. A seemingly simple story, the structure of the film is shaped around a series of buttons that fall from a young girl's dress; each revealing a lesson she has learned along the way. This innovative approach to storytelling showcases traditional narrative techniques in a new way, while still highlighting the brand's values.

However, what if this story did not intend to promote? How would it look? Would the dress still be the center object? How would Varda's voice manifest in alternative formats, such as video games, TikTok posts, or animation? Thankfully, we have many examples of her work and voice throughout her many feature-length and short films, and her voice remains distinct. The central question then becomes how she chooses to wield her voice in various contexts.

Finding the structure for your story can be a bit of an adventure. For some, an empty whiteboard can be very exciting. For others, having some sort of template or originating structure is a more comfortable experience. Either way, the search for the right structure for your short is well worth the investigation.

STRUCTURES FROM AROUND THE WORLD

Film structures can be crafted through many different elements, including visuals, sounds, themes, and experiences, as well as more concrete elements like words, sentences, paragraphs, and pages. Interestingly, film consumption operates at the intersection of attention, language, and time. The viewer's attention span and the platform on which they consume media have led to the creation of various time standards for media. How long can we capture someone's attention and keep them there? For television, a household-based medium, running times are shorter than theatrical-length films, because capturing the audience's full attention is easier in a black box theater space. Now, in the post-modern, post-digital era, where distractions come at us every thousandth of a second, we observe a trend towards shorter and shorter content.

Short films' abbreviated length makes them perfect for experimentation and consumption. The seemingly infinite formatting possibilities of short film are based on one of the fundamental tools of filmmaking: its ability to shape time in a different reality. The way we do this is by manufacturing new structures for new realities.

Here are some common ways that filmmakers have structured their films; a few I discuss further below this list:

> Cycles and Patterns
> Songs and Music
> Devices as Dividers
> The Puzzler
> Thematic Construction
> Thematic Chaptering
> Title Cards
> Character Introductions and Departures
> Emotional Constructions
> Themes
> Collaging
> Location
> Time Stamps
> Anthology
> Quotes, Lettering, and Story
> Looping
> The Classroom

Traditional three-act structure tells us how to organize conflict-driven, goal-oriented stories, but every story isn't built that way. Stories are told in segments and for shorts, typically in short prime number segments. While the story segments are commonly two, three, and five, there's no rule determining this. Who says that human life only exists in three acts? Every organism has a different life cycle, and within different belief systems, numbers carry different meanings. Both seven and four are significant numbers in Judaism, Hinduism, Buddhism, and Islam!

Cycles and Patterns
Bara Hiralova's *Cimpoiasca*

Bara Hiralova's two-minute animated music video follows a young girl who is visited by a dragonfly-like insect, whose wings lead her into a dream. The essence of this animated short lies in its playful exploration of numbers, with patterns intricately woven throughout. Starting and ending with the girl tucked in bed, this video takes us along as she dreams of a journey through a mystical forest. With the help of a magical elixir, she summons other girls; one girl brings two, two girls bring a third, and the cycle continues, whimsically revealing a numerical pattern.

The fun of the film is how Hiralova plays with numbers. This is reflected in multiple ways. For instance, when four girls appear, their faces form a diamond shape, and with five, we witness them dancing and swinging their legs in sets of five. In terms of form, the sequences are led by a piece of classical music—similar to a music video. Every time a new verse is introduced, a new girl is brought into the story in a new and creative way. This short eschews rigidly segmented sections, allowing the film to flow effortlessly as it introduces each new character, culminating in a total of five girls before the protagonist awakens. The significance of the number five is subtly foreshadowed from the beginning with the appearance of five seeds, five branches, and five trees!

Thematic Construction
Amar Hernandez's *Morabeza*

Thematic construction is one of the most common ways we see structure established in a film, particularly with experimental films. When there are many different images or visual material, we look for other kinds of continuity: similar emotions, similar expressions, or similar themes. Sometimes, thematic construction can be traced through music or a written narrative.

Morebeza's quiet, poetic two-minute meditation has a documentary-esque feel as it reflects on the theme of kindness that permeates this experimental film. Through the words of a poet's recitations, viewers are introduced to the beauty of Cape Verde and its people. The poet's words, which appear alongside the images, tonally connect through color and texture. This is a great example of thematic construction where the director allows the rhythm of the words and music to dictate the pacing of the images.

Thematic Chaptering
Jenn Nkiru's *Rebirth is Necessary*

Segmenting films by creating chapters through titling or aural titling is a common tool used to structure films, especially documentaries and experimental films that use less linear structures. Jenn Nkiru's ten-minute experimental short, *Rebirth Is Necessary*, uses chapters, quotes, and sometimes names to separate the thematic sections of the film: beginning, death, beauty, community, and awakening. The film is remarkable both for the number of sequences and archival footage used and how Nkiru shapes it together to tell a story of rebirth for the Black community. I counted at least nine different sequences cut together throughout, and that doesn't even include all the archival footage. The organization of these vast quantities of media is a marvel, and an indicator of the intuitive strength of the editing and direction.

Thematic chaptering really depends on the director and editor, their strong grasp of the film's theme, and how they want to communicate it. In documentaries, the organization of the material may be based on specific topics. Documentarians often edit around the ideas of a conversation or interview. However, in an experimental film, you will use various forms of media and select those in coordination with your theme for that chapter. Music can be useful for laying out and organizing pacing and rhythm in these cases.

In defining the chaptering, Nkiru organized the different sections of the film with these tools: quotes spoken aurally but sometimes presented visually as title cards marking sections of the film; music shifting and changing by section; and dialogue, used to reinforce the themes of each chapter. There are turns and shifts in this ten-minute film, occurring every one to two minutes, creating at least six sections in this impressive work.

Emotional Constructions
Dana Washington's *Under Bone*

Organizing films based on emotions is also a common tool used for structural devices. Dana Washington's *Under Bone* uses emotional constructions to demonstrate a woman's relationship with grief. Washington made both a documentary version and an experimental version of the film. The documentary version reveals core emotions, which act as turning points for the experimental version. Washington does use captions but relies on emotional landscapes and poetic language to move us through the story as we watch a character in three different settings wander, dance, fight, embrace, and release balloons into the sky.

In thinking about form, five distinct experimental sequences surround four documentary sequences that could be said to reflect the five stages of grieving. The first and the fifth act as bookends for the middle of the story. Washington also effectively uses a strong music soundscape to accentuate the emotional shifts.

Devices as Dividers
Peter Huang's *Five Films About Technology*

Sometimes, filmmakers will use objects to structure their films. Peter Huang's hilarious *Five Films About Technology* links five one-minute shorts to make social commentary about the presence of technology in our lives. What's fun about the segments is that they are linked, not only through technology but also through relationships, as we explore different technologies through meeting parents, siblings, and friends. Each segment introduces a new device and character in a kind of "tag, you're it" game, before moving onto a different segment with that new character and their technology. In terms of form, six animated title cards separate each of the sequences, which take place in different locations with different, but related, characters.

Huang creatively uses the title card to give us the number of the sequence, a written and drawn theme, and sometimes the character name. Huang also further connects the sequences by using the same song as an additional audio unifier. The title cards, each caringly imbued with information, don't act as bookends as much as prologues that set up the sequence. Less than five minutes in total in its original form, a more expanded version of this short was developed into a TV series called *Nine Films About Technology* in 2021 by Huang. This early foray demonstrates the possibilities of what you can do in such a short amount of time.

Marking Boundaries and Places
Brandon Lake's *Tin*

Changing locations in a film is also a common way to structure a film. The jazzy animated Claymation romance tale *Tin*, by Brandon Lake, plays with structures of two and four to emphasize the pairing of the two characters in the film. Changing spaces marks the structural shifts in the film through emotion that is accented by color and a terrific jazz soundtrack. The story unfolds through, and is shaped by, the protagonist's various locations and moods, including his apartment, the fire escape both with and without the other character, and his imaginative journeys.

Contrasting Time and Motion
Eulalia Carrizosa's *What Does Your Mother Do?*

Although I watched Eulalia Carrizosa's *Y Su Mama Que Hace* with only Spanish dialogue, by the end, it was easy to see what Carrizosa's focus was from a purely visual perspective. Starting her film with the mother getting up before six in the morning, Carrizosa applies a faster camera speed as the mother achieves the feats of making breakfast, getting her children to school, and seeing her husband off to work. Throughout all this, the children and husband remain at normal speed. Its commentary on the matriarch's responsibilities is clear and impactful.

When using devices that play with time and motion, you must create visual or aural anchors of the world to remind us of which storyline we are in. When time is distorted, viewers may lose their place in your film. This structural approach bears similarities to the looping structure in some respects. To effectively communicate the contrast between storylines, Carrizosa includes anchor points such as the stairs, the stove, and her robe. These elements help to keep the audience grounded in the reality of the day and time.

In terms of form, Carrizosa employs two storylines: the mother's and the rest of her family's. These two plotlines are juxtaposed to tell the story. The structures she uses to organize the film revolve around tasks, such as the mother preparing to nurse a baby that we never see. This technique of playing with time innovates a simple structure, aligning two storylines together to illustrate one character's experience alongside the others. A third storyline, serving as an epilogue, focuses on one of the children, returning us to the question posed in the title.

Anthologizing Stories
Larry Achiampong's *Relic Quadrilogy*

Some films are anthologies—collections of films that are connected through similar themes. Horror films, like *Tales from the Crypt*, assemble three or more shorts linked by a common theme that, together, achieve a feature-length runtime. We have also seen other genres do the same in recent decades. New filmmakers love this approach as a means to getting their name on a feature-length film. However, some short films themselves are anthologies of shorts.

Larry Achiampong's *Relic Quadrilogy* visits our future in this four-episode set of Afro-futurist shorts. According to Achiampong, these shorts examine "the intersection between pop culture and the post-colonial position." They are anchored by the repeating structure of a traveler, played by different characters who wear the same astronaut suit, exploring different locations in the U.K., while a narrator provides context for the social issues related to the tremendous landscapes we visit.

The Puzzler
Michael Omonua's *Rehearsal*

Telling storylines out of order is a common storytelling device used in feature films. This technique is also employed in shorts, but it is often more effective in longer shorts than shorter ones. The intent is to create tension in the film by withholding information at the beginning, thereby creating mystery and opportunities for reveals. In Michael Omonua's *Rehearsal*, we are introduced to a group of people who appear to be preparing for something, although we don't know what. By catching them in the middle of this act, with very little information, we are forced to dissect and examine the story as information is parceled out to us in bits. We learn that this group of people are actors brought in for a spiritual community. The lines of reality become blurred for us, as the viewer, as we start to question what's performance and what's real.

In terms of form, Omonua opens in the middle of an action to intrigue us and draw us in. This is an important part of using the puzzler tool. If the opening sequence doesn't have something immediately attention-grabbing, we won't be sufficiently motivated to solve the puzzle to reach the end. As we go deeper into the film, the director reveals rehearsal tapes for some of the cast. Three storylines weave together: the rehearsal tapes, the rehearsals themselves, and the actors' interactions. In a puzzler paradigm, one could use more than three storylines, but with more, additional anchors are required to keep us rooted in the reality of the story. Omonua deftly reserves the audition of the character introduced at the beginning for the end of the film, captivating us with our own curiosity.

Looping
Travon Free and Martin Desmond Roe's *Two Distant Strangers*

Looping may be a commonly overused construction in experimental or narrative films, but it can be effective if used in an innovative or deeply emotional way. Looping structures tell a story that repeats because there is a lesson that the main character needs to learn. Travon Free and Martin Desmond Roe's *Two Distant Strangers* confronts the topic of race and freedom when a man tries to break out of a cycle to prevent a violent ending.

In terms of form, you have to set up the first scene before we get to the looping. Additionally, the very first scene must establish a few different anchors to the narrative to allow us to enter the cycle of looping. Things that break and characters who have specific lines or actions are both often used to illustrate this looping idea. After the first scene is complete, subsequent scenes should be shortened so that only new information is delivered. Scenes grow shorter and shorter as they change, and we start to comprehend the repetitive nature of the story. The challenge of looping is making sure that the reader never gets so far ahead of the story that they want to abandon it because they already know the ending.

The Classroom
Kamran Shirdel's *Women's Quarter*

Documentaries may develop narrative storylines of introduction, body, and conclusion but can go in many directions. Often, a character-driven narrative, a documentary may follow a single person through different times or locations that structure the film. But it may also be organized around a question. For an ensemble piece, you may want to choose a different approach.

Kamran Shirdel's *Woman's Quarter* sets up an introduction, body, and an ending that uses song and a combination of pictures and live-action to shape the structure. Songs accent the beginning, middle, and the end, but most of the body of the story is structured by meeting each of the women in a shared event that occurs in a classroom. The camera settles on a face and then tells that woman's story. This was a suitable approach for Shirdel, who wanted to focus on making sociopolitical statements through his work by commenting on the struggles of these women in the Red Light District of Tehran in the 1960s.

Shirdel's film uses a classroom-type approach with the anchoring narrative that sees all the women in a classroom. The second storyline visits each woman individually to tell their story.

Narrative Exits & Experiments

The Chorus
David Lynch's *Six Men Getting Sick*

Although the above tools focus on traditional shorts in narrative, experimental, documentary, and animation forms, these tools can also apply to other content forms. They can be used for commercials, music videos, social media, and cross-genre forms.

David Lynch's *Six Men Getting Sick* loops six times to focus on process and repetition. His next experimental short, *The Alphabet*, utilizes climaxes in the story of a young girl completing the song of the alphabet and finishing with one of the most memorable vomiting scenes in cinematic history.

In terms of form, Lynch's *Six Men Getting Sick* composes six identical parts as we watch the animation create and recreate a looping narrative, like a chorusing play over a resounding siren.

The Collage
Beyoncé's *Formation*

While many songs may not have a crescendo that easily identifies as a climax, narrative music videos will construct climactic events or a climax of montage shots towards which the film builds. Part-experimental and part-narrative music videos still communicate strong themes and structure around lyrics.

Beyoncé's music video, *Formation*, directed by Melina Matsoukas, serves as a strong example of a narrative played to lyrics; it applies a collaging structure that suggests a build up to a fight—a confrontation that the director illuminates through images of police, black pride, and protest. Her climactic build, up to the final sinking police car, completes the prior sequences of her singing from atop a police car in the middle of a lake—a conclusive final act. Looking closer, you can see many of the sequences in the video are their own storylines—whether they have two scenes or five.

Transforming Characters
Julian Bass' *Favorite Heroes* TikTok

Social media has, single-handedly, shifted how we think about short content. On Instagram, story video shorts last fifteen seconds. Snapchat started with ten seconds before increasing to sixty. TikTok started at fifteen seconds, increased to 60 seconds, and now allows for three full minutes of short content. These boundaries keep shifting to allow users to create unique ways to tell story. The central building block here is time. Notice how social media platforms have created boundaries for the structure, but also how consumers and media makers have forced shifts in what they want to see. Both makers and consumers have made demands around that building block of time, and platforms have reorganized to serve the needs of their consumers.

In 2020, Julian Bass, the college student TikTok phenom, caught the attention of big studios like Disney because he changed how we saw story through his superhero transformation TikToks. In twenty-two seconds, he created stories that had a visual structure of five segments: three superhero changes and two bookends. His TikTok content wasn't limited to fifteen seconds because he created a different length to serve his story. Your story should always dictate your structure and not the other way around.

At the other end of the spectrum, Berlin Film Festival Jury Grand Prix award-winning director Béla Tarr crafted his seven-hour *Sátántangó* epic; a feature which was structured into twelve chapters, often spread out over three viewings. Tarr described this structure as mimicking the chapters of the novel on which the film was based, structured on the steps of the tango; where movements are six steps forward and then six steps back.

So, outside of boundaries of time, what are some of the other elements that will influence the structure of your story? Certainly, resources will always be an issue that will affect access, money, locations, casting, and crew. But within the confines of the short, media makers are finding that the limitations of short content are forcing them to think more creatively.

The Promotion of Place
Arie Esiri's *Because Men in Silk Shirts on Lagos Night*

Creativity is one of those topics I love to discuss in my classroom because, as a young person, I was taught that creativity was relegated only to practicing artists—painters, illustrators, sculptors, and other classical disciplines. As an adult, however, I came to realize that artistry is not defined through a task or even a skill. Artistry is defined by the artist's commitment to the craft. I learned that scientists, businessmen, and even foresters could be creators. It also helped me realize that creativity is not art. Creativity is defined by your ability to create when you lack resources; limitations and boundaries can facilitate creativity.

So, if you find yourself in a conundrum regarding an idea, one approach to solving it is by adding limits. Think about going into a grocery store and someone saying you can have anything you want, anytime, anywhere. You wouldn't know where to begin. Given a boundary however, perhaps anything *within* a ten-minute time frame. . . this will set you in motion. The boundaries of advertisement, time, and place certainly shaped the night shoot in Tafawa Balewa Square—in which Arie Esiri places male characters in silk shirts. The Square is integral in establishing not only the character of the Lagos setting but also the sophisticated Afro-futuristic feel that would promote designer Maki Oh's designs.

Intersecting Form and Function
Ja'Tovia Gary's *The Giverny Document*

During a conversation with one of my mentors, I was reminded that structure, much like many aspects of our lives, is tethered to existing systems. Language itself is a limiting structure. The English language boasts nearly one hundred thousand words, and the size and content of lexicons vary significantly among other languages. As someone who often hears bilingual speakers say, "There is no word for this in English," I am left contemplating how my access to language may deprive me of the richness in expressing a feeling, detail, or an experience. This serves as a reminder of the personalized nature of limitations, which are often shaped by individual perspectives. While some boundaries may appear restrictive to you, they can always be expanded by other viewpoints and experiences.

Ja'Tovia Gary's provocative collage of images, *The Giverny Document*, appears only in segments online—one part of the art installation, *The Giverny Suite*. Part-documentary and part-experimental film, the trailer that appears on YouTube features Gary interviewing Black women on a street in Harlem and asking them, "Do you feel safe?" Recently recorded footage is interwoven with archival footage of recognizable musicians and artists speaking about their lives in America and commenting on the "creative virtuosity of Black women." This juxtaposition demonstrates the power of combining formats within a work.

TECHNIQUES AND TOOLS

THE IDEA AND THE LOGLINE

Haukur Bjorgvinsson's *Heartless*

In the ideas chapter, you may have completed the exercise of writing an emotional logline. There are many kinds of loglines and various formulas for writing effective loglines. You'll find some that are more exploratory, while others are more action or goal oriented. Generally, your logline should be a one-to-three sentence summary of your story. The logline is important because it becomes an entryway for communicating your story in a brief, simple form. The most effective loglines are easily digestible, providing enough, but not too much, information about the story, intriguing the listener or reader. Consider the logline in the pyramid of story development here:

Idea

Logline

Synopsis

Treatment

Outline or Beat Sheet

Script

What's great about a logline is sometimes, loglines can reveal structure. Whether you look at the clauses in a single sentence or examine the two or three sentences of your logline, pay attention to how the logline itself may inform the way you segment your story. Haukur Bjorgvinsson's *Heartless'* one-sentence logline (written on *The Short of the Week* page) about a young couple torn apart by a lottery system can easily be broken down into three sections: beginning, middle and end, or even setup, conflict, and resolution. It's a great reminder that structure can be simple, or it can be complex and even messy at times.

THE ORGANIZING CHAOS OF THE TREATMENT

The "treatment" is best applied after completing the work of character, world-building, and synopsis.

This treatment can take the structure of your choosing, but I like to begin by suggesting you write your story in prose form on the page, the requirement being that it must have a beginning, a middle, and an end. Then we get to see what happens.

I encourage students to write three to five paragraphs and then do a little digging. Sometimes, the story requires more, and that's okay, but I try to ask them to keep it down to a page or two of prose. This will be a messy exercise, but it's about getting your thoughts down on paper. Try not to worry about it making sense and just focus on getting the ideas out. Then, walk away.

When you return, look for the naturally occurring breaks. Not only where you yourself put them but also around the shifting of ideas. Remember, structure is about finding the shifts in the chaos.

THE EVOLUTIONARY OUTLINE

Kat Candler's *Hellion*

Outlines, also referred to as less developed beat sheets, have a bad rap, but they are one of the most useful tools to the screenwriter. Outlines are an excellent way to keep focus and keep track of your story. The outline will sketch a skeleton of the story by sectioning out ideas, beats, or concepts. Charts, notes, beat sheets, index cards, maps, Venn diagrams, or sketches are all potential outline tools for your story. They act as a reference or a guide, much like how a painter might lightly pencil in some details before they paint. This outline can help create a trajectory for the story by keeping you from meandering and helping you identify faults in the storyline. I've referenced screenwriter John August's sequence outlines from his website, but I especially love Kat Candler's *Hellion*, for shorts.

Early in her career, Kat Candler wrote an article for an outline that she created and graciously shared with new writers. One of my favorite takeaways from this article, "The Art of Short Filmmaking," was that she would post the theme at the top of her computer (more on theme in the theme and premise chapter!). Whatever your style, you must find a way to stay on track with your story's purpose. Whether by posting a picture, a problem, or a question, find a tool that keeps you centered and moving toward a specific resolution.

In my early years, I used index cards to outline my story. Many writers use various other tools: colored pencils, scribbles on post-its, or screenwriting software highlighters. Other digital screenwriting software may offer tools to analyze a script and deliver various reports that help you to visualize your storyline. These are extremely helpful for a feature, but still have great utility for short films, especially if they are a longer form short. I love creating colorful charts to help me discern other plots.

OUTLINING THE ACTS

George Sikharulidze's *Red Apples*

The base idea of the outline starts with identifying your structure first and then creating segments for these sections. Whether your short has four, sixteen, or seventy-five acts, it's about:

- ➜ Identifying what is the focus of each act
- ➜ Writing out the beats within each act
- ➜ Ensuring that the beats lead up to the focus of each act

The relationship between beats, scenes, sequences, and acts are critical in the industry. Beats, also known as rhythmic beats, movement beats, or sound beats, are the base of writing a dramatic scene. The organization looks like this.

Actions make Beats
Beats make Scenes
Scenes make Sequences
Sequences make Acts
Acts make Stories

The relationship between the beats, the scenes, and the acts will unify the purpose of each act so that you reach a centering conclusion. In George Sikharulidze's *Red Apples*, the first act sets up Lilit's virginity at her wedding, the second act questions Lilit's virginity, and the third act sees the question of her virginity resolved. This last act further serves to make us question the validity of this archaic and disempowering issue of virginity where women have no control over their bodies.

An approach I learned from John August is to see outlines as evolving documents, much like drafts that you date or number. As you discover more of your story, you might find yourself using multiple outlines. Writing a draft will sometimes lead me back to a more detailed outline as I figure things out along the way.

The Turning Points

Andrea Arnold's *Wasp*

Another way to approach thinking of act structure is by exploring turning points. In traditional three and four-act structures, we talk about various turning points, or plot points, within a story. These are the fundamental events that we expect to see in the goal-oriented plot of a feature film—at least according to Syd Field, Chris Vogler, Blake Snyder, and others. I've also seen some great shorts adhere to a strong goal-oriented structure. Kat Candler's seven-page short, *Hellion*, showed me that you can create three-act structure no matter the length. I also love Andrea Arnold's *Wasp*, a longer short that also adheres to the traditional structure with a buzzy climax that has everyone on the edge of their seat.

Inciting incident
Turning Point One or Plot Point One
Midpoint
Turning Point Two or Plot Point Two
Climax or Crisis
Resolution or Denouement

You will find descriptions of these turning point elements in many traditional screenwriting books. While the titles may vary, the ideas tend to be similar. Here is what they may look like for a short narrative.

The Determined Student's Journey

Another way to think about the inciting incident is that it is a moment on the character's timeline that starts this small story. That moment can be an ordinary everyday moment.

Inciting Incident: In one of my classes, we studied the movements of one of my students whose alarm had not gone off. This inciting incident propelled her into a wild journey to get to my class on time. Along the way, she encountered various characters, such as her landlord, an Uber driver, and even her iPhone! While this scenario may appear trivial to us, I was touched that, to her, the stakes were quite high, and she overcame numerous obstacles to make it to my class instead of just skipping! Inciting incidents are the events which occur that disturb our sense of normalcy, throwing us into chaos and a search for balance.

Turning Point One or Plot Point One: In this classroom example, my student faced the choice of going back to bed, but she was determined to still make it to class. She took a decisive step forward into act one of her journey! This served as an important example of stakes, priorities, and motivations. We tend to procrastinate only when the stakes are low enough that we don't mind the consequences. In her mind, missing my class was a high stake. She shared the issue (the alarm hadn't gone off), players (herself and her iPhone), and goal (to get to class on time) of her first act. Her second act includes new characters (her landlord), places (the world between her bed and school), and quandaries (her phone wasn't charged, nor could she use her charger, so she couldn't call an Uber). Discovering her phone was not charged (the event) prompted her next move, marking the beginning of act two. Her decision to persist instead of surrendering represented turning point one.

The Midpoint: For my student, the inciting incident was caused by the electricity going out. This new realization complicated what could have been a simple solution, like calling Uber, into a more heightened one. The electric outage explained why her alarm hadn't gone off and her phone hadn't charged, requiring alternate actions. The scenes between the turning point one and the midpoint usually tend to be hopeful or lighter moments in the story. As tension slowly builds towards the climax, the midpoint event establishes the new reality or change for the character. After this, they must proceed in a new or different way due to the introduction of obstacles or information that alters their approach to attaining their goal. The midpoint is also often seen as a point of no return, where they have more to lose by trying to go back than moving forward.

Turning Point Two or Plot Point: For my student, this was about going to a landlord that she didn't have a personal relationship with, to convince them to help her get to school. This was her low point as she was reluctant to ask for help. In this goal-oriented structure, turning point two presents obstacles that make the goal harder to attain, perhaps even out of reach, which, in turn, might entail a shift in tactics. The scenes between the midpoint and this turning point should give us unexpected information that will make things more difficult for the character. We think of this event as something that throws the character into greater tumult, which is exactly what happened when her landlord initially said no to her.

The Climax: For my student, this is where she had to return to her landlord and pull out all the stops to convince them to help her get to my class. I'll never know exactly what she said, but it likely had to do with the reason she wanted to get to class. For story purposes, I'd like to imagine it involved themes of community, acceptance, or appreciation, as these are emotionally and dramatically resonant. This decision to fill in story gaps is called dramatic license. The climax is where the character's hidden secret is revealed. It is, in many ways, a mirror opposite to what happens in the inciting incident's act one. The class she was going to miss now becomes the class for which she fights.

However, climaxes are tricky and, as mentioned earlier in this chapter, can befuddle new writers. Climaxes can be big fights or events, but they must resolve the issues of the first act. Often, a mistaken climax will veer away from the story's origins instead of connecting to them. This is why we must maintain clarity throughout the emotional journey of the characters, even if the external goal shifts. Also, it's important to note that during the climax, the character may or may not achieve their goal, and that's okay! As in the real world, we don't always get what we want. Although audiences are generally drawn to hopeful stories over bleak ones, what's more important is to make the story truthful, otherwise the audience will feel cheated by the resolution.

The Resolution or Denouement: For my student, this was arriving to class in an anxious and worried state, only to discover that I was simply happy that she had made it. So, there was a great ending. As a class, we gathered to hear the story and spotlight it as a way of studying structure. We were all quite amazed at her determination to learn.

Decisions, Decisions, and Events

Meli Tuqota's *You, the Choice of My Parents*

Before we leave turning points, I want to clarify one important aspect of understanding the relationship between decisions and events. For my student, the failing alarm clock (inciting incident) and the uncharged phone (turning point one) and discovering the electricity was down (midpoint) were all events. The turning points act as decisions the character makes in the face of these events. You need to create specific, problematic, and sometimes escalating, events to propel the character forward in the story. Turning points are identified by the choices that the character is forced to make in difficult circumstances. The example I use in class involves walking in a straight line to a wall, which would force me to "turn" and go in a different direction. In this example, I am forced to make a decision. Your narrative short will be all about choices.

Meli Tuqota's animated film follows a reading of a poem against images painted on fabric. Different colored paints permeate the fabric, similarly to real life, creating a weaving effect that feels tangible in a novel way. Even though it's a poem that tells the story of a woman brought into a marriage against her wishes, she still makes decisions about the acts she commits, fully aware of the compromises she makes against her own desires.

Changing Places in the Geography of the Heart

Journeying
Nora Sarak and Dominik Krutsky's *A Poem About Love*

Nora Sarak and Dominik Krutsky's experimental documentary hybrid, *A Poem About Love*, is a tender, reflective illustration of how the emotional geography of our hearts can structure movement in the story. In *A Poem About Love*, we follow the director's experience of coming to a new place out of love for her partner. It's a poetic and meditative multimedia film that is shaped by the director's spoken narrative and her visits to different spaces in her new home and life. It reminds us that there are no perfect roads; just like there are no perfect structures. There are only the roads we find. *A Poem About Love*, with its journeying structure, is a reminder that as long as you keep your "story moving forward," that itself reveals a structure.

"Change is more incremental than time."

I heard this from a scientist on a panel I attended for the National Science Academy's Science and Entertainment Exchange. As a screenwriter interested in science, I always loved attending these panels. This organization was interested in drawing entertainment writers together with scientists to create more collaborative work. This scientist shared this phrase, and it has stuck with me for reasons I still can't explain. It relates directly to the idea of story moving forward.

Life is about change.

When creating a structure, the most important thing to remember is that you move story forward by creating change in the various segments of the film. Whether it be through character or place, whether it is good or bad, monumental or incremental, persevering or momentary, there is change. Something must be changing in the story on every. Single. Page. Something must be different. Tangibly, we often visit change through the evolution of character. With every occurrence in our lives, we react to change: whether it's the phone ringing, someone coming to the door, or a vase falling and breaking on the floor. Our lives exist as a construction of changes. When the story is not moving forward, nothing is happening.

Change in our lives is seemingly random. Or is it? In our stories, structure is about articulating movement towards something. That something often has to do with emotion, desire, and personal theme.

The Sly Comfort of Monotony

Structure can help you construct your practice. The practice of craft, however, must be cultivated consistently. Unsurprisingly, many of my favorite artists and writers have established rituals in practicing their art or writing. Establishing a ritual is a requisite technique for teaching the mind and body how to re-engage with your process. However the writer-artist must be ever wary of the pitfalls of monotony: doing things in a rote manner, abandoning being present in your process, or making steps without moving.

Coming out of film school, I had a period of being in an artistic desert where I was writing and revising but not creating any new films. I had many excuses to explain this, none of which were true, including the notion that I was working too hard. Toni Morrison's ritual of rising in the dark mornings to write before she took her kids to school and went to work set me straight on that! I found myself occupied with tasks that created the impression of progress, yet failed to move me in the right direction. It's perfectly common for artists to experience periods where they're not producing their best work. Every writer can't pen a masterpiece with every attempt, and not every actor delivers a flawless performance every time. These phases are often referred to as "dialing it in." Within these moments lies a pivotal juncture in an artist's life. Here, the prospect of change ignites a flame of possibility, and the world often provides opportunities for progression when one decides to seize them.

For me, this significant gap in creating work lasted years. It was easy to create the illusion that I was doing many things because, in this world of multitudinous devices and distractive opportunities, we can be busy doing nothing at all. Monotony can look a hundred different ways, but only you can recognize it in yourself. I thank the books, *The Soul of Money* and *The War of Art*, the poets Lucille Clifton, Rainer Maria Rilke, and Pablo Neruda, and my work at the public library for helping me find my way back.

I always try to encourage my students to interrupt monotonous structures. Everyone's structures are different, so this can look different for everybody. For me, it was communing with bodies of water, taking trips to museums, traveling to new places far and near, visiting old friends, enrolling in new classes, working new jobs, and going on long walks. Director Joel Schumacher's journey of making the independent feature, *Tigerland*, was an inspiring story for me at that time. Monotony is seductively comfortable but, sometimes we require time outside of our habits before revisiting them with a renewed love or passion.

PRACTICE AND PLAY

1. Write a list of the major turning points in a classical Western structure for your film: include status quo, inciting incident, turning point 1, midpoint, turning point two, climax, and resolution.
2. Go through your script and identify the purpose of each scene. Write the purpose on an index card. Order them on the floor so you can see how each scene leads to the other and how some branches reach out. (This will also help you recognize irrelevant scenes that aren't moving story forward.)
3. Write a structure for your story around three, five, and eight segments. Which one fits best?
4. Reimagine your story as a part of an anthology of the character's life. It could be an anthology on heartbreak, on motherhood, or on mentoring. How could you revisit your story as a series of vignettes? Write an outline of your story as an anthology.
5. If you were to chapter your story, what would each chapter title say? Break up your story into emotional or thematic elements with titles.
6. Identify a prop or object in your film and use it to segment different sections of the story. Decide how the object can be shifted or changed as a tool to demonstrate different emotions in each segment.
7. Take the climax in your current story and use that as the inciting incident for a new story. Create a new climax for this new story.
8. Find a local building or space that has meaning for you. Create a new structure for your character by placing them in a new location in six time periods and allow them to interact within each one.
9. Identify a needed resource, a person, place or thing, that your character requires in the story. Remove it and see what happens when you retell the story.
10. Revisit your map of your character's journey from the world chapter. Connect your character's emotional growth to their physical location.
11. Apply the loop tool from the Cycles and Loops section to your story to create five loops. What changes in terms of setting or character in each loop? And why?
12. Structure an interview as if you are documenting a character's life in your story using social media time limits, such as an Instagram story, TikTok, or Snapchat. What is the interview topic for each segment?

TYING THEME & PREMISE:
PURPOSE AND INTENTION

Purpose
*—The reason for which something is done or created
or for which something exists*

Intention
—A thing intended; aim or a plan

TO WRITE; OR, NOT TO WRITE

Writing is a tool that we can use for many purposes. But how did writing evolve and why? To enshrine an idea or tradition, to communicate, to express how we feel, to accomplish a task, assignment, or job, or to get something that we want? Is writing a conduit to our emotions, desires, and expression or an instrument of achievement and access? As a youth, I wrote many journals exploring why I felt this way or that. As I grew older, I learned that writing could be more purposeful. Writing was a tool that helped me to earn better grades in school, made my mother proud, and promoted me to special honors. I learned that there were different styles of writing: beyond journals there were essays, short stories, letters—and poetry. It was much later that I found screenwriting, the form that enraptured me as a writer.

One of the first scripts I wrote after I left film school was a story about two women who were dancers in Miami. Both characters were based around my experiences living in Miami—both dancers who became friends. One of them in particular was a combination of a young teacher I knew and a dear friend I had at the time who made me feel at home in this new city—who helped me feel that I belonged. I was lonely and living in Los Angeles at that time and struggling to make friends. I suspect writing the story became a comfort to me, returning me to a warm and vibrant world where I had felt loved and treasured by the Cuban-American community—and by these women in particular. When I shared this script with another co-worker, he cried, not because of any specific character, but because of it as a whole. It wasn't until much later I realized what I had done. I had infused my feelings for these women into the character. I had approached these characters with the love and comfort they had shown to me and that was what affected my co-worker. This is what it means to write with intention.

Purpose and intention are elements of writing that we discover as we age and develop intellectually. We slowly discover that writing can do more than just sit on a page. It can help with expression, connection, and relationships. Writing can bring attention and affection. Writing can win arguments, disputes, and political races. Writing can introduce you to other histories, cultures, and ways of thinking.

When you think of purpose, I want you to think about the reason guiding it. You are thinking about the specific *why* that you are embarking on in this journey of making. That could be making a film for a job, a course, or even a contest. In the short form chapter, you will learn that different forms exist for different purposes: to market, to advocate, to play. For example, if I think of making a video game, the purpose ostensibly revolves around gameplay. Courtney Cogburn's *1000 Cut Journey* is one of several emerging social commentary virtual reality games (*I am a Man* and *Passage Home* are two other examples) that allow the viewer to experience racism as a person of color. However, it is her Ted Talk that reveals to us her personal connection to the game and some of her motivations for making it.

However, intention is something different completely.

Intention is what is happening *behind* the words. We get a glimpse of it when Professor Cogburn speaks in the Ted Talk. When she discusses her relationship to the game, we wonder if she made the game to protect, to shield, or to uplift her son. You can also think of intention when you think of the trillion ways your parent might call your name. Each time they say it, it has a different and distinct meaning depending on whether you are in trouble or about to be smothered in affection. In our everyday speech, intentions are often embedded, even if they go unnoticed. Consider the insincerity behind someone's casual use of "sorry," where their true feelings may contradict their words. In our writing, this same idea applies. Stories are never only about the physical *why (purpose)*, they are also about the emotional *how (intention)*.

Purpose and intention are the foundations for a lifelong pursuit of storytelling.

LOCATING PURPOSE AND INTENTION

When we share a film, we offer our audience a diversion from everyday reality. In the making of that film, however, we draw from our own experiences, and in doing so, attempt to wrap a moment into a digestible engagement that leaves the audience feeling different and, hopefully, better than before. This escapist venture is most successful when we feel transformed in some way. We are attracted to this new existence in a pursuit of themes that we recognize, and these themes come from your emotional experience. How these themes mix together is like a unique recipe for your purpose and/or intention.

A recipe of intention:
A tablespoon of loneliness
A cup of forgiveness
A teaspoon of family
A dash of discovery

Which ingredients would you choose? In your short film, purpose and intention are the tendrils that wrap your ideas together into a complete event. Like a novel, a script requires a well-defined conclusion. This ending serves not only to wrap up the story but also to provide a sense of resolution that resonates with the audience's emotional experience. Often that ending ties your purpose (*form*) and intention (*theme*) together.

Your purpose and intent exist as guides; leading you through a forest of storytelling elements and keeping you on the right path, not only for you but also for the audience. They want to feel that the experience has led them somewhere exotic or tender, or made them feel better about their lives. Why else would we comb through infinite streaming platform options for an hour looking for something interesting to watch?

In my experience, shorts with a clear and meaningful intention behind their storytelling often deliver some of the most personal and impactful narratives. I've witnessed truly magical films come out of filmmakers who were writing stories to their brother, mother, or another loved one. Stories that embody honor, protection, care, and fear resonate deeply, touching the heart in uniquely selfless ways, as they stand as one-of-a-kind gifts of expression. These stories are embedded with such emotionally potent intention that they can make the viewer feel showered in feelings of love, courage, boldness, grief, and terror. This only happens when the intention comes from a cultivated personal and generous space.

When someone watches your film, episode, or experimental work, they are, at the very least, gifting you their time and attention. You want to give them a gift back, and this gift is more sincere when it is given with honest intention. This gift doesn't necessarily have to be something grandiose. It can be as simple as wanting to bring laughter or comfort, letting viewers know they're not alone. Your film inherently carries a portion of your intention, but establishing a firm foundation of intention and purpose starts with understanding your beliefs, values, and themes.

Lessons, Values, and Theme

As we grow up, we are offered many lessons in the world. Some of these lessons are specific to learning skills (read, writing, arithmetic). Other lessons are about learning behaviors (social norms, customs, and traditions). We are also taught lessons around values (family, love, justice); principles that guide us on what is important. Our value systems tell us about what we need, what we can lose, and what we cannot do without. Perhaps more than anything else, our value systems shape who we are as decision-making organisms. They mold who we are and who we will become. Within a story context, these can be referred to as themes.

When we talk about films and stories, themes are the values that we associate with a particular film. Sometimes themes are presented as lessons to learn, such as in the case of myths, fables, or folktales. Themes may be exhibited through personified animals that symbolize nature or humanized deities that tell us how to live. Sometimes they can appear as warnings or harbingers, but they can also be themes that exist within entertainment as belief systems. Whether the theme persists as a cautionary tale or a reflection, themes demonstrate what matters in the film. Why is this story relevant or significant? This is the silent question that runs through your audience's mind when viewing a film or reading your script.

So, What's It About?

When a person asks this question, they are trying to get some sense of the core purpose or relevance of the film. The answer typically revolves around theme. That answer will demonstrate the core emotional elements that anchor your story. Marketers know this too, which is why thematic elements like joy, love, or hope often appear in advertisements. Sometimes, you will notice themes in the synopsis or logline when you flip through movies on your streaming service. The characters and plot of a story are crucial, but fundamentally, people yearn for connection, and something as universal as theme is essential for fostering understanding and facilitating that connection.

The Braiding Denouement

Once you have discovered what the central theme is for the film, it becomes your job, first as writer, and later as director, to tie all the strands together. Think of a braid; you must weave together the different strands to create the whole. Tying them together creates cohesion for the braid, preventing it from pulling apart easily. This is how you want to think about theme—as one of three strands that tie the story threads together: theme, purpose, and intention. These are the elements that tie together all the other building blocks of the story, from plot and world, to structure, tone, and mood, to the conclusion (or denouement). These elements will be stronger if they are shaped by a single idea.

Themes are Universal

Film themes are observably universal because, when examining differences between cultures, languages, and places, we can easily identify similar principles. We recognize two people embracing as "love." When we witness a generational group together caring for each other, we see that as family. When we follow people being tried for stealing something that didn't belong to them, we call that justice. We visually recognize these themes because we know them and can identify them. However, these principles aren't the same for everyone.

Just as our bodies possess a distinctive composition, so too does the combination of values and principles that shape our lives. These codes are determined by much of the world we visited in the earlier chapter; our society, our family, our religious beliefs, and so on. We each have a particular code that guides us, and that code is determined by not only our values but also their weights and balances. When can the code be broken? When can it be bent? This code defines us and influences how navigate the world. It defines our interactions, connections, and relationships. Embedded within these principles is our personal character, the inner voice that tells us whether we should help, ignore, or steal from that person lying in the road. It embodies our morals, serving as our compass in discerning right from wrong. This compass reveals our personal themes, the ones closest and known best to us.

> *"Personalizing the film is very important."*
> SIDNEY LUMET, *MAKING MOVIES*

PERSONAL THEMES

Personal themes are the ones that we know better than others. Growing up without my father after my parents' divorce, loss and abandonment became themes that I came to know very well, more than I ever wanted to. I found these themes embedded in many of the movies I sought out as a youth. Steven Spielberg's *E.T.* resonated with me like few other films had, so it was interesting to learn, years later, that the film had themes of divorce, family separation, and loss. I only began to notice them as an adult.

Personal themes are value systems that have taken root in our psyche. Whether it is feeling less than (validation), suspecting we are being underestimated (underdog), or wanting to win someone's attention (approval), these are personal themes from which we can draw. When we tell stories from emotional places, films become their most potent, their most resonant. That doesn't mean every film will impact everyone equally, but certain films will resonate with certain people. You'll also find that love, arguably the most recognizable emotion, is where most films carve their themes.

Many artists use themes in their work. Mexican painter and visual artist Frida Kahlo worked in themes of the human body, death, and identity; often reflecting some of her own life experiences. Similarly, jazz and blues singer and lyricist Billie Holiday often sang songs about the struggles of Black-Americans. As a director-producer casting my own films, I quickly learned that actors were often drawn to particular themes in the work for which they auditioned. Even though it is work, sometimes it reflects passion and personal struggle.

SHIFTING CHANGE

As human beings, we are always shifting and changing as we grow and evolve. This is the same for the personal themes that guide us. As a child, our themes might hover around acceptance, adolescence, and discovery. As an adult, some of these themes might change as our relationships expand, grow, and disappear. If we have children, motherhood might become a prominent theme. If we lose the love of our life, loss might become a prominent theme. If we are harmed, safety might become an urgent theme. Personal themes will always shift. We are always works-in-progress, doing the work of living as best we can. That doesn't mean that some themes might not lead us through our entire lives. In the actors' world, they call that a spine, and spines are important for characters. We might discover that we will always be driven by curiosity, acceptance, or a lack of love.

Here is a list of common themes that show up in short films:

Acceptance
Love
Passion
Renewal/Rebirth
Individuality
Death
Darkness
Despair
Hope
Retribution/Revenge
Redemption
Non-conformity
Community
Justice
Forgiveness
Validation
Intimacy
Family
Discovery/Transformation
Nature
Race
Connection
Gender
Health
Loss/Grief
Maturity
Adolescence
Sexuality
Identity
Playfulness

WHAT DO I WANT TO SAY?

So, what's valuable about knowing your personal themes? Why can't you make stories about themes that aren't important to you? You can, but when you choose to make a film that is guided by your personal themes, it provides an anchor to the story, a grounding material that infuses the film with an emotional reality. This emotional reality allows others to connect to the story in a deeper way. The film stops feeling arbitrary and feels specific, even if you can't put your finger on exactly why. The film begins to feel real on some level because it is real—it becomes real with true emotion infusing it, such as in Lynne Ramsay's *Small Deaths* or Nuotama Frances Bodomo's *Boneshaker*.

I believe most artists' work develops from personal themes. The reason you like this video game instead of that one is personal taste, but that personal taste is bred by your experience, values, and thoughts, all connected to personal themes. However, sometimes a film can become muddled with themes.

In our lives, it seems we experience an infinite number of moments. From these moments we gather different themes: from work (responsibility, determination, family), to play (joy, freedom, childhood), to going around the corner to the convenience store (sustenance, convenience, community). Themes are always dropping out of the sky. It's hard to say that a single theme remains more important than others because we, and our values, are always evolving. One theme might be relevant in this moment and another theme may become more relevant in the next. Reading Paulo Coelho's *The Alchemist* meant more to me as an adult, with its themes of perseverance, than the first few times I read it in college where I mainly identified its themes of adventure. With time shifting constantly, each moment portrays some unique experience that may pull some new emotion forward.

However, in a film, and especially in a short, like a fable or fairy tale, it's better to concentrate on one theme.

That concentration can provide clarity and purity in focusing on what the artist wants to communicate. Rungano Nyoni and Hamy Ramezan's short, *Listen*, ably positions the title to guide us through a film with themes of disconnection—although the themes of violence, immigration, and discrimination also populate the film. However, you can only provide this guide or direction to the viewer when you yourself have a grasp on not only what the film is "about," but what precisely it is you want to say.

THE DRAMATIC ARGUMENT—THE PREMISE

In writing, a common tool that writers will discuss in thinking about written story is the dramatic question. This is a central question that may guide the writer on their way, like a touchstone, keeping them on the right path of their story. In the structure chapter, I discussed how easy it is for the writer to wander off the main storyline in their story and for multiple storylines to occur as subplots. Kat Candler's trick of posting a note at the top of her computer was one of my favorite activities that she shared. If you recall, that note was the theme of her short.

Great bodies of literature have often been produced searching for the answer to an urgent question. In the theater world, the dramatic question describes the central conflict in the story. In *Macbeth*, a question might be "how far would we go to achieve great power?" In *The Bluest Eye*, it might be "what happens to a child who is not taught to love herself?" This question can be a driving force in the creation of written work. It is often filled with thematic elements and can serve as a guiding principle for the writer and for the characters in the story.

Now, if you take this dramatic question and shape it into a statement, we will call it, as Egri does, a dramatic premise! However, this premise is not just any statement. It is a personal statement, and because it comes from a personal space, the artist should have some meaningful relationship to it. I like to think of the premise as a stance, perhaps even an argument, because even though it is a statement, it should be as profound as a firmly held belief by the artist. Great bodies of literature were not produced on a whim, they were written because the writer had an urgent thought, one important enough that the writer chose to invest heart and soul in the task. That is how you want to think of the premise.

The premise is what makes your film as unique as you. It is the driving force for your film. Your ideas, your concerns, your passions, your curiosities all come together to create a body that moves toward this single idea. In my experience, the more personal themes that infuse your story, the more impactful it will become. While this doesn't mean that storytelling must solely stem from personal experiences, it does consider that even a story you choose, still comes from a personally grounded perspective. Consequently, if you decide to take on a story that you have no personal connection to, that story might suffer from this lack of grounding. In this case, you might seek to create connections.

In my earlier years, in one of my jobs, I was asked to create connections with strangers whom I'd never met as a form of marketing. At first, this idea felt ridiculous to me, but it's actually helped me a great deal as a communicator, educator, and artist. I've found creating connections to be very possible, even in the most unlikely scenarios. We are all different, but if you look hard and long enough, you can find similarities, and this will always lead you to compassion.

Artistry, Honesty, and Truth

Honesty is one of the most challenging parts of artistry. To be honest in your work is to know who you are and accept your strengths and failures. You show compassion to yourself, even as you might try to improve. For some of us, this is easy. For others, it may take a lifetime of discovery. Think of it this way; how can you portray a character who is honest about their shortcomings if you haven't been honest with yourself?

As a young screenwriter, I wrote a script about a woman looking for love. My readers liked my writing, the world, and many of the supporting characters, but no one liked the main character. No one seemed to understand her. I revised and revised it, but it didn't make a difference. As an older writer, I now realize that no one understood her because I didn't understand her! I was still grappling with the themes of the character, which mirrored the themes I was wrestling with in my own life. I couldn't tell her story honestly because I wasn't being honest with myself. The ending didn't make sense for her. It was something *I* wanted for the character, but we don't always get what we want in real life, and in this story, as I had written it, the truth was that she would not find her love. Forcing characters into situations we want never works because it's not honest. Even if we don't understand why, our subconscious picks up on that, and we translate that as a false note.

When we cannot be honest with ourselves, this will sometimes lead us to overprotect a character. This character will come off feeling false and uneven. This happens commonly with new writers. When we feel too vulnerable, that desire to hide our vulnerability will translate to the character in a way that shields them. This might appear as the character being inconsistent, having a journey that is too easy, or resolving a conflict when the character hasn't earned it. My character's story ultimately rang inconsistent and hollow no matter how many times or ways I returned to it. I needed to grow a little more to understand my own themes and values so I could pass them on to my character.

Uncovering a personal theme in your work will, for some, come very easy. For others, it may take some work, but this is work that I believe great writers have done in self-examination and self-reflection. I find very young and very old writers frequently can access this honesty in a way that's very powerful.

I also believe that, at times, there are some themes that we simply find too raw to confront. There may be moments when our spirit cannot handle dealing with this or that theme and more healing needs to occur before the writer can come back to it.

TOOLS AND TECHNIQUES

INTERNAL AND EXTERNAL JOURNEYS: WORK WITHOUT AND WITHIN

Childish Gambino's *This is America*

When discussing story development with my new writers, I talk about the internal and external journeys. The external journey refers to the plot, the physical journey we witness the character traversing on screen, filled with concrete places, things, and interactions. This journey highlights specific goals: leaving a job, capturing the villain, winning the battle. Even in shorts, these rules still apply. While the goals may look the same, shorts tend to focus more on drama than expensive special effects or extravagant action sequences, especially in the case of budget-conscious filmmakers.

The internal journey describes the character's emotional journey, returning us to theme and premise. When you've identified the physical objective of the character's pursuit, now you must determine what it represents. Is leaving the job about finding validation? Is capturing the villain about redemption? Characters are driven by the principles that we investigated in the character chapter. What are their needs, fears, or joys? The answer to these investigations ultimately tells us about the internal journey the character must make and, hopefully, the arc they will accomplish.

As a music video, Childish Gambino's experimental *This is America* creates multiple narratives as we watch Donald Glover tell a story within a story through lyrics and scenes. In this video, the internal journey is so emotionally heightened, exaggerated, and externalized—referring to so many contemporary allusions—it is impossible to miss what the song expresses about the challenges facing Black people, and Black men in particular, in their search of freedom.

Demonstrate the Premise Arc

Earlier, I mentioned Lajos Egri's bone structure for character development. I also have embraced his first chapter on premise. In this chapter, Egri uses several existing plays, including many of Shakespeare's, to demonstrate the idea of premise in a play. In his formula, the premise can be broken down to just a few words, with two thematic words that he separates with a verb of action; for example, love overcomes distress, forgiveness leads to freedom, or fear resurrects destruction. What I like about this tool is that it that it encourages *thematic* consideration of character evolution.

A strong premise will help to elucidate the arc that takes place in your story. It is also through this premise that we will see the evolution of your themes. For example, if you decide that your premise is "Family heals old wounds," you want to figure out how to get there. This premise suggests that a connection to family is essential for healing and moving forward from an earlier emotional wound. So, what does the beginning look like to demonstrate this arc? Perhaps for the main character, there is no family in the beginning, and they are surrounded by family in the end. Then, the arc would be about reconnecting with family. Another example could be a character grappling with unresolved emotional wounds who initially exhibits destructive behavior, only to transition to healthier behavior by the end.

We focus on opposites to create the arc in a relationship of absence and presence. Does it make sense that we seek that which we do not have?

If the character seeks a family in the end,
then family will be absent in the beginning.

If the character seeks healing at the end,
then destruction will be apparent in the beginning.

What the character seeks as a goal in the end,
that goal will be absent in the beginning.

Andrea Arnold's *Wasp*

As another example, in director Andrea Arnold's *Wasp*, the mother character initially yearns for the freedom of singledom so she can date her old flame. By the end, she has learned the cost of this pretense. This shift exemplifies the character's arc through themes of family, freedom, and love. In the beginning, she perceives her children as obstacles to her romantic aspirations, but she eventually learns that her children mean a good deal more to her. In the hopeful end, she has a chance to find love *with* her family.

In the character and world chapters, we discussed arcs in developing your story. Whether you create arcs in the character or through the world, remember that change is a fundamental aspect of life. We expect arcs because life is always changing; nothing stays the same. Change lies at the core of our existence, even more so than time. So, when visiting a story, be aware that arcing the story is something that the reader expects and awaits.

INVESTMENT, THEMES, AND FOUNDATIONS

Kasi Lemmons' *Dr. Hugo*

As you launch into the opening sequences of your story, you may not know precisely "what" it is about. However, as you approach the end, you'll glimpse some kernel of truth that reveals its emotional essence. What I want to highlight most here is that this emotional reveal isn't only about what it means for the character; it's also about what means for you as the writer, as your emotions serve as the emotional foundation for the story.

One of your hardest journeys as the writer is uncovering these connections, and then deciding how much of yourself you want to reveal. Like actors with performances, and like directors on set, you serve as the foundation for the themes in the story. If you give little, there will be little for the reader to absorb and carry. Opening yourself up to these themes and feeding them life through the pages of your story is how we best imbue emotional reality into our stories.

As an actress first, director Kasi Lemmons probably knew the shorthand of personal investment after her work in features like *Candyman* and *Silence of the Lambs*. The personal voice she brought to *Dr. Hugo*, as a child looking at the adult world through curious eyes, laced her deep affection for Southern culture and made this film remarkably distinctive.

Now, what happens if you tell stories that do not have thematic investment? I don't think they will have the same weight, gravity, or impact as those that do. When you think about the shorts listed here, consider how some of them were made decades ago by directors who may no longer be with us. These shorts have endured because of this thematic investment. Not every filmmaker will make this commitment to investment, and not every film carries special meaning. You get to decide just how much you want to invest in each film.

Thematic vs. Personal Investment

I want to be careful to also distinguish between what I call thematic investment and personal experiences. I've had students who have written stories that are filled with stories that are deeply personal: of their lost love, of a difficult family, of an awful friend. Writing a story that allows you to unload some of your deepest concerns is a type of journaling. While journaling is a wonderful writing tool, it's one that serves you in a private space. It does not follow the formula I mentioned earlier: think, make, share.

A thematic investment is about creating a foundation for others to find footing. It is based on the notion of giving. Art, at its base, is about sharing, which makes it a selfless act that is without conceit or expectation. When you make a thematic investment, you are infusing this story with themes that are personal to you. That being said, you are not telling a story that you would tell a friend, hoping for validation and support. That story, as intimately personal as it is, centers around what you need, as opposed to what you can give. Expecting your audience to heal you is treacherous territory for any artist.

Limiting Subplots and Widening Storylines

Rungano Nyoni and Hamy Ramezan's *Listen*

When I think of the biggest difference between features and short films in terms of themes, I think about subplots. In a feature, we get to explore relationships and lives of characters whom we meet. In a short film, we simply get to meet them. Subplots (subordinate plots) and supporting storylines (supporting plots) offer opportunities to explore themes in various ways. Subplots are smaller plots that take us down a different road through a sequence of scenes; there is a beginning and end to that plotline. Think of storylines as lines we are exposed to but have not developed to the extent of subplot.

In a short film, the maker will have less time to explore other narrative lines but it can be done in efficient ways. In narratives and documentaries, we can create truncated single-scene plots or subplots that get divulged through conversation or other media. Characters and what they discuss can open up subplots. In Ramezan and Nyoni's *Listen*, we are introduced to a series of storylines that we *could* explore in a longer film: the story of the police officers, of the translator and the child, and of actions referred to off-screen regarding the main character's husband. The title *Listen* is effective at directing us toward the theme in the film, only for us to see the multitude of ways that characters do and do not listen and the crisis this creates within the film.

Note how the more abbreviated the film, the less time we have to explore subplots and other storylines. In proof of concept shorts that are trying to propel forward a larger feature that is already written, this can become a fault point. Sometimes, the writer will feel the need to incorporate many of the themes and subplots in the feature film but providing too many ultimately loses the reader or viewer. In a short, we want to keep the focus on the most urgent ideas that serve the main plot and save the development of other plots for the longer form.

Aural and Visual Representations

Gareth Dunnet-Alcocer's *Contrapelo*

One way to make a theme clear is to represent it in multiple ways. Themes can commonly be expressed through basic storytelling elements that you maneuver on screen. If you want to tell a story about fatherhood, you show fathers. If you want to tell a story about nature, you show bodies of water, fields, or maybe wildlife. If you want to tell a story about love, you show affection or intimacy.

A strong film will go deeper than this, creating layers, as we see in Gareth Dunnet Alcocer's *Contrapelo*. In interviews, Dunnet Alcocer questions issues of masculinity and fatherhood. Beyond showing fathers and sons, what else might we use to communicate that idea? This is where aural and visual representations might be used. There are some obvious ways, such as showing pictures of family or having conversations about fatherhood, but there are also more subtle ways, like perhaps a prayer card from a patron saint of fatherhood, a news article on absent fathers, or even using music with lyrics that mention fathers.

Some of my favorite films will find more subtle or indirect ways. Perhaps in the film there is a book title in the background that refers to fatherhood or maybe the TV displays a newscast showing a group of cubs being led by an adult lion.

Narrate the Theme's Journey

Bi Gan's *A Short Story*

There is a marvelous subset of narrative films that are basically poetic exercises, where we follow a character or characters under the guidance of an omniscient narrator who tells us some story elements that we need to know. This narration can be used in a multitude of ways: to convey character development, foreshadow what is coming ahead, or provide backstory. Playing with narration is a fun exercise because it can be very tightly tied to the story or just loosely connected. Either way, the narration will influence our comprehension of the visuals in the same way that editing bridges a connection between them, even when there is no apparent connection.

While this tool breaks an often-followed screenwriting rule of avoiding narration, when used in a novel and innovative way, it can be effective. Creating contrast in imagery and dialogue can lead us to poetic delights. The downfall of most ineffective narration is that it is too straightforward and reiterates information that we already see on the screen.

Bi Gan's whimsical fable, *A Short Story*, narrates the journey of a black cat who, after providing a last wish to a scarecrow, embarks on a journey to find out what is "the most precious thing." The poetic narration offers the "weirdos" histories of these but also reinforces the themes of a magical black cat and its quest.

SETTING THE UNEXPECTED OVER THE LITERAL

Amat Escalante's *Amarrados*

Placing your story in an environment that is thematically connected but unexpected is another effective tool commonly used especially in the fable, fairy tale, and magical realism genres. Bi Gan's *A Short Story* marvelously reveals that a room is much more than a room. The theme of traveling mirrors the black cat's pilgrimage and makes us question where we are, where we are going, and where we have been.

Likewise, the stark opening of Amat Escalante's *Amarrados* sets up the bleak realism of the story as we watch a young homeless boy in a gray windy landscape struggle against bonds at the top of a mountain. The film continues with dark themes of abuse, despair, and corruption as narration fills in the gaps. However, this opening could have taken place in any location of the story: a room, a lake, or a hallway.

Escalante's decision to open above the city, near the gray sky, adds to the themes of loneliness and helplessness that envelope the film. It also provides a different landscape than the literal one we might imagine a homeless boy might wander. Thematically, that choice imprints a more indelible impression of this boy's lack of safety and security, of yearning to belong, of struggle. Tone and mood can also be applied as thematic elements to allude to premise and theme through visuals but also through words (which you'll learn more about in the Language chapter).

DETAILING AND SPECIFYING PERFORMANCE

Marcelo Martinessi's *La Voz Perdida*

Sometimes, you can aid a performer in reaching a thematic space by revealing to them what the themes are in the film. This might come in a meeting before the shoot or in a rehearsal where the director may share some insights into the character. However, in a well-written script, this will be expressed in the writing, and the actor can reap and harness these themes like a fresh crop.

In the same way, words can also suggest imagery with the use of poetic devices. Referring to a group of kids as "a flock" is very different from referring to them as "a herd" or as "a murder." The different images this conjures not only helps the actor associate feelings and emotions with this group of kids but also helps the reader as well.

Marcelo Martinessi's *La Voz Perdida*, part-documentary and part-narrative short, opens with a woman listening to a news report. Descriptions and dialogue of the "wounded," "battle," and "blood" establish the world while simultaneously setting the tone and mood for a film about loss in the wake of the Curuguaty Massacre.

Performance, Dialogue, and Subtext

Lily Baldwin's *Swallowed*

Dialogue and subtext are excellent ways to insert theme into your story, but they can be tricky. Dialogue that references theme too directly will come off as cumbersome and clunky, or even condescending to the reader. If it is too obvious, it will play like a school lesson. A great technique is using conflict, like an argument or disagreement, to deliver the theme in a less obvious way. The dialogue can also indirectly reference the theme. Instead of arguing about motherhood, in Lily Baldwin's *Swallowed*, a conversation about breastfeeding, care of an infant, and illness, indirectly suggests to us the conflicts around motherhood, even if the word 'mother' is never used.

Strong actors will know how to use subtext in any given situation. Talented actors can inject life into some of the most trite or cliché lines through subtext, but a strong writer can help them get there by allowing the writing itself to imply the conflicts of motherhood.

Is the Personal, Political?

Alice Diop's *Toward Tenderness*

Alice Diop's documentary short film, *Toward Tenderness*, follows her frank and vulnerable conversations with four young men about masculinity and relationships. The short documentary delivers a searing statement in a short amount of time. It leaves us contemplating the complex relationship between masculinity and love. However, this illuminating and sometimes devastating rumination in the film stems from Diop's clear and profound premise. Diop's curiosity about her subjects is evident in her thoughtful and non-judgmental approach to portraying them. We feel the despair of some characters and we feel hope for others.

In interviews, Diop has been open about her political statements in her films, but many other filmmakers look to avoid exactly this. However, when you make a film, you are inherently taking a side, even if it's by *not* taking a side. I believe it's challenging to present statements that appear neutral or align with current trends while still expressing a strong feeling. Films serve as extensions of ourselves, reflecting our statements, visions, and thoughts; they embody our themes. They are inherently personal.

It Does Matter

Sometimes I've recognized in my students a tentativeness in wanting to be big in a world that endeavors to make everyone small. This struggle can lead them to diminish the strengths of who they are and who they can be. I find myself having to remind them, "What you say matters. What you do matters." So be mindful. When you include a throwaway scene that encourages casual destruction or a camera angle that makes us belittle the character, are you aware of what you're saying? A colleague's student once wanted to make a film that would decimate tons of ants. What does that say about their appreciation for life? What you see and hear in every frame matters.

It's important to analyze the roles of power and control through form and choice and how they are utilized. Your film is not only a film, it will, intentionally or unintentionally, make social commentary on the world-at-large. The subconscious, remarkably, absorbs a lot of what we see and hear when we watch a film, even if we're not aware of it. While the influence of subliminal advertisements of the 50's and 60's was debunked, it remains undeniable that media consumption guides your thoughts. You can resist these influences, but how often do we choose to wield the tools to identify, examine, assess, and then reject them? Not often, as it's more convenient to absorb than to act.

As filmmakers, I believe we have a social responsibility for what we put into the world, akin to our duty to preserve the planet and its ability to sustain life. We can claim that what one person does doesn't mean anything, but that just isn't true. If it's strong, clear, purposeful, and unwavering, one person's voice can move mountains. Many films create grand change for both the better and for the worse. Media is a powerful tool. Consider this when you tell your story.

Theme and premise are the most important parts of your story and hidden within them is your voice. What are you saying? What does it mean?

PRACTICE AND PLAY

1. Identify your personal themes by making a list of your ten favorite movies, books, and TV shows. For each selection, write the three themes that stand out to you. After doing that for each item in each category, review the lists and highlight the three most repeated themes across all categories.

2. Write five of your personal themes. Then go back and try to visualize each one as a tool or a symbol, i.e., love is a heart. How would you visually represent each theme on the screen?

3. For your story, consider how your character's themes will evolve as an arc. If they start with loneliness, will they end in belonging? Write a thematic arc for your character by reflecting on your own personal arc. Where have you recognized your own thematic evolutions?

4. Visit how your theme can be expressed through multiple ways. Write a scene for your story that conveys theme through character behavior, the production design of the scene, and the dialogue.

5. Draw your character's favorite themes as elements of a self-portrait. If needed, revisit Egri's Bone Structure to recall them. Use any accessories, clothes, shoes, jewelry, body paint, etc., to express these themes. Also, consider how the items are worn.

6. Reflect on your story's environment and how weather, season, and atmosphere can be used to depict tone and mood. Draw the home and the exterior environment. Then write the scene using thematic words to convey tone and mood you've established in the picture.

7. Describe a space that is important to the character and include specific objects that are pertinent to the character. Write two scenes that describe the arc of the space based on your premise and the character's

evolution. How do the space and these props demonstrate the shift in theme from beginning to end?

8. Write your premise as a lesson you would tell a young child who has meaning to you. Limit it to five words or less. Picture telling the child why they need to learn this lesson and how it will aid them in the future. Write this down. This is your purpose in telling the story and adhering to it as your touchstone.

9. Take the premise you wrote earlier and switch it. Instead of "love overcomes all," write "all overcomes love." Write a new scene(s) that demonstrates this shift.

10. Take a camera phone and take a picture of ten of the favorite things in your bedroom right now. What personal themes stand out? How would you describe your evolution as a character through a one-line premise? Write this new premise.

11. For an interview situation, take your character and put them in a room. What would you place in their background to establish pertinent themes? In what location could you place the interview to establish those themes?

12. Look at your script and identify some of the current thematic images. Make a montage of these images, consider their themes, and narrate a storyline or a poem that plays over a set of images that you've connected together. Remember to be playful with narration and to make thematic, not literal, connections.

LANGUAGE & STYLING:
WRITING TO FREE THE IMAGINATION

Poetry
—Writing that formulates a concentrated imaginative awareness of experience in language chosen and arranged to create a specific emotional response through meaning, sound, and rhythm.

THE SCREENPLAY: POETRY IN ACTION

Screenplays are an intriguing form of writing. You must learn how to write visually and precisely, while also delivering information in an efficient way. Unlike fiction, you cannot delve into rumination; the comfortable, thoughtful meanderings of the mind. Unlike plays, you cannot have page after page of dialogue without paying attention to the environment and the perspective of the camera. The best approach I have found for thinking about writing a script is reflecting on how you approach poetry.

While many writers and readers out there may gasp at this comparison, the teens I teach poetry workshops to at the library believe poetry is too complicated, too high-minded for them to enjoy—I love surprising them! On the other hand, the most esteemed aesthetes may think that writing scripts is a step down from the intricate study and mining of language that poetry requires. Then there are those who have stumbled upon the truth: screenwriting is simply another way to write, and like all forms of writing, learning one makes you better at writing any of the others. Secretly, I believe that screenwriting borrows a little from them all!

In fiction, essays, and memoirs, we often ask readers to do more work when reading. We may string together a tumble of adjectives in long sentences. In contrast, scripts, like poetry, require detail and brevity. Their limited word counts mean they are often read quickly and sometimes not too closely, especially if your script is being reviewed by a new intern tasked with coverage. Consider how many scripts are swiftly scanned by an executive who has twenty more to read by day's end. You want your script to make an impact, so you must guide the reader through it. Otherwise, you risk them abandoning the script altogether. Approaching this process like poetry, where *details matter*, will significantly enhance your writing.

What I also notice when comparing poetry and screenwriting is that each pays attention to form and structure, as well as the visual and the auditory elements. Both focus on emotional growth. What poem have you loved that didn't take you on an emotional transformative journey, whether it was delight or grief, love or lament? Poems are powerful in their potential to make us feel things in such a compact amount of time on a page. They leave us feeling different, awakened, renewed, or surprised. Isn't that how you want someone to feel when they read your screenplay?

POETRY & SCREENWRITING: EMOTION & IMPACT

When I ran into my old college graduate Teaching Assistant on campus one day shortly after graduating, I recall mentioning that I was considering going into film. It was the kernel of an idea that I had no notion how to pursue. I was watching a lot of movies, and they seemed to be calling out to me. On that day, I seemed to be asking permission or seeking encouragement when I tentatively asked her about going into film. It seemed so antithetical to me at the time. I was surprised and inspired when she casually replied, "Lots of poets become filmmakers!" like it was the most common thing in the world. The suggestion that film and poetry shared a deep connection freed me, and ultimately, became the motivating principle that allowed me to pursue my love of film.

Discipline & Excess

In my syllabi for short screenwriting, and for screenwriting in general, I like to recommend that students read poetry, not only because of these ideas of efficiency, emotion, and sensory connection, but because, like poetry, screenwriting asks for specificity, succinctness, and precision. In this process, it requires a discipline that other forms do not demand. A script will require rules to be followed and standards to be acknowledged, even if you attempt to bend or break them. Like poetry, screenwriting often asks us to choose our words with precious care, to ruminate on the novelty of their connection, and to not waste time with excess.

The House of Literary Form

I compare the script to the poem, but that is just a beginning of thinking about its form, because the script in many ways is the new kid on the block of literary form, having supposedly arrived in the early 1900s. With its late arrival, I suspect the script borrows from its other writerly siblings. It borrows the paragraphs of fiction, and the scenes of the play; it carries the spoken dialogue of the song, and the throughlines of the essay; it dallies in the inner life of the memoir with its voiceover and the sentimentality of the letter with its closing. In this century, we have now also seen the script mimic our texting. The script is an intriguing form because it is at once present, but also evolving with time and technology in a refreshing way.

Perhaps what makes the magic of the script so sacred is that it is *performable* and comes to us with the desire to live in the present moment. We find ourselves gathered around a script often awaiting the moment to be whisked away. Still, it reads as an incomplete document because it doesn't only live on the page and in our imaginations as fiction does. Like in a play, it lives on the lips and within the limbs of those who translate its vision, and in the revered consciousness of those who convey it.

Yet it is also leanly efficient as a blueprint document of intense scrutiny and concision. Technicians of all kinds, from the performers to the crew and executives—the camera person, the designer, the manager—must study this document to execute artistry *and* construction. Therefore, the words of the script must often do double duty, delivering theme and emotion, but also imagery and action; and that is why word selection becomes so important.

It's no accident that you will often find the most memorable and affecting scripts filled not only with a lyrical, exquisitely chosen vocabulary and a plethora of poetic devices such as metaphor, simile, personification, and allegory; but also with the clunkiness of scene headings, delineated shots, and editing transitions. Writing a screenplay is an exercise in balance because you must learn to write for both the artist and the builder.

Understanding this will equip you in the best way to write your short script. A good way to start down this path is to become close with your dictionary and choose words selectively.

THE DISCIPLINED WORDSMITH

When I started writing poetry, I would often keep a good dictionary and thesaurus nearby. Many novelists do the same, and some of my favorite authors will name their beloved dictionary as if it were their favorite children. Simply put, writers do this because, if they need to convey more information using less words, they need to have access to more words! It's also good to have a remembrance of what words can do—more on that below. Great writers sift through words to consecrate a perfect tangle of feeling from them, and while you may not do that at first, a little practice will help you get there.

Great screenwriters will do the same. I like to think of a great screenwriter as a disciplined wordsmith, a writer with an infinite capacity for sculpting phrases and sentences into delectable sounds on our tongues and imprinting unforgettable images on our brain. While this skill may be inherited by some, most of us are challenged to develop and refine it with each piece of work we shuck out of our pencil or keyboard, through the rigorous craft of revision.

Revising begins with revisiting the old parts of speech of our ancient yesteryears, and finding a way to redirect them in a different direction. As disciplined wordsmiths working in screenwriting, we do not have the time or space to write in the verbose language of fiction, memoir, or nonfiction. We want to find more efficient and effective ways to suggest ideas to readers, choosing our words carefully for emotional impact and sifting out excess information that we don't need.

WRITING TO FREE THE IMAGINATION

As a short screenwriter, your goal is to write the script that ignites the director's creative resources. That means writing to free the imagination. Some scripts I've read are so detailed that they feel limiting. This is what we call a "writer-director" script, and receiving this note is not a compliment. It indicates that you've included too many aspects, leaving insufficient freedom for good directorship to take place.

What is good directorship? A great script is one that breathes. It provides suggestions and inspiration for the director while still giving them room to bring in their own voice and vision. A great, memorable script offers a fertile landscape for images, themes, and emotions to frolic. This allows each reader's imagination to bubble up and overflow with ideas, making the director, actor, DP, designer, and crew eager to get involved.

Writing a script that encourages the freedom of imagination is about allowing room for the story to evolve organically, guided by the essence of the film. Making a film is always a negotiation with the surrounding environment, in collaboration with the script and its technicians. A good director will be prepared to shift and adapt as problems, issues, and opportunities arise. However, a strong script can facilitate this process by fostering openness and promoting a range of ideas through its word choice. Interestingly, we find this freedom through specificity rather than limitation. Instead of describing every movement of a character step by step, we might use a verb with specific action and connotation, serving the dual purpose of conveying theme and emotion while inspiring action and imagery.

STYLING YOUR GRAMMAR FOR SCREENWRITING

Approaching styling is a great way to consider how screenwriting is distinct from other forms of writing. To do this, we revisit grammar in this chapter because it is the nuts and bolts of your writing. However, this doesn't mean that all screenplays will look the same, because they do not, and should not. By understanding some of the screenwriting style standards, you can develop your own personal style of screenplay writing. This will also help you recognize if there is a particular screenwriting style that is your strength.

Personal styling is important because often, the industry treats screenwriters like doctors, calling them in to repair a script. Like regular doctors, screenwriters have specializations. So, one script may need a dialogue doctor, a female character doctor, a structure doctor, or a world development doctor to spruce it up. While this rarely happens with short scripts, it is common with feature films, and sometimes, television shows. Shorts are the perfect canvas to develop your styling because the stakes are lower, allowing you to experiment more freely.

Understanding parts of speech and how they can effectively be applied to the sentence structure of screenwriting will better equip you in the screenplay writing process. You want to construct an effective and efficient reading process that keeps readers compelled to turn the page, balances tension and pacing, and cajoles them to keep reading to the end. Additionally, it allows your personal voice to develop and shine.

In this section below, I will reference some films for discussing language and styling:

TECHNIQUES AND TOOLS:
THE ART AND PERFORMANCE OF LANGUAGE

SUBTLE SIGNS OF BEGINNINGS AND ENDINGS: PUNCTUATION

Punctuation
—the act or practice of inserting standardized marks or signs in written matter to clarify the meaning and separate structural units.

The script is a surprising document when it comes to the practice of punctuation. These special marks can lift us into spaces of clarity and, more importantly, can lead us into directing action for cast and crew. The functions of commas and colons, periods and points can carve structural corners for screenwriters. They are also emotional touchstones for performers and craftsmen in this very efficient space. The remarkable act of punctuating anything is about placing emphasis or structure on the language by pulling a word, or group of words, into a more prominent space.

LANGUAGE & STYLING

For the Love of Script Punctuation

:

Colons announce starts, open doors and investable spaces.

()

Parentheticals give direction.

"" ''

Quotations invite other texts and colloquialisms.

'

Apostrophes build relationship.

.

Periods tell us about finality.

?

Question marks summon curiosity.

,

Commas communicate turns and continuing.

;

Semicolons indicate shifts and lists.

-

Dashes lead to abrupt shattering.

!

Exclamations demand emphasis and intensity.

. . .

Ellipses open windows to galaxies of possibility.

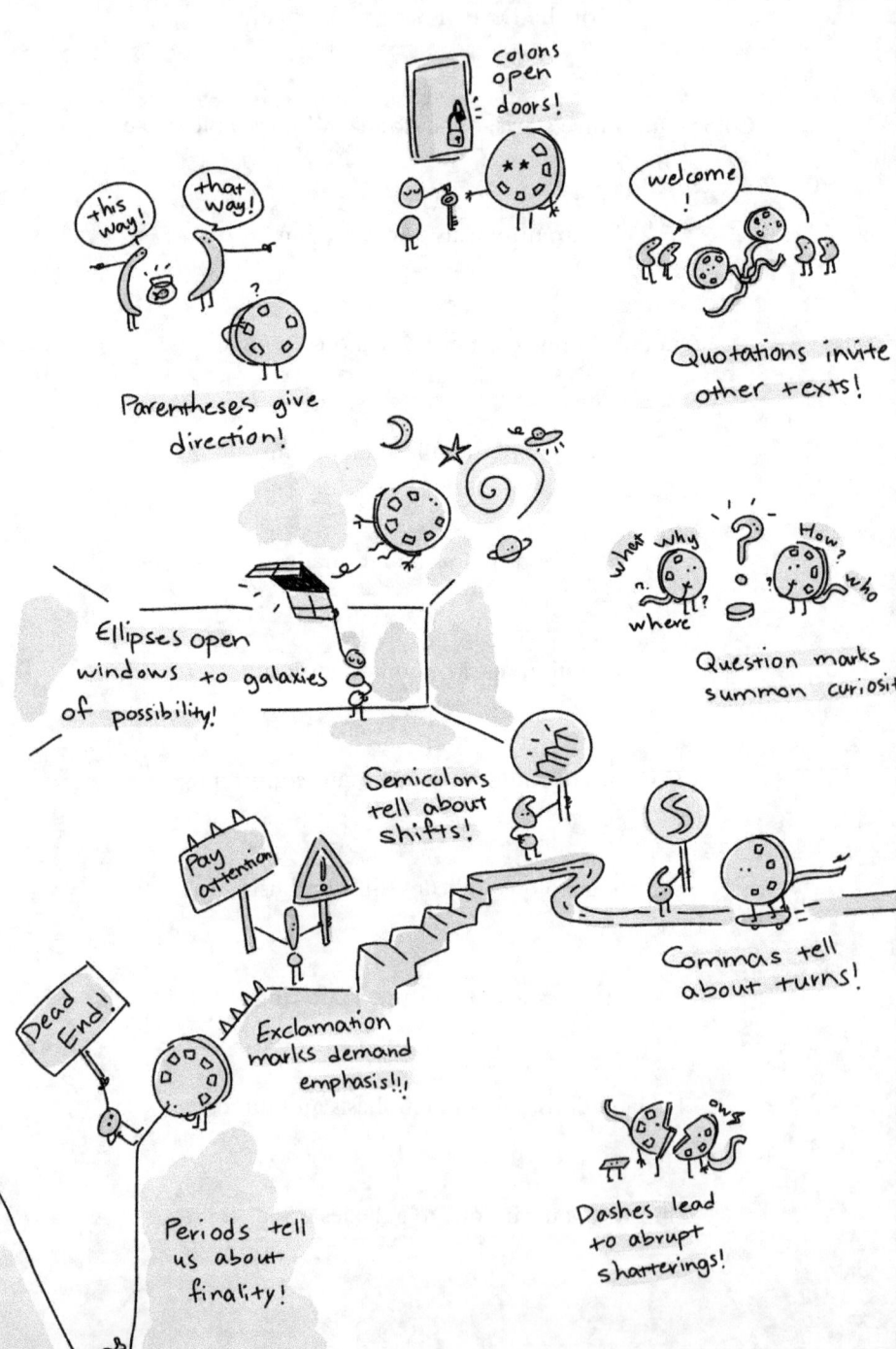

Marks Making Sparks and Meaning

What do each of these unlikely symbols convey to us from their figurative planets? Discovering in Keith Houston's short article, *The Mysterious Origins of Punctuation*, how punctuation, in its earliest beginnings, was not merely a vehicle for language but a vehicle for perception, was most intriguing for me. It was about crafting meaning. This makes it all the more pertinent to the world of drama, where perspective is everything.

Colons tell us about what's coming and act often as preparation for transitions; we commonly see them in description and dialogue, but they are also applied to formatting transitions, text messages, and shots:

FADE IN:
INSERT:
DISSOLVE TO:

Periods tell us about closings, resolutions, and completion. They are, in a way, the essence of punctuation because they are shapers of emphasis, of impact, of beginnings, and therefore of endings because we cannot have either a beginning or an ending without it.

Beat.
CUT TO BLACK.
FADE OUT.

Parentheticals commonly act as reminders, normally outside of the context of the story, to create structure or clarity. Parentheticals tend to communicate directly to the performer in a script. When overused to emotionally direct the actor, this becomes problematic because it confines the actor.

(Continued)
(to the Mother)
(softly)

And then there is punctuation that inspires the performer. With the examples below, notice how the meaning changes with the punctuation:

Ellipses are radiant in their ability to ask our imaginations to fill in the blanks.

> I thought you meant...
> She told me...
> What if...

The emphatic dash will tell us about abruptness, forcefulness, or interruption.

> I thought you meant—
> She told me—
> What if—

The exclamation can do the same by heightening in either a positive or negative way. This doesn't necessarily mean yelling or shouting, but it does mean something to the character.

> I thought you meant!
> She told me!
> What if!

Consider how these same phrases shift with commas, an invitation to continue in a different way.

Punctuation are the tender and delicate moments in the script that many new writers treat cavalierly. These moments in your script are tell-tale opportunities for adventures in performance. Embrace them.

Tooling our Fascinations: The Good Line

Barry Jenkins' *My Josephine*

An exercise I love to use in class is retooling a line. I ask students to rewrite a single page or a short passage of their script by using verbs and poetic devices. In one case, the class was filled with second-language learners, and I felt the inward groan of the group of them. To navigate this, I broke it down into small steps and they had to come up with one small example: one good line.

Watching them post their before and after lines, I was thrilled. One of my students was especially elated! The new line she'd written was pure magic! Not only did she know it, but the other students knew it too. She had felt that because English was a second language, it could not be done. Somehow the translation wouldn't work, the words were too different. What we discovered together was that poetry works for everyone, across languages and cultures.

Some of my favorite scripts are simply swimming in poetic devices. Surprisingly, they are not always scripts that are "high art" or highly dramatic. I've found good lines in action, horror, and comedy films. There's no genre requirement for writing a good line. They can occur at any turn. When certain words are spun together, they create a blanket of wisdom and elation that transforms into magic when actors deliver them on the silver screen.

This is the screenwriter as disciplined wordsmith in our midst. She will take a personal fascination and she will wield the image, symbol, or hyperbole like no other. Good lines can occur in feature films, television, and yes, even short films. Does this take hours and hours of rewriting and laboring over your script? Perhaps. If every script has one good line, that to me is a small miracle. If you have a small miracle, aren't the ten drafts time well spent?

Here are three beautiful lines from one of my favorite lyricists of screenplays, Barry Jenkins:

> Every flag, its own dryer. A delicate tumble. Low heat.
> Sometimes, you can't help but stare at them.
> . . . like you should be in love with something.

After reading this script or watching the film, how could you ever think of a laundromat the same way again! The pauses, the rhythm, the alliteration and consonance, the imagery and emotion. Aren't you just shivering with feeling?

However, I don't think it's about searching for this grand eloquence. On the contrary, I think it's about falling in love with your script, your story. If you don't fall in love with your story, who will? It's absolutely true that there's a bit of geekdom that can happen when writing your script, and I profoundly encourage that. It's when you fall in love with something that you can see it for what it is, weaknesses and strengths, and want to go the ten drafts to help it grow to its fullest.

Note that you can find the full script for *My Josephine* in Claudia Hunter-Johnson's *Crafting Short Screenplays that Connect* and the short is captioned online.

SCRIPTING WITH ACTION: VERBS

Verb
—a word that characteristically is the grammatical center of a predicate and expresses an act, occurrence, or mode of being, that in various languages is inflected for agreement with the subject, for tense, for voice, for mood, or for aspect, and that typically has rather full descriptive meaning and characterizing quality but is sometimes nearly devoid of these especially when used as an auxiliary or linking verb.

Verbs are the spice of a writer's life.

A verb is so much more than an action.

Verbs in a script are often used to direct action for cast who are using the script not only as a literary document but as a blueprint for enacting the film. Due to its function as performable work, script description and action are usually written in the present tense and active voice (more on tense and voice below).

Let's pause for a moment and revisit the verb in language—a brief refresher on this essential part of speech. When communicating, we use verbs to connect objects and actions. We apply verbs to connect people, places, and things and what they do. These verbs are called action verbs: i.e., sit, walk, expand. We also use verbs to connect people or objects and how they feel: i.e., feel, be, seem. These verbs are called linking verbs.

In a script, it is stronger to use action verbs than linking verbs because of the relationship to performance. However, the other reason for this is that action verbs can convey multiple meanings, unlike linking verbs. The often overused "being" verb doesn't have any connotation because its job is simply to connect two things or ideas.

Being Verbs: is, are, was, were, being, am, be, been

The action verb will often carry connotations, a feeling that is invoked in addition to the word's meaning. Simple verbs like "run," "move," or "act" don't tell us that much emotionally; however, the verbs "skip," "assault," and "arouse" do. These verbs not only have connotations around them, but they also have imagery! They are specific in their actions and suggest situations that we can change through contrast.

"Skip" has a lighthearted connotation, while "assault" has a negative connotation. We think something bad has happened when "assault" is used. "Arouse" has a connotation that could go in many directions, but we get the sense that something has awoken. In this way, the verb we select becomes important, not only for its meaning but also the feeling we associate with it. By reflecting on the connotations of the words you use, you can build structures of resonant feeling in your script. You can also leave poetic tonal trails in your script when you use words in unexpected ways.

Verbs are wonderful at creating characterization, tone, emotion, and more. They can paint mood (different from verb mood) and atmosphere. The mood of the girl who is "leaping" contrasts with that of the girl who is "crawling" and the one who is "begging." These verbs each conjure a new feeling as we think about the character and her situation. The professional writer's most commonly used instrument in their toolkit is their verbiage. Strong, distinct verbiage has the power to cut right to the emotional core and suggest to the reader the character's feeling in performing an action.

The other magnificent thing about verbs is that you can layer a bridge to your actors. Much of the actor's working process involves verbs as tools of action, intention, and behavior. Actors love verbs, and verbs are tools that they often use in performance. While we may think that adjectives like sad, angry, or happy are effective in writing a story, a verb is stronger at suggesting these feelings, because it can act as an emotional descriptor while also suggesting performance. The more specific the verb, the better.

Deliver Cool Tones and Light Moods

Lkhagvadulam Purev-Ochir's *Snow in September*

Think about the effect of using "skip" in a dark scene that deals with murder or applying "assault" in a bright, cheery ice cream parlor. Consider the difference between using "arouse" to describe a dark room with shadows or a pink room surrounded by ten teddy bears. Specific verbs can be used to shape mood and tone. So, if I portray a girl "skipping" through an ice cream parlor, we get the sense of a lighthearted comedy. If I portray a man getting "assaulted" by a villain in a dark room, we get the sense of darkness, evil, and horror. The imagery around "arouse" could go in either direction depending on the context. Is it the sleepy "arouse" of a silly teen or the desperate "arouse" of someone who was knocked unconscious and trying to find his bearings?

Sometimes, we might choose to create intentionally contrasting poetic tonal moments. In that case, staging the "assault" in the ice cream parlor offers a refreshing twist. In Lkhagvadulam Purev-Ochir's tense teen drama *Snow in September*, the director disassembles everything we expect about teen love in a single intimate scene with an older woman. The contrast of ages, approaches, and even the words in the conversation create a memorable film. Understanding how you can use verbs will help you to set the tone of your film.

What Time is Tense?

Verbs also help us tell time in our speech. Tenses establish when something happens. Was it in the past (jumped), is it happening now (jumps), or will it occur in the future (will jump)? There are also *perfect* tenses that tell us about something that happened previously and is continuing, while *progressive* tenses suggest action that is ongoing. However, in a script, the main tense we want to use is present.

Present tense verbs suggest the action is occurring in the present, which makes the action easier to perform for a "live" performance, even if it is being filmed. The other reason I believe that using present tense is effective in screenplays is that present tense, also referred to as "simple present" is the clearest and simplest tense to understand and read. Perfect tenses get the reader wrapped up in a time warp trying to discern whether the action occurred in the present perfect (has jumped), past perfect (had jumped), or future perfect (will have jumped).

Present tense also allows for the faster reading normally applied to a script. Unlike a nice 500-page fiction book where readers curl up on the couch to disappear into it for hours, scripts are often skimmed for performance. There is a swiftness associated with that process. When you look at the spareness of a play, you get a sense that it feels somewhat incomplete without performance. We expect that the actors will bring it alive in a novel way. While plays tend to be more dependent on dialogue, a screenplay will be more description-heavy. In that description, we find cinema, but we also find action in behavior.

Present progressive tenses (is jumping) will often show up in scripts and can be problematic because they are vague in indicating the duration of an action. However, they can still be useful at times. Past progressive (was jumping) and future progressive (will be jumping) tend to appear less often but are also verbs that require careful monitoring. The more complex the verb, the slower the reading becomes as readers struggle to discern timing in the story.

Whose Voice is it? Active or Passive?

When writing scripts, in addition to using the present tense, it's important to use the active voice for main verbs. There are two primary voices, the active and the passive. Active voice refers to a verb that allows the subject to perform the action (she jumps). Written out, it is easy to see the action in the present and identify the subject. We can recognize an active character who is engaged in movement. Movement for characters in a story is important. Passive voice, on the other hand, can be challenging for the script reader.

Passive voice describes action that is happening *to* the subject (She was jumped). Passive voice will often use auxiliary or helping verbs which makes them easy to detect: typically variations of the being verb. (She is jumped, they were jumped, he has been jumped.) Notice how passive voice automatically uses more words to accomplish the action.

Interestingly, passive voice is often used in speeches and politics to hide information, like who exactly is doing what. Likewise, in scripts, it asks the reader to work harder to determine who is performing the action. Even more deleterious to the script is that a script that has a pattern of using passive voice might suggest a character who is passive. This character may not be moving forward in the story in an active way, making choices or decisions, or compelling the narrative forward.

To make this clearer, consider an inactive character in your story as a character who allows all the characters around them to make the decisions. In this circumstance, this character becomes less interesting than the other character because they have stopped making choices, taking chances, and moving, both physically and mentally. While these occurrences are common in everyday life, in a short film, we condense time and actions to highlight the most powerful and impactful moments. This allows characters to make difficult choices that drive change and development within a brief timeframe. If no decisions are being made, there is little action occurring, and if there is little action occurring, the story isn't moving forward in a compelling way. How long will we wait for that character to move again? With that guardian of technology, the remote, not long! Your character must move because, in life, we live and we move.

WRITE THE SPECIFIC LIFE

In early chapters, I shared this urgent idea of the specific. The more specific our writing is, the more it leads us to good performance and elements that the cast and crew can rally around. Verbs are our most useful tool for making our writing more specific, authentic, and connective because they can concisely convey so much action, emotion, and imagery. However, this doesn't apply to all verbs. Many different verbs exist that perform various functions, even within the wide category of action verbs. Therefore, I like to categorize verbs when discussing their application in scripts, using the categories "least specific," "specific," and "highly specific."

The Umbrella of Least Specific

I keep verbs like "speak," "move," and "touch" in the least specific camp. These words don't conjure many images because they are so wide and inclusive. Many actions could apply to them, making them generic verb descriptors. For example, "move" could encompass anything from a slight shift to a jump. However, using a thesaurus, we can dig into "move" a little more and end up with verbs like "push," "squeeze," and "walk."

Scaling Down to the Specific

Now, the movement becomes more specific in terms of the type of movements. We can visualize them more vividly. For example, we can picture a "push," and with the connotation, we get some sense of aggression. The context of the full sentence will determine whether the push is friendly, teasing, or hurtful. Did he playfully "push" her, or did he roughly "push" her out of the way? In this example, we use adverbs to help convey the context. However, if we go up one more level, we can recognize highly specific verbs that don't necessarily need adverbs.

The Siphoning of the Highly Specific

"Shove," "edged," and "barged" reach high specificity because they do three things: they tell us the act, provide visual detail, and relay a feeling behind them. "Edged" gives a sense that someone is trying to be small or get through a small space. The movement itself is small. "Barged" tells us that something large is entering and won't stop, regardless of what's in its way. "Shoved" describes something making a way by moving something else out of the way. It suggests selfishness and a lack of courtesy, as does barged, but not necessarily from a huge figure.

This is a lot to think about, and a big question you might have is "where do I find all these wonderfully specific verbs?" Well, the verb list in the appendices of *The 25th Anniversary Directing Actors* is a great place to start. Before we leave the world of specific, let's talk about these other parts of speech that help deliver detail and nuance.

SPECIFY IT AND MODIFY THEM: THE ADJECTIVE AND THE ADVERB: WHEN IS IT TOO MUCH, TOO BROAD, OR JUST ENOUGH?

Adjective
—a word belonging to one of the major form classes in any of numerous languages and typically serving as a modifier of a noun to denote a quality of the thing named, indicate its quantity or extent, or specify something as distinct from something else

THE SPECIFICS OF ADJECTIVES

When I ask a writer to be more specific with a character, place, or object, I am asking them to use an adjective. Adjectives are wonderful descriptors in their ability to illuminate an object. We receive more intel about this person, place, or thing, making it more relatable and valuable to us. "Apple" and "juicy apple" summon different feelings. The latter wants to tease us a bit to get to that apple as soon as possible. The "moldy apple" will evoke the opposite feeling!

Adjectives tell us "which one," and let us know how one item is different from the other. Increasing specificity means providing more information about a person, place, or thing and making it more distinct. Consider "the little dog," "the tall woman," and "the large house." However, while applying these adjectives is helpful, the items still feel pretty broad. We can use more adjectives, or more complex adjectives that convey more meaning or connotation, to increase specificity. Highly visual adjectives can also accomplish this in an efficient way.

The tiny dog. The lofty woman. The immense house.

Notice how these adjectives still convey the same ideas but with a little more detail; they are more specific. These adjectives provide detail in distinction, indicating how the dog is small, the woman is tall, and the house is large.

The toy dog. The leggy woman. The Victorian house.

We can even take it one step further. These adjectives also convey deep meaning; for example, the "toy" dog suggests playfulness, the "leggy" woman suggests casualness, and the "Victorian" house suggests formality. Can you see how this disciplined approach allows you to accomplish much with less? Let's approach it from another angle.

A Little or a Lot?

Is there such a thing as too much description? This question frequently arises among new writers. The key is to strive for balance. Efficiency is crucial; you want your writing to flow smoothly and be easy to navigate. Additionally, excessive description can overwhelm the reader. When bombarded with too many details, readers may disengage. Therefore, it's essential to choose words that pack a punch and deliver maximum impact.

Let's look at the described subjects in longer ways and even with excessive detail.

The small, tiny dog with tiny pink ears, one standing and one flat, bright oval brown eyes and a button nose was barking in a high-pitched tone.

This sentence isn't incorrect, but it is indulgent for a short script where every line counts. Do we need to know about the pink ears and that one is standing and one is flat? Do we need to know that the eyes are oval in shape? The button nose is cute, but along with the other information here, it doesn't seem relevant. The reader starts to ask: *What am I supposed to see here? What information is important?* By cutting down information, you are making relevant information easier to grasp. Also, can you imagine the animal wrangler and costume designer trying to get this right?

What if we try it this way?

The small dog that was a Chihuahua was barking loudly like a bird in a high-pitched tone.

Again, this sentence isn't wrong, but the idea can be accomplished in a much shorter sentence. Let's try: "the chirping toy dog."

By suggesting "toy" dog, we eliminate the need for both small and Chihuahua. By using "chirping," we replace "barking loudly like a bird in a high-pitched tone." Why is this important? Shorter efficient sentences make room for more story to occur within your pages! In a short film, this means a lot. We just showed off what a skilled and disciplined wordsmith you are. Now, let's talk about "chirping" and how we landed on this verb.

The Participle
—a word having the characteristics of both verb and adjective

Action verbs also make wonderful adjectives. They are called participles. Participles are adjectives we typically recognize by the suffix "-ing" or "-ed," as seen in examples like "squinting eyes" or "scrunched face." When we create a participle out of a verb, we allow the action to become the element that brings specificity to the object. So, rather than bringing attention to something that we can sense, we bring attention to what the object does.

The chirping toy dog.
The giggling leggy woman.
The towering Victorian house.

Notice how the specificity here includes detail that provides characterization and mood.

> *The chirping toy dog* suggests a comic tone. If I changed it to snarling, we think something more dramatic.
>
> *The giggling leggy woman* suggests romance. If I changed it to cackling, we think something darker.
>
> The towering Victorian house suggests horror. If I change it to floating, we think something fantastical.

These are good reasons to make the participle your literary friend.

The Modification of Action: The Adverb

Adverb
—a word belonging to one of the major form classes in any of numerous languages, typically serving as a modifier of a verb, an adjective, another adverb, a preposition, a phrase, a clause, or a sentence, expressing some relation of manner or quality, place, time, degree, number, cause, opposition, affirmation, or denial, and in English also serving to connect and to express comment on clause content

Adverbs can be dangerous when overused in a script. Like adjectives, adverbs are modifiers and are therefore also prone to overuse. However, unlike adjectives, which modify nouns, adverbs modify adjectives, adverbs, and verbs; they tell us how and how much.

The mime shifted softly.
The ship turned abruptly.
The owl hooted loudly.

These adverbs are helpful in giving us more detail about how a verb was performed. This is what they look like when we decide to emphasize how much.

The mime shifted very softly.
The ship turned too abruptly.
The owl hooted so loudly.

The modifying words do accomplish a lot in determining the intensity of "softness," "loudness," and "abruptness" of how actions occur. Like with adjectives, there is a caution surrounding the increased activity around the verb.

The aspect that comes into play when modifying verbs is performance. Actors take these words to heart and translate them into action. Each individual actor may be pushed further by the adverb, effectively directing their performance. However, this may not align with the script's intention to leave room for interpretation by the director. This isn't to say that writers should never use adverb modifiers, but it's a call to monitor their usage. The best scripts open doors and release the imagination.

PROPOSING CONNECTORS AND MULTIPLIERS: THE PREPOSITIONAL RELATIONSHIP AND THE FAMILY OF CONJUNCTIONS.

THE RELATIONSHIP CONNECTOR: THE PREPOSITION

Preposition
—a function word that typically combines with a noun phrase to form a phrase which usually expresses a modification or predication

Prepositions are convivial relationship building words. Prepositions are always making connections between things, places, and time.

The teacher, writing at his desk.
The artist, painting on the canvas.
The student, walking under the bridge.

Building relationships is an essential part of navigating the industry, and it's equally urgent in navigating the words within a script. Consider how prepositions establish relationships between a teacher and desk, artist and canvas, student and bridge.

In stories we are often asked to create relationships because they help us understand behavior. We look for relationships between people, but we also look for relationships between things. Whether this relationship is momentary (The girl smacked the ball with the mitt) or something deeper (The woman brushed his tears with her hand), prepositions help us create these connections.

In a script, we will often find sentences teeming with prepositions, these great connectors: with, on, to, along, by, before, after, and so on. They are immensely valuable to the writer, but like many other elements, must be used with attention to balance and moderation. A sentence that has too many prepositions might cause confusion. Conversely, a sentence that avoids the prepositional overcrowding will blossom with literary intimacy!

Another noteworthy aspect of prepositions is their ability to denote direction or location in space. This is crucial for visual writers in helping readers locate objects or characters within a scene. Prepositions such as next to, behind, inside, below, over, and under provide much-needed visual orientation.

Sometimes, when reading a script, I tell a student, "I am not sure where things are located. I cannot see the character in the space. I cannot visualize what is happening." In such cases, examine your prepositions. Have you used too little or too much? Other prepositions are great at specifying time: before noon, at noon, afternoon. These are all functions of prepositions.

What I also love about prepositions is their ability to establish relationships with inanimate objects (we will also discuss personification later in this chapter). The more visual the objects, the better.

The pin in the apple.
The tape on the house.
The hands in the sand.

Notice also how these prepositional phrases have also become descriptors, adjectives specifying the subject.

However, these also work with emotions in very poetic ways:

The anger in her eyes.
The sorrow in her skirts.
The thrill in her fingers.

Building relationships between unusual things is a core tenet of poetry that can also be used in screenwriting. It keeps things fresh, novel, and intriguing for the reader.

JOINING SUBJECTS, PREDICATES, AND PEOPLE: THE NOUN, THE CLAUSE, AND THE CONJUNCTION

FOLLOWING YOUR SUBJECTS: THE PROPER NOUNS AND PRONOUN

In grade school, I recall learning about nouns as the first part of speech. Nouns are easily identifiable as the "who" or "what" in the sentence. They are the essence of our story, whether they represent characters, locations, or elements like weather. Ultimately, your story revolves around what happens to the central character in your narrative. What's exciting about characters is that they can encompass not only people but also animals, objects, and things.

The proper noun is the specific name or title of your character, such as Sally, Monika, or Juana. It may also be Prof. Hernandez, Mr. Akiti, or Ms. Bravebird. In scripts, characters may or may not be named. Sometimes, we might specify the character as the Yellow Ribboned Girl, Tall Thin Man, or Hooded Figure. While not every character needs a proper noun, actors often excited to play named characters, as a name adds depth to a character.

Pronouns offer another way to talk about your subject and avoid repetition in your sentence structure. However, they can be overused in scripts, leading to confusion.

For example, if there are two or more women in a scene, only using "she" could quickly become confusing. If there are multiple groups of people, then "they" will be hard for a reader to follow. Therefore, it's important to check and ensure clarity in the use of nouns and pronouns, even if it seems obvious to do so, to ensure the audience can easily identify who is who.

This is especially important to remember at the beginning of a scene.

The Long and Short of Phrases and Clauses

Phrase
—a word or group of words forming a syntactic constituent with a single grammatical function

Clause
—a group of words containing a subject and predicate and functioning as a member of a complex or compound sentence

When nouns and verbs come together as subjects and predicates, they form a clause, which serves as the foundation of sentences. In a script, clauses are like lustrous strings of information, linked together like elaborate bead bracelets and necklaces. The right combination can produce something beautiful, while the wrong combination may leave us weighed down by too much media, too little information, or simply a mismatch for the story.

A phrase differs from a clause in that it tends to be shorter and often lacks one side of the subject-predicate relationship. Prepositional phrases, as seen above with prepositions and their relationships, are one type of phrase. However, there are also noun phrases, verb phrases, and others.

The candle in the ceiling (prepositional phrase)
The amiable nail (noun phrase)
Traces the turnstile (verb phrase)

Phrases can be very effective as a literary element but should only be used sparingly and in tandem with clauses. We are taught to expect movement (subject and verb), so when there is no movement or feeling, we get lost. If someone says they are confused about what is happening, look for clauses and phrases. A prolonged string of phrases can disorient readers. Short phrases are excellent for breaking up the monotony of long clauses and adding accents here and there, but they are truly accessories to the clause. Working together, phrases and clauses make paragraphs elastic!

The Coordinates of Conjunctions

Conjunctions
*—an uninflected linguistic form that joins together
sentences, clauses, phrases, or words*

The conjunction is the joiner, forming connections between clauses. Common coordinating conjunctions frequently seen in scripts include "and," "or," and "but." However, there is truly a rainbow of conjunctions to choose from, including single conjunctions as well as phrases categorized as subordinating conjunctions.

Conjunctions can also act as adverbs suggesting time, feeling, place, and action. "Presently," "currently," and "momentarily" all suggest time, while "despite," "although," and "however" suggest a contrasting idea. Omitting conjunctions is also a creative option.

The heart beat, and the heart leapt, and it cried. (with conjunctions)
The heart beat. The heart leapt. It cried. (without conjunctions)

The example above, without conjunctions, is a common feature in scripts. This staccato style is great for shaping rhythm and pacing. It falls under the familial category of literary devices, which is another significant umbrellas of language styling.

THE UNBEARABLE LIGHTNESS OF LITERARY DEVICES

Vier Nev's *A Mind Sang*

In the early part of this tools section, I shared how to approach different parts of speech in your scripts, from verbs, adjectives, and adverbs to nouns, conjunctions, and prepositions. Now, we are going to build upon those ideas to share how you can use these varying parts of speech as devices to elevate the reading of your script. Literary devices, also called poetic devices, are used throughout fiction, memoir, letter-writing, and of course, poetry. We will find them in essays too, but more often in personal essays than critical ones.

These literary devices are used to add variation, color, and richness to your writing. When using literary devices, a sock will never just be a sock. This sock can be described through a comparison, hyperbole, or even personification. This sock can be as soft as a baby's bottom (simile), go the extra mile (hyperbole), or scratch us into oblivion (personification *and* hyperbole!). These tools are important in the writing of your script because they allow the script and its objects to come alive in an innovative way. If we can make this sock into a character, or even simply an object with meaning, it becomes a tool that encourages diversity in writing. This is the livelihood of creative writing, and this is how great screenwriters win the hearts and minds of their directors, producers, and crew.

Vier Nev's *A Mind Sang* is a playful experiment on our perception, using a plethora of visual devices, from symbolism, imagery, visual metaphor, and more. We watch shapes emerge, disappear, and reappear anew; we are constantly challenged to ask questions about what we see and why, with fluidly shifting information.

So, let's start with revisiting some of the more popular devices that show up in scripts:

Allusion
Allegory
Alliteration/Consonance/Assonance
Hyperbole
Imagery/Symbolism
Irony
Metaphor
Onomatopoeia
Personification
Rhythm
Repetition
Simile
Staccato

I have already mentioned some of these, and I'm sure you're familiar with at least a few others as well.

Lemohang Jeremiah Mosese's
Behemoth: Or the Game of God

Allusions are references to other people, stories, or objects that are swathed with deeper meaning. Applying allusions in a story is a short-handed way to communicate a bounty of information. We can do this through dialogue in an obvious way, but also through description and the inclusion of books, newspapers, and news reports in the film. The background of the film can become vital to helping set information. So, adding "Malcolm X," "Mother Theresa," or "Helen Keller" to story brings immediate associations to the story. It helps set up some of the background or potential theme of the story. The only caveat is that everyone might not recognize the allusion if it is too obscure. Here, personal background plays a part. For example, some might know Helen Keller for her disability, but not for her political leanings.

The powerful allusion to God, or a higher divinity, is made evident in Lemohang Jeremiah Mosese's *Behemoth: or the Game of God* by a preacher who is dragging a coffin through fields and streets amongst shadows and silhouettes, natural light and darkness. The image is provocative and disturbing against the slow-moving landscape. We can't help but think about who brings life and death to us in this moving short that references Cain, from the biblical stories of Cain and Abel.

Other great allusions in Barry Jenkin's *My Josephine* are the references to Napoleon and his two wives, one of whom is named Josephine. In Jenkins' brief notes on Vimeo, he quickly and simply references that the events of September 11th and Napoleon were inspirations for the story. However, you can glean this when taking into account the date of the film, the presence of an American flag (as a form of symbolism), the Muslim characters who speak Arabic and English, and the discussion of Napoleon. The allusion to the character of Napoleon, a military leader known for his part in the French Revolution and other conflicts, allude to the martial themes in the film. For my students, many of whom were quite young in 2001, these connections are not immediate. However, as someone who was an adult during September 11th, I immediately perceived this allusion, increasing the film's intriguing and compassionate commentary.

Maysaa Almumin's *J'ai le Cafard*

Allegories tend to describe entire stories, but can also apply to characters. They mark story elements that come to represent deeper meanings. We often see them in lessons and moral tales, but sometimes we see them in characters or places. Maysaa Almumin's *J'ai le Cafard*, a French saying that translates to "I have a cockroach," animates a woman's depression as a cockroach that takes over the woman's life, to the extent that her bedroom becomes an unforgettable space.

Nuotama Bodomo's *Everybody Dies*

Hyperbole is exaggeration, and we tend to see it often in exaggerated circumstances, such as comedies. In written form, a hyperbole might be phrased as "I was so hungry, I ate the whole house." In Nuotama Bodomo's *Everybody Dies*, the game show setting acts as extreme hyperbole, criticizing the innumerable avoidable deaths of young black children in American society.

Nebojsa Slijepcevic's *Real Men's Film*

Imagery is figurative language used throughout scripts to provide visual details and description. In the dialogue-less *Real Men's Film*, the images of children wielding weapons is all that is needed to organize an affecting climax in the storytelling. When combined with symbolism, these images add another layer of depth and meaning. So, a "stiff empty cup" can be an example of imagery; however, in a story about loss, this empty cup could be used to reinforce themes of grief and emptiness. Imagery and symbolism are the foundation of understanding and applying cinematic language, this idea that story can be told through sound and visual storytelling.

David Darmadi and Lidia Afrilita's *Diary of Cattle*

Metaphor and **simile** compare two unlike things; however, simile is differentiated by the cue words like or as to signal the comparison. "Her words were wounds," is a metaphor and "her words were like wounds," is a simile. This figurative language is also heavily used within script-writing and can add so much detail and suggestion around theme. Consider phrases such as "their wounding words," "their scathing comments," and "her haunting song." David Darmadi and Lidia Afrilita's short documentary *Diary of Cattle* brings us to cattle that are living alongside and inside a landfill. The juxtaposition of these two images creates a visual comparison that is at once daunting and disturbing, rendering words unnecessary.

Svilen Dimitrov's *Rew Day*

Onomatopoeia, the fun device that mostly shows up in comics and animation, can also add some color to more formalized scripts, although some writers prefer to steer clear of it. Onomatopoeia breaks down noises into written sound, such as the "creak" of the door or the "click" of the lock. The "squawking" of birds and "buzzing" of flies that open Svilen Dimitrov's *Rew Day* could have been written into the script. Onomatopoeia is common in action sequences, with words like "boom," "wham," and "slap," and interjections like "ouch!," "doh!," and "oww!" Onomatopoeia is used often in horror, action, and comedy scripts. They can be useful in creating rhythm and pacing. I also love onomatopoeia for its affection and appreciation of sound design.

Ivyy Chen's *Isle of Chair*

Personification is one of my favorite examples of figurative language because it allows the writer to animate all sorts of things to emote mood and atmosphere. It also frees up the writer from the rope of passive voice in the process. "They were shoved into the room by the heavy door," can become "the door shoved them into the room." It's great for animating objects that can produce sounds, such as "the chair creaks," "the wind bellows," or "the pencil scribbles." It also enhances descriptions of relationships and energy, as seen in phrases like "the room swallows," "the garden invites," or "the trees shelter." In Ivyy Chen's *Isle of Chair*, chairs are personified as the main characters of the story as we discover an island of chairs varying in form, shape, and size. In action writing sequences, this becomes invaluable in creating conflict not only between people, but between places and things.

PERSONAL STYLE: THE PERFECTLY IMPERFECT SENTENCE

Like other forms of creative writing, the script is the sum of its parts. Every sentence will not use an action verb, present tense, or active voice. Every paragraph will not have imagery, personification, or assonance. This is all okay!

Variety will always add some spice to our lives, and in a short script, should be approached with moderation, keen attention to space on the page, and always in service to the story. You want to acquire the knowledge to reflect on how to approach issues when they arise. Know that these suggestions will always encounter an alternative and an exception that will invariably delight us.

What I wish for you to take away are the core ideas behind what this chapter offers: that language tools can be used in a multitude of ways to accomplish different tasks in the writing process. Like any good utility, there will always be another way to use it; while directions may provide one approach, any good handyman knows there are many others.

Your mind is the most important tool in any endeavor.

There is no perfect script, just as there is no perfect sentence. Contrary to what we may expect, art does not need to be a competition. Simply put, there are words that will move each of us for different reasons. We've often been taught that perfection is the mother of success, but imperfections are what make us unique, lovable, and irreplaceable. They make us human.

After practicing these techniques, take note of which language tools are easy for you and which ones are hardest. Hopefully, you will discover something new. Ultimately, these exercises, I hope, will reveal to you glimpses into your personal style of writing, whether that involves unleashing a glorious vault of action verbs in your sentences or transmitting a deeply embedded ritual of metaphor and hyperbole. Neither is wrong or right. Understanding the basics of how to wield these tools will help you to tap into a free imagination, inspiring your own distinctive voice on the page. That is what will make your script stand out.

PRACTICE AND PLAY

1. Search for being verbs (as helpers or main verbs) in your script and circle them. Identify their purpose in the sentence: are they linking, helping, or creating passive voice? Then replace them with action verbs.
2. Take one action paragraph. Make it more emotionally impactful by condensing it to half the size and use more specific verbs, participles, and literary devices.
3. Take one longer dialogue segment, around monologue length, and create stronger breathing, rhythm, and pacing through commas, ellipses, dashes, and periods.
4. Take a scene with a character in her room. Create relationship between this character and objects in her room using prepositions.
5. Take one description paragraph of five to seven sentences in your script and practice pacing by applying staccato and turning three sentences into phrases for emphasis.
6. Find a sentence that is four or five lines long in your script. This can be dialogue. Practice using hyperbole and allusion with that sentence to make it an easier and simpler to read.
7. Look for a sequence in your story where your character interacts with an inanimate object. Reduce the words in the scene by applying examples of onomatopoeia and personification to illustrate their actions.
8. Find a scene with a single character where no action seems to be happening. Think about how that character feels. Use personification with items in the space or room to illustrate how the character feels.
9. Take one sentence with a character and a less specific verb. Consider the character's emotional state. Practice transforming it by replacing the less specific verb, a specific verb and a highly specific verb.

10. Look at the opening paragraphs of your short and identify tonally how you want it to feel. Add three elements of metaphor, simile, symbol, or imagery to that opening paragraph to help set the tone for the short. Then consider how you believe that symbol or image will change by the time we get to the end of the story.
11. Identify a part of your script that someone said was confusing. Look at prepositions, conjunctions, and phrases. Can you identify if any of these are the culprit? Rewrite the sentence with a good balance of clauses.
12. Find a sentence in your script that feels ordinary. Play with conjunctions and punctuation to create action and intention. Look at where you can apply punctuation for depth and reflection or to forward action or emotion.

THE DISCOVERY OF STORY:
DRAFTING AND REVISING

The Draft
—Prepare a preliminary version of a document

Writing my first significant short film, when I think back to it, is one of the experiences I most hold dear. Not because of the result, but because of the process. Just like many of my students, I truly struggled to find my story.

I was writing daily in the library, gradually learning more about my characters each day. However, it was a foray into the wilderness that began to yield blossoms. As I wrote more, new branches of subplots started to unravel. I began a story about one character but found myself drawn to other characters in her midst. Subsequently, the main character I began with became the supporting character in the new narrative I began to explore. Later, I found myself sitting in an advocacy organization's office, asking questions I didn't even know I had about these characters. Ultimately, this journey led me to discover the story of a character grappling with remorse after committing an act of violence. It was a revelation that unfolded only through persistent writing, even when I didn't know the end or fully understand the journey I was on.

Writing is rewriting.

Every single one of my writing teachers has said this, but I don't think I fully understood it until I was deep into my adulthood. A draft is not simply a bunch of pages, it is a threshold, an invitation, a step into an adventure of self-discovery, challenges, triumphs, disappointments, and revelations. It will be turbulent and rough, but it can also be rewarding, filling you with promise, if only you dare to commit to the process.

THE MYTH OF INSPIRATION

For a long time, I believed this myth of writing when it moves you. That's a wonderful hobby, to write when you feel comfortable or joyous. However, if you have a plan to work in the industry as a writer, you are deciding to sacrifice this luxury of writing when it is convenient or easy. After reading a lot of different writers, from Anne Lamott to Charles Johnson to Maya Angelou, I discovered that if you want to make a living from it, writing is work.

You don't wait for inspiration to hit;
you create it.

I've heard a variety of opinions on writing as work; some say it puts too much pressure on creativity, while others feel it's their calling. But if you choose to make a living from writing, you must create or find the reality that will support your writing. This could involve a ritual, such as a scheduled time or place, a sensory experience, like lighting candles or incense, a specific location, such as a retreat or private cabin, or gathering with a group of people, like a writers group. By teaching your body and mind to recognize the art of writing, and committing to it in the long term, you'll discover the practice that best suits you. Finding your practice makes the ground fertile for real progress to begin!

THE WRITING JONES

Writing, like many artistic processes, is about simply that; the process, not only the result. Oh, the struggles I have witnessed (and experienced!) in seeking to comprehend this idea! How can we possibly let go of the result to embrace the process? How can we believe that the result doesn't matter in a capitalist, Western, results-driven world where final numbers, test results, and scientific fact matter? Perhaps it's because we also live in a world where exceptions occur every day; where miracles and impossibilities seize us and shake us when we least expect them; because "never" can happen today.

Rewriting is akin to that. Consider rewriting as a journey of discovery, much like life itself. We may believe we have a grasp on it, only to be greeted by fresh insights, challenges, and expanses each new day brings—many of which we never even fathomed. Crafting the script can unfold in a manner reminiscent of the enchanting worlds found in *Harry Potter*, *Labyrinth*, or *The Wiz*. Yet, it can also manifest as an extraordinary experience, akin to the mind-bending narratives of *Ganja & Hess*, *Everything Everywhere All At Once*, and *The Matrix*.

What we think we know is never quite what we actually know. What we think we can do is never quite what we can actually do. Writing can push us to profound heights and harrowing lows. I often feel that, writing draft after draft, I am surprised to find precisely what my story is about. Sometimes I wonder what would've happened if I had stopped and had not gone far enough.

When you stop writing after that first draft, you deprive the script of its marrow, the bitter honey of what this script has to offer. Certainly, there will be boredom and struggle; but that only carves out space for thrill and marvel. You keep drafting because there is more to *investigate*! There is more to learn about yourself and the people around you! Remember this idea that you are endlessly fascinating. Let that drive you.

PROCESS EQUALS RESULT

So, what exactly does it mean to commit fully to the process? I believe that it may be akin to searching for that missing charm (or another misplaced crisis-causing anecdotal item). How many times have you tucked away this charm, and then when you need it you can't find it? Yet it suddenly appears when you least expect it, or after you've abandoned it altogether. Or maybe, it appears when you calm yourself down, uncork the tension, release all that anxiety, and discover it's been in the same place all along.

I suspect that the process and result for the writer is similar to those for directors and actors. When we overly fixate on trying to achieve a certain result, we inevitably put shutters on our eyes. We allow ourselves to only see one perspective and one vision. This is the antithesis of creative work, intuition, and listening to your heart. What we don't realize is that fixating on results can limit the potential for other ideas and opportunities to arise. It also prevents us from improvising during those magical, serendipitous moments when creative solutions bloom. That is what we don't want to miss.

> *The result is not what you think it is.*
> *The result is what you discover.*

We can be so driven by establishing the result that we fail to see the brilliance of what lies in front of us. Herein lies the necessity of process. We must allow the journey, the adventure, and the excavation to unveil not *the* result, but *a* result—one that enriches and expands us, recognizing that there are many possible outcomes. If I were to formulate it, it's not so much process versus result, but rather, process leads to an accumulation of results. Ultimately, isn't that what we want as artists? The accumulation of many works, not just one.

Is this creativity only related to the artist's process? I don't think so. I can recall my struggles in my calculus class in college. Calculus was elusive, and I found myself completely challenged by "finding the right answer." My impassioned young professor tried to explain it to me, but I needed an explanation in layman's terms. It was finally my kind teaching assistant who sat down with me and shared the process for arriving at the solution. He generously broke down what was happening behind the numbers so that I understood the steps and how to execute them at each level. Learning a process allowed me to complete not only one problem, but several throughout the course, allowing me to complete the class.

On the Train, In the Park, At the Window

For many years growing up, libraries were my favorite space to write. As an older writer, I've tried to nurture my creative process in different spaces, from my home to the neighborhood park. Through this process, I discovered that it wasn't so much the spaces that guided me, but rather my emotional connection to them. This opened me up to better understanding my own personal rituals of writing. I learned that writing is not simply a process of putting a pen to paper; much of it happens away from the page.

I recall a conversation with a prolific colleague who had already authored ten books spanning fiction, essays, and children's stories. When I asked him where he found the time to write, given his busy schedule, he simply replied, "I write everywhere. On the train, during my commute, between errands, even while attending my kids' games. I'm always writing." His words resonated with me, reminding me of something I knew but hadn't fully embraced: the importance of keeping a notepad and pen handy wherever I go, and of reserving mental space specifically for writing notes to revisit later. We've all been so seduced by our electronic devices, it's easy to forget that, as human beings, our brains are doing more work than we'll probably ever know.

THE ODYSSEY OF DRAFTING

Drafts represent the earliest and continually developing stages of your script. They are new renditions, new iterations of your story, akin to early prototypes. In these early drafts, we apply many fundamental writing techniques in the development of story, but more importantly, we are developing our voice, sifting and sorting through what exactly we want to say in the story. These two things are in many ways happening simultaneously—which is why we often think of drafting as a messy process. In many ways, drafting should be a messy process—coming out the chaos feels so much more earned when we do that.

The Marathon of Ten Drafts

❶ Your **first draft** is a triumph of completion, raw and pure, clumsy but impassioned.

❷ The second draft is a quiet meandering through the field of disappointment as we hope we've made a strong next draft but realize we have a ways to go.

❸ The third draft finds us diving deeper into the abyss of questioning after we receive feedback.

❹ The fourth draft has us unearthing uncut jewels of "character, world, and quest" that we will shave and polish into something pure but imperfect. . .

❺ That we refine and revisit in a draft five that unifies themes.

❻ Draft sixth forces us to recall some of our original ideas and challenge our original assumptions.

❼ The seventh draft explores the story from the vantage point of what we knew then (past drafts), what we know now (current drafts), and the "what if" of what we don't know (future drafts).

❽ Drafting the eighth of these versions feels Herculean and like a climactic point as we muddle through issues of predictability, cliche, and convenience.

❾ Draft nine fulfills the promise of breakthroughs we never imagined.

❿ **The final of draft ten is the pinnacle of revelation we never knew we'd achieve. And then we often start again!**

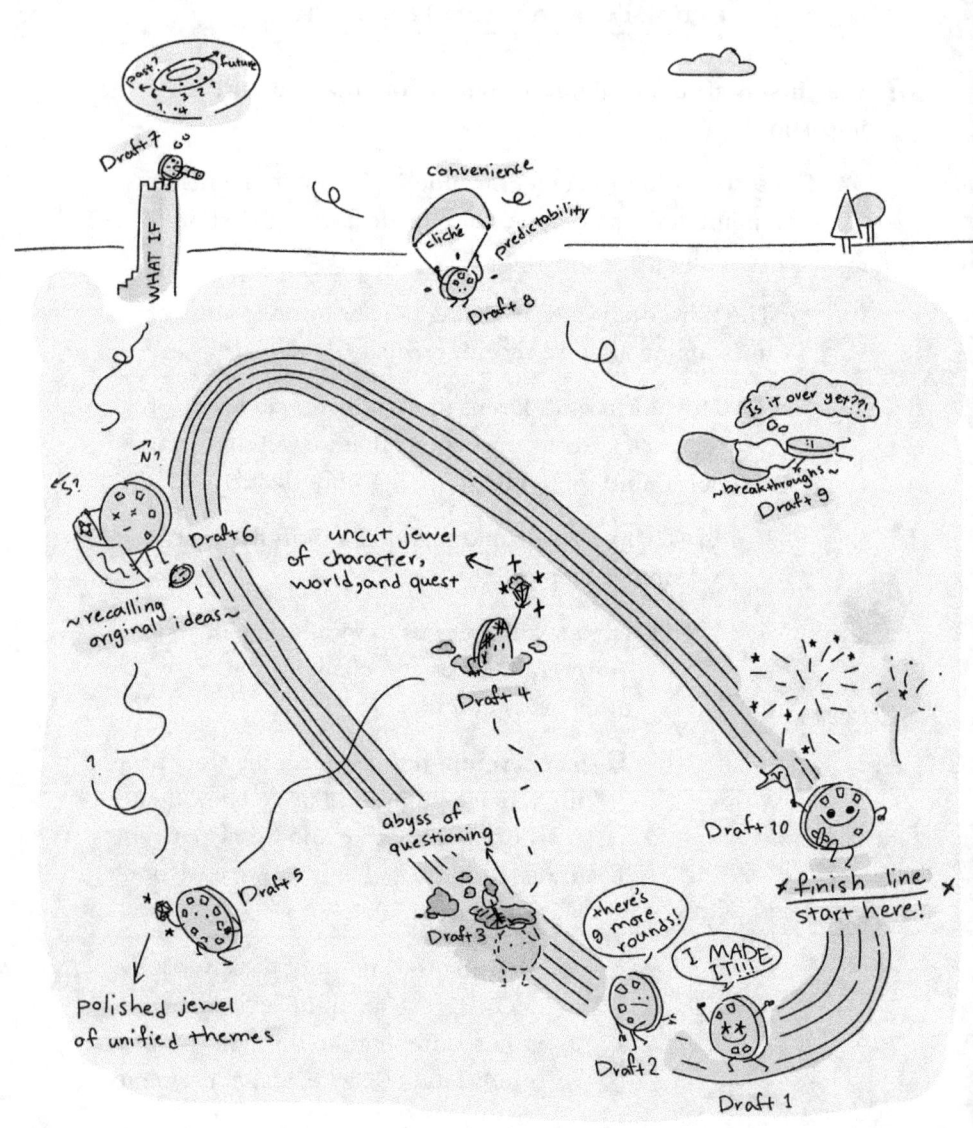

The Marathon of Ten Drafts

Ten drafts is a basic number for a script, and these ten drafts should be thought of not as daunting, remedial tasks, but as quests of experience, opportunities to grow, and ushers into expansion.

While you may formally not always have an exact ten drafts, there may be other ways to think about drafting. For example, developing your story through many of the exercises in this chapter, such as the bone structure, the rule buildings, and the first scenes and last scenes, can profoundly impact the development of your story. If approached with significant attention and sensitivity, these exercises may help you maneuver through this odyssey of drafting so that you might arrive to the revelation sooner. However, the first draft is always very special. Like a first kiss, a first day at school, or a first swimming lesson, it's an awkward, stumbling foray into the darkness that holds a unique beauty.

The Authentic Beauty of the First Draft

The first rule of drafting is never lose your first draft. Only you know what that is. Like your first love, which might not be the person you kissed first, or had intercourse with first, or even married first, your first draft is the birth of a star. Everyone knows their first love because it touched us in tender spaces we never knew. Similarly, the first draft should never be forgotten because there is something eloquent and profound about the accomplishment of this imperfect beauty. The first draft can be quite raw and powerful in the fumbling of intense emotion and sheer will. It is the messy marvel of ideas and feelings, all tumbling out onto the paper in a way that betrays that we don't know what we're doing. We just knew we had to do it. That delicate chaos holds within it the core of our passion that led us to this place, and the potential for that chaos to organize into something meaningful and persisting.

There is nothing quite like the first draft. Yes, it is the first of many drafts. If you stop after the first draft, you will miss the fullness of what this relationship has to offer.

The Edit & Revision

Edit
—To alter, adapt, or refine, especially to bring about conformity to a standard or to suit a particular purpose

Revise
—To make a new, amended, improved or up-to-date version of

One of my first "real" jobs came in college when I worked for the University of Chicago Press. I was an assistant copy editor, which translated then to a proofreader. As a proofreader, it was my job to look for potential *edits* in the language and writing that affected the comprehension of the idea on a sentence level. My job was always to aid in the comprehension and understanding of what the writer wanted to say, and to ensure that their idea was delivered in a clear way. That included looking at grammar and punctuation, as well as misplaced or misspelled words. My favorite curiosities were commas because the rules were all so different.

This is different from a *revision*. In a revision, you affect story. Revising means that you are changing ideas in the story. Perhaps you want to develop a storyline further by adding scenes or lines or reducing other scenes or lines. The change could be as significant as changing character dialogue, or as minor as changing a movement. It could even be capitalizing an object to add prominence to it, which is different from capitalizing a character's name because you forgot to do so—that would be an edit.

Why is it important to know the difference? This is because in a script, you will apply both. It is best to not do both at the same time. Attempting to correct (*edit*) uses a different muscle than trying to enhance (*revise*). One is drawing on your knowledge of rules, and the other is asking you to draw more from intuition. There will be some overlap, which is why I believe writing is an art and a science.

The Domino Effect: The Page One Rewrite

Every draft is a page one rewrite. This is another writer's anecdotal gem I didn't understand until I was older. This means that in every draft, you want to be open to the possibility of changing the script at any point in the story, not for any random reason but because every script is a conglomerate of dominos. When you change one area of the script, even something very small, it can and will have an immediate impact on the rest of the script. Especially in a short, one small change can be deeply affecting. I've had many students who have been surprised by how one small revision changes the feedback they receive from classmates. It's surprising, but should it be?

In a poem, we could certainly expect and understand how the shift of one word in a work, where every word means so much, could cause great shifts. But isn't that so in life too? Isn't it the small details that can affect us so much even though we are loath to admit it? The tiny gestures, the looks, the pauses? I suspect it's simply that sometimes we move so fast we don't see them, but they are there. So, this means any revision you make creates a new draft, although that revision may be major or minor.

Electronic Drafts and Title Pages

It's important to know how to organize your drafts in this world of electronic devices and saved documents. When you create a new draft, you also want to save and categorize it so you can easily refer to it. Many writers may need to return to an earlier draft, so it's not always the best idea to rewrite over old drafts. Every time you create a new draft, you want to save it, and identity this new version in the document and on the title page. You will need this information later as a reference if you need to go back to an earlier draft. This happens more often than you would think.

On your title page, you can see draft listed by date, by number, or both, i.e.., Draft Date 7/3/20 or Draft_v3.2. In a feature film scripts, colors will be used to help illuminate new drafts, but for shorts, simply noting it on the title page will suffice.

The first number represents the significance of the change. You want to change to a whole number draft every time you create a draft with major changes that may not be easily replicable. The number behind the decimal indicates minor edits, like fixed misspellings or minor deletions.

On the title page, you can add draft date or number either in the contact info space or under the title. When you save a new document, you should acknowledge the change, i.e., LittleRedsPie_Draftv.2.6. This tells us how far you've developed the draft and how many significant changes have been made to the script. Remember, 10 drafts for a script is average, so 10.8 is a lot of drafts!

Summoning Revisions and Surface Reveries

In my early writing years, when I received script notes from someone, I would run back to my computer and apply them immediately and mechanically without thinking too much about it. Certainly, I would make an evaluation, but it was admittedly a superficial one. I now know that surface evaluations are insufficient; they merely skim the surface of the issue. Surface edits can lead you astray from your narrative because you aren't following *your* story; you're following someone *else's* opinion, perspective, and idea of your story. They are essentially edits, and as I wrote above, an edit is not a revision.

When I edit, that is usually a process of polishing; a mechanical act of applying rules and standards of grammar, punctuation, and format. I usually do those before I send the script to a company, contest, or actor. However, when I begin a revision, it is often because I feel that something is unfinished and it is summoning me. While it's true that this urge to revise might stem from a note I received, I've had to learn to trust my instincts more. Not every note is valuable, not every writer understands your story, and not every suggestion aligns with your vision of the script.

As an older, more seasoned writer, I invite and embrace the notes, let them wash over me, and allow my subconscious to do a lot of the work. I wait to see if the notes have resonance. Do they stir something within me? I don't rush to make changes, except in the case of a looming deadline. Stories grow and expand like a little seed. Little changes affect a lot, and I want the story to grow in a healthy direction.

Surprisingly, when I have won an award for a script, I've never felt, "OK, I'm done!" Even when I've had a script for years, sometimes I'll still feel like there's something not quite right. Revisions come from a personal place that I believe is akin to the art of self-improvement. If you believe that you could be better at something, it's similar to the feeling that something in the script is seeking to be changed, altered, or improved. It is summoning you to make it better.

These moments of revision might come to me in the early waking hours, on my way to work, or during the late nights when I am preparing for bed. Often, they occur during moments of peace. They are these tiny, little voices that compel me to return to my work. When these ideas approach, I'll turn them over in my mind, and once in a while, make a discovery! I try to write them down mentally and physically, because they are often fleeting. These moments are amazing. I imagine that every writer or artist has experiences like this.

THE WILDS AND WILDERNESS OF WORKSHOPPING

Before you start workshopping, write down on a post-it why you're writing this story. It can be a word, phrase, or sentence, similar to Kat Candler's theme. This post-it needs to be your anchor in the sea of critique. While criticism can be very helpful, it can also be overwhelming. It is easy to forget that this story is *your* story and is ultimately about you and the things that move you. Make this vow and keep it close and visible while workshopping. This is why you are writing.

I love the process of workshopping and enjoy grabbing hold of other books that discuss new techniques in the writing and workshopping process. However, the result of the workshop can sometimes be challenging. I believe this is the case for all writers. Comments that you receive that seem to confirm issues you have already identified in the script are the easiest to absorb. Things get tricky when you receive feedback that makes you question yourself and your idea. New ideas can be finnicky because sometimes, they can offer new concepts that may sound fun and exciting and even "why not," but ultimately take you further away from your script.

THE CHIPPING AWAY OF CRITIQUE

Criticism can often chip away at the original idea in the same way. In my earlier years, I remember working with a set of producers on a writing project and completely losing my handle on the project. I applied notes because I felt I was supposed to, not because it elevated the story. Even though I knew the producers were earnest, this was a negative experience.

On the other hand, I had one student say to me once, "I received so much great feedback; which ideas do I enact?" It's such a wonderful experience receiving robust and well-intentioned feedback, but you want to find an effective way to sift through it.

Your premise is your sieve.

When you have a good hold on what you want your story to be, this will help you identify feedback that builds towards your larger goal and helps you to discard the feedback that takes the story in a different direction. If it doesn't make it through the sieve, it may not be an effective note for your story.

Mailing in Feedback

So how do you avoid these kinds of rabbit holes? I don't think there's any one way, but if you're asking for feedback, before you apply changes to the script, first start by asking questions. Find out why someone is suggesting a note. What is their reason? What is their basis? What is their evidence? The more they answer, the more it can reveal if it is a personal issue or an issue of story.

If you are asked to provide feedback, questions serve as your greatest resource. Asking the writer questions will help you to align yourself with the writer's desires and get away from your own perspective, which will influence how you absorb the script. The best feedback is given selflessly and humbly, not for you but for the good of the writer.

In my classroom, my students often build scripts within a community, and I take time to set rules for a safe space by asking for the kind of feedback that is effective and the kind that isn't. In that way, we consecrate the space for everyone in it; however, my students also carry a pre-existing knowledge of their stories from exchanges over the term, which also aids in helping the community understand the writer's goals.

While most students get excited to *receive* feedback on their scripts, I believe that *delivering* good feedback is a great indicator of a true storyteller. Not only does it mean they know how to analyze story, but it also suggests they comprehend tools and concept outside of their own perspective. This means they understand that storytelling, at its core, is a selfless enterprise. Isn't that what the best actors do in a story? Aren't they giving us so much of themselves in a selfless way, without protection, without caution? Aren't they givers of their hearts and souls?

TECHNIQUES AND TOOLS

The Twelve Screenwriting Elegant Exercises

When approaching your first draft, which I will describe here as the rough draft that you've edited into a somewhat more elegant form so you can share it with others, there are some specific steps you can apply. This commonly quick and slim editing process happens to all writers, and as

I've worked with new screenwriters, I've found that there are some common pitfalls that my new writers will fall into, so I've singled them out and summarized them here as the Elegant Exercises. This is a great exercise for approaching proofreading and editing.

> The Tentpole Paragraph
> The T Factor and the Days of Future Past
> The Broken Lens of Belief
> Feeling, Explaining, and The Mystery of Exposition
> Heading Into and out of the Scene
> The Long and Short of It
> The Weight of Massive Detail
> To Be or to Not Have Been
> The Doing Nothing of It All
> Getting in Late, Leaving Early
> Capitalizing on Your Strengths
> Punctuating and Pointing to the End

1. The Tentpole Paragraph

One of the most common edits I identify with my new writers who have written fiction before is editing the tentpole paragraph. The tentpole paragraph is the long, grandiose paragraph that will often take the space of half a page to a page in a script. There are no breaks, little punctuation, and a lot of description. It is a specimen of spectacle. It looks big and exciting, but when you look inside, there is not a lot happening.

To avoid the tentpole paragraph, you want to consider the first rule of writing paragraphs in a script: paragraphs are singular ideas, moments, and most importantly, visual guides. Write paragraphs as shots.

Every time you break the paragraph, you are directing the reader's attention to a new visual idea and moment. For this reason, you will rarely see paragraphs that are longer than four or five lines in a script. If you do, this is a flag to check out what's happening. Think of this not as a rigid rule, but more as an indicator and a warning of a lack of visual direction in the story.

2. The T Factor and the Present of Future Past

Another common note for new screenwriters is recognizing tense (T) as a vehicle for writing for performance. In fiction, stories can be told in the past, present, and future. We can share what happened before the character arrived, while the character was there, and what will occur with the character in the future. This often happens with the use of an omniscient narrator. However, screenplays are written in the performable tense of the present and active verb. Changing the tense causes confusion for the performers, technicians, and readers.

Some common signals of tense issues include adverbial phrases and clauses, especially those that delineate time, such as using "when," "after," and "before." Writing that the character "will" do something "when" or "after" another event occurs is predictive of the future. Similarly, using "before" refers to things happening in the past. Other signals we might recognize are "if" and "then," which are conditional.

However, in a script, we want to try as much as we can to keep action in the present, for the sake of the performers. They can't perform the past or the future, only the present.

3. The Broken Lens of Belief

Many screenwriting teachers will talk about the use of camera angles like "zooms" and "dollies," and phrases like "we see" or "we hear," as being problematic. In the scripts that I use in my classes, these phrases pop up intermittently, and I know this confuses my students.

The issue is not so much the phrases or camera shots themselves, but the fact that new writers will often use them awkwardly and in a way that does not move the story forward, but instead, distracts us from the story. The distracting thing about applying this phrasing is that it disturbs our "suspension of belief." While this is a phrase we recognize mostly for moviemaking, the same idea applies when reading a book, and certainly, a script.

Reading a poetry book, novel, or script are escapist experiences, and when we sink into them, we want to leave the turbulence of the present world behind. However, clumsily inserted camera angles, zooms, and dollies, and overuse of interjections of "we see," are the kinds of things that constantly remind us that we are not a part of the story. It reminds us that the story needs to be executed, that it isn't real. Stories are all about the realness of this new and thrilling reality.

Experienced screenwriters won't use these cumbersome phrases often, because they don't need to. They've already acquired an arsenal full of language, poetic devices, and action verbs. They don't depend on these clunky phrases to do the work for them. Early on in my classes, I find myself often critiquing these little disruptors in my students' papers. They are writing crutches, and when students have learned how to walk, I get excited for them to run to this exciting new literary reality.

4. Feeling, Explaining, and the Mystery of Exposition

The most common element that shows up in making this transition to screenwriting is abandoning the idea of telling, so you can *show*. Alexander Mackendrick talks very vividly about this idea of developing a visual language; about learning how to communicate without needing to explain everything using words or dialogue.

Making the transition to expressing feelings through action rather than words can be daunting. My students often use phrases like "she decided to," "she wanted to," or "she thought." I often ask "How can we *enact* her decision, share what she wants by *revealing* her desire, or hint at what she thinks by *demonstrating* her frustration?"

Moving away from explaining is one of the most difficult parts about shifting to a screenplay. There is always some exposition in a screenplay, but good screenwriters develop their visual language to accomplish this. Signage, other media, and symbolism are all other strategies outside of behavior that can achieve this.

5. Heading Into and Out of the Scene

Scene headings and transitions are other aspects of screenwriting that often require practice for early writers. Many new writers struggle to determine when a scene begins or ends, and how its beginning and ending are established on the page. A new scene begins whenever the time or place shifts. Therefore, every new scene should include "INT." (for interior) or "EXT." (for exterior), the location, and the time, which is usually written as "DAY" or "NIGHT."

INT. OFFICE—DAY

However, many of my new writers will remember the few times that they have seen a scene without one element or another. They will take this as screenwriting law.

OFFICE—DAY or INT. OFFICE

These are subheadings, and they are appropriate with the proper setup. A subheader like "OFFICE—DAY" is best used when we have established an entire space, like a building or floor (INT. MANAGER'S FLOOR—DAY), but we want to direct attention to a particular part of it. Other times, you will see "INT. OFFICE." This is not actually a subheader; it is an incomplete header. It means that the writer expects you to know the time of day and to refer to previous headers. However, as writers, we want to prioritize clarity and understanding over style or assumptions about the reader's knowledge.

Ensuring that your scene headings are complete will never harm the story but will help to alleviate any confusion that may occur later. Scene headings ground us in some of the location reality of the story, and we depend on these little words to keep the read crisp and brisk.

Conversely, the end of a scene will be marked by a transition. In the days of physically cutting film, transitions of "CUT TO:" were commonly used. The transition was used to define the exercise of cutting strips of film footage to link sequences together. "CUT TO:'s" were simple, but there were also "FADES," "DISSOLVES," "CROSS DISSOLVES," and more.

Here, I want to impress upon you that each of these transitions communicates time. A CUT TO: (or its absence) indicates going directly into the next scene; FADE UP TO: indicates the start of a new period; DISSOLVES indicate a lengthy amount of time has passed. Intentional usage of these and other transitions assists in accomplishing the shorthand of script language that allows the reader to move quickly and easily through the story.

6. The Long and Short of It

In the chapter on literary devices, I discuss the importance of writing efficiently in scripts, using compact and impactful details and descriptions. There, I mentioned the literary device of staccato, where a series of short sentences or phrases is employed to shape rhythm. Staccato is also a nice device to break up how words appear on the page. Like long paragraphs, long sentences are also rare in scripts.

Long sentences with multiple clauses or phrases that stretch across four, five, or six lines are another red flag. Long sentences require more time, thought, and comprehension from the reader. When I see long sentences, I recognize them as signals for a prolonged reading experience, prompting me to seek ways to break them up. While there's no formula for a perfect pattern of long and short sentences, screenwriters aim to create spaces on the page where readers can breathe, both mentally and physically. Remember, a script aspires to a brisk, engaging experience regardless of genre. Without a mix of long and short sentences, you may slow down that read, making it a trudge instead of a glide.

7. The Weight of Massive Detail

One of things I love about writing prose is the potential to dive into the minutiae of description. We can dedicate pages to describing something as ordinary as a chair, mountain, or leaf. Unfortunately, such lengthy descriptions don't occur in scripts.

As discussed in the language and device chapter, details in a script are written concisely and precisely. Precision, accuracy, and intentional word selection are key. Less is more when it comes to detail in a script. When describing important elements in the script, provide something memorable, visual, actionable, or revealing about this person or object.

Another issue I often recognize with excessive details is that the detail swallows the story. When you find a paragraph of massive description, you will often find that story has stopped moving to accommodate all of these details, many of which are not relevant or interesting to readers.

8. To Be or to Not Have Been

Helping verbs and being verbs, both visited in the language and devices chapter, are easy prey for my editing pen! In my students' papers, they often lean into these being verbs because they are comfortable and easy. However, they can also be boring and repetitive. As a writer, you want to showcase your dexterity not only with the story but also with language! So, I encourage you, as a developing writer, to recognize these simple verbs and to challenge them with action verbs that can provide more visual and emotional impact. Additionally, being verbs can signal passive voice or incorrect tense, which are red flags for a story that may have taken a downturn or stagnated.

9. The Doing Nothing of It All

As I said before, typically, when a page has massive blocks of paragraphs or dialogue, there is usually very little happening in the scene. If there is a full page of description or dialogue, and I can describe it in one sentence, like "the character wakes up," or "they're talking," that's a problem.

Sometimes, new writers will get so excited about a scene that they spend all their time there. We can recognize this as a detour from the story and a way of dragging down the movement of the narrative.

In a short script especially, massive blocks of paragraphs with description or dialogue feel off putting, disrupting the expected flow. What you are looking for is action, change, or development, no matter the genre, no matter the form.

10. Get in Late, Get out Early

This is a note from my former screenwriting teacher, the impressive Rafael Lima: "Get into a scene as late as you can, leave as early as you can." The idea behind that is that you don't want the reader hanging out idly. They have reached the destination (the end of your story) ahead of what is written in the script, and they are bored like a child waiting to get picked up by a late parent. A bored child is ready to get into trouble by doing something else!

Getting into a scene late makes the reader hurry to catch up. This makes them read faster and with heightened anticipation. Exiting the scene as early as you can leaves them on a cliffhanger. Where does the cliffhanger break? Right after the climax of the scene, of course! Like a story, every scene has a climax, and as the writer, you should know what and when that is. If a scene drags on without introducing fresh ideas or developments, our reader becomes the bored child waiting on the late parent.

11. Capitalizing on Your Strengths

In the language chapter, we touch on formatting, with capitalization being a particularly perplexing aspect for many. There are so many rules around capitalizing, and the truth of the matter is, many professional screenwriters have chosen to follow some rules while disregarding others. So here, let's review the foundations of this tool.

Capitalization in a script is about suggesting something or someone is important or that something needs to be done. When you capitalize something, it means, "Hey, look over here! This is urgent!"

The fundamental rules of capitalization should be applied: capitalizing proper nouns of people, places, and things. Additionally, in screenwriting, other rules pertain to capitalizing characters we encounter for the first time (for casting purposes), sounds (for the sound editor), shots or perspectives (for the cinematographer), and the actor reading the dialogue. Occasionally, items such as a magical box or a special hat may be capitalized (for the costumer or set designer). However, excessive capitalization can lead to confusion for both the reader and other collaborators, as it prompts questions like, "Why was that capitalized?"

Keeping in mind that capitalization serves to highlight components of the script requiring action can serve as a useful guide. Nonetheless, I often find myself addressing both undercapitalization and overcapitalization in my students' work.

12. Punctuating and Pointing to the End

In my syllabi, I often include a section that reminds the class, "even though we have left English class, we haven't left the building of English language." Grammar and punctuation rules still apply. I covered some of the punctuation practices in the language and devices chapter, but I want to mention that I often find that new writers forget what to do with periods, question marks, colons, and commas in their scripts. The hundreds of people who may read the script, including the actor performing it, depend on them for beats, intentions, and pauses. A good talent manager I worked with in the past spent endless hours proofreading one of my pilot scripts for punctuation. I was shocked, and then deeply appreciative, of this work. Punctuation is an essential aspect of communication, whether spoken or written. If you cannot demonstrate that you comprehend and can apply tools of language, you will have a difficult time convincing anyone in a decision-maker's seat that you can write a good story.

THE FIRST READ OF THE ROUGH DRAFT: QUIET, CLEAR, AND OPEN

Reading through your rough draft is an important process. Getting a sense of how it reads and feels when you read is simple but amazingly useful at this stage. Find a good comfortable spot and read it from the beginning, taking notes of how you feel at different points: which parts feel slow, which parts make you feel impatient, which parts confuse you, which parts get you excited, and which parts seem to soar?! In this first full reading, take note of *where* the issues are, but focus less so on *what* the issues may be. You can start to determine who the culprits are later.

The Next Reads: The Determination

Here's where using the steps from the determination process from the personal investigation chapter can help you: imagining, examining, inquiring, discovering, reporting, and conceiving of the next draft. You may not need to use all of the steps; perhaps even only using one might work. If you're having issues discerning how to revisit a problem area of the script, these steps will help. Ultimately, what you're looking for is the conception: what idea do you have to address issues in the script?

The Elemental Passes

In Pilar Alessandra's workshops, she likes to direct writers through the process of revision through passes. A pass means that as you go through the script you focus on one element instead of trying to fix the script all at once. This is an effective strategy when discussing feature scripts, but it is also useful in short films. In a "pass," you might focus on subplot, world-building, or character. Perhaps the pass concentrates on developing location or illustrating theme. With this method, you don't have to try to do everything all at once.

The Backbone and the Spine

One essential element to return to when revising is your outline or beat sheet from the structure chapter. This beat sheet or outline is the foundation and backbone of your script. Your first beat sheet may not be your last, and as you delve further into the many layers of the script, you may find yourself uncovering new things and writing new drafts of the beat sheet. Regardless, returning to this skeleton of the original idea of your film is useful in fleshing out what you have accomplished and what still needs to be developed. A similar exercise is checking in with the logline of your story: do the structure and themes of your logline tell the structure and themes of this story?

The Big Event Three and the Big Turn Three

When looking at a three-act short, you want to consider what the big turning points are. Mostly, when we talk about this traditional structure, we talk about these three elements: inciting incident, climax, and resolution. Notice how these elements can also be considered the significant three events in the life of your character within the film. If the inciting incident creates the disruption, the climax sees the character confront the issue stemming from the inciting incident, and the resolution sees the character resolve it. If you line up these big three events, they should all revolve around the same issue. For example, if the loss of love is the inciting incident, the fight for love is the climax, and the return, or deeper absence, of love is the resolution.

You can also use this tool for the other big three, the turns: turning point one, midpoint, and turning point two. These turning points prompt shifts in tactics or escalations in stakes as the character makes choices. When examining the big three turns, check to see if your character is making choices and decisions. Collectively, these make up your structural turning points. Do you observe your story thematically evolving through these turning point decisions and events?

Plants and Payoffs

Hala Matar's *Moncler x Salehe Bembury*

Some other areas that are important to address when reviewing your script are plants and payoffs. Perhaps you "plant" a ring that is significant at the beginning of the story, introduce a recurring mannerism, or assign your character a unique colloquialism. Questioning how these qualities are distinct will lead you to asking why it's there in the first place. Once you've realized why this inclusion is necessary, you must then have it "payoff." A payoff could include the ring holding the answer to everything the characters sought, the mannerism helps them break into the bank, or the colloquialism getting them captured by the cops. Note that payoffs can be good and bad! Hala Matar's less than a minute commercial *Moncler x Salehe Bembury* is excellent at introducing the product in a reflection of a pond. This pond reflection encompasses brand, the audience and the "nature" aesthetic, eventually creating a returning loop that pays off.

Remember that elements in your short script cannot be random or arbitrary. If you include them, do so for a purpose. Check that these elements that you've chosen to highlight are paying off in some way in the script.

That's My Pattern and I'm Sticking to it!

Patterns serve an essential function in the screenplay. We expect each script to abide by general standards of the screenplay, but also each script must carry its own uniqueness. You as the writer establish this individual pattern of rules and then must commit to retaining this pattern for the entire script.

Identifying consistencies and contradictions is crucial during the revision process, whether within the story itself or in its presentation. These can be found through attentive reading. It might be a character who does something that doesn't feel quite right, and you can't put your finger on why. You can use any element to explore this, from character to world-building to formatting.

Establishing rules not only aids comprehension but also enhances the overall readability of the script. When you abandon a structure that you have set up, you risk disrupting the reader's immersion. Text messaging is one common example, There is no one way to handle text messaging in a script, but once you have determined your preferred structure, you must adhere to it consistently.

Charting Uncharted Objectives

A simple objective tool for evaluating feedback for revision and editing is creating a chart. If you are in a class or a writing group where feedback is being delivered by many members of a group, it is worthwhile noting all the feedback, not so much for the individual feedback, but for the consistency of the feedback. Make a chart with these six major categories: world, character, plot and structure, formatting and organization, language and devices, and theme and premise. Review the feedback and mark each time a piece of feedback relates to one category. It matters less what was said, than the element that was referenced. When you start to witness several marks in one category, that is a good signal to revisit that element in your script.

Ode to the First Lines

Beginnings are such austere and ethereal spaces. They must be crisp and specific, but at the same time whimsical and branching. They are an explosion into an unknown that only you know. The first page is where it all starts, the life of your story.

In earlier chapters, I mentioned the urgency of the opening scenes and the necessary establishment of character, world, and quest as well as relationships, stakes, and obstacles. I have also shared that in a short, where space and time are limited even further, opening scenes should be considered to be half a page or less.

I want to emphasize in this revision chapter the powerful intention of the opening lines. Strong opening lines in scripts dictate the quality of the reading experience. In those three lines, we can be encouraged to read your script or to abandon it.

Consider the first three lines of your screenplay. How can these three lines in particular establish the world, the quest, and the character? How can they set up genre, tone, and mood? How do they use visual storytelling and literary devices to foretell what the story is about and what will happen later in the story? How can these three lines deeply engage us in the event of your story? Three lines in a short film are a lot. Make them count.

Serenade to the Final Page

Goodbyes are so memorable. When we say goodbye to someone we care about, we often look for clues and hints that maybe this is not an end, that this may be the beginning of something new. A strong end is a story that offers the potential for a new beginning. There is something very human about this desire for endurance and hopefulness, and a good end can suggest that, even in death.

When you reach this last page, think about this door that closes, but can still be opened. Have we seen a character who has traversed one sequence in their life, and is now ready—or not ready—to enter the next? Have we seen a world transformed? Have we seen plots and possible subplots resolve? Go back to the first page to compare how these two scenes feel next to each other. Are they from the same story?

Look at this last page. Does this page all by itself say something about endings? A funny thing that regular script readers will do with scripts is they will look at the beginning, and then quickly flip or scroll down to the end with a first reading. I don't find myself doing that in books, but I almost always do that with scripts. Knowing that someone might look there first, how can you make that last page feel like an awakening, a transformation, or a long journey's end?

I still love "FADE OUT." It's not something you often see in scripts these days, but I love how it mimics the closing of a door and the lights going out, whether in a movie theater or in a bedroom before night. It's a comfort.

THE FINAL FRONTIER: THE NURTURED SCRIPT

In the end, how do you know it's a final draft? To be honest, I don't know if there ever is a final draft! Often, my drafts are a function of deadlines and submissions. The process of rewriting can sometimes feel infinite. To me, a final draft is the one that I feel best represents my vision at that time. It reminds me of how filmmakers will often revisit their films decades later and revise them. There are some tangible and story hallmarks to look for that I've discussed above. At the end of the day, you are the writer, and only you know when it's truly ready. When it's ready, the last thing you will do is proofread.

Proofreading is the thing that I watch new writers struggle with, but it's one of the essential parts of the final draft. Proofreading works best if someone else proofreads for you or if you change mediums, like from computer to paper. Another good technique is reading the entire script aloud.

This is why it's important: a well-proofread script will declare that the work has been cared for, assessed, reviewed, and polished. It speaks to your professionalism, or regrettably, your amateurism or carelessness. Just think about how much money and time goes into a production of a show or a movie, and then imagine asking a producer to read your error-laden script. How comfortable do you think that producer will feel in giving you a six-figure project when you couldn't find the time to proofread this project?

PRACTICE AND PLAY

1. Revisit your draft using the Twelve Elegant Exercises edits to revise your draft.
2. After your first read, examine how you feel. Consider how you want your reader to feel when they've finished your script. How close are you to this goal? Mark the spaces that felt slow or frustrating to you.
3. Try the elemental pass first with characters, then world-building, then theme, looking at the scenes.
4. Read your last page. How does it make you feel about the rest of the script? Does it make you feel like you want to go back and read from the beginning. If not, how can you revise it?
5. What's your pattern? Look at three or more previously written scripts, focusing on their beginnings and endings. Do you recognize your patterns? Can you define them? What does your pattern avoid?
6. Search for the structural turning points in your story. If you are using three act structure, can you find the Big Event Three and Big Turn Three? If you are using a different structure, are you hitting your marks for the turning points in the story?
7. Consider the theme that you identified earlier in the story. Find examples of how you have incorporated these themes: through dialogue, sound, and visual representations (symbols, similes, metaphors, imagery).
8. Visit your first ½ page and the last ½ page of your script. Compare the two. Are they mirrors of evolution?
9. Think about your last revision of your beat sheet and check in with the first draft and your beat sheet. Have you stayed on track with your original intention?
10. Examine the major events of your story: the inciting incident, the climax, the resolution. Trace the development of a character, a set piece, and a prop in these Big Events Three.
11. In the morning, read your first three lines. In the evening, right before you go to bed, rewrite them making them symbolically foreshadowing, tonally predictive, and emotionally impactful.
12. Identify the spaces that are where you write the best and the tools that make you feel the most comfortable. Take some time to dress this space and make it more comfortable for your writerly self.

THE SHORT FORMS:
SHORT LANDSCAPES OF THE STORYTELLER'S IMAGINATION

WELCOME TO THE SHORT FORMS!

Which One?

One of my popular short content pieces was a South Los Angeles project which I envisioned as a transmedia project with narrative, educational, and community outreach elements. When I started working on the narrative piece, I originally envisioned it as a comic, then as a short film, and eventually, a video game. By the time I made the project, I had created various versions of it in many different structures. I'd come to write it as a short, an hour-long TV drama pilot, and then finally, a web series. I'd also visited it as a drama, as surreal superhero fare, and then as dramedy. In the end, the web series dramedy is what got the film produced.

Does that mean that the other modes were incorrect? No, but it does mean that there are elements I can't control that are deciding the fate of the project, and sometimes, timing is everything. I'd never imagined that the project would evolve through all of those structures over the course of all those years, but it taught me one thing: That storytelling is a fluid process.

NAVIGATING THE SHORT FORMS

Now that you have explored various approaches to your story, the question of how to tell the story arises. Know that you are simply a storyteller, and the function of the story is something that you may change or shift. In my early years, I allowed others to dictate how it should be told; in my later years, I learned that as the storyteller, I could expand my choices. As a professional, this flexibility would be required of me often. I could tell the story in a myriad of ways.

You Tell the Story

You are the illustrious bard of this story, and how you tell it is up to you. In this conclusive chapter, I will share with you some of the different structures of short media. In each section, I will introduce you to the form, beginning with the traditional bodies of narrative, experimental, and documentary. Then, I will try to capture how to approach each short form/concept from a writing standpoint, as well as highlight the differences. In each section, I will also make suggestions about why each form might be effective for you, as you attempt to uncover which form works best for your idea!

The Narrative Short

Mariama Diallo's *Hair Wolf*
Roseanne Liang's *Do No Harm*
Ali Asgari and Farnoosh Samadi's *The Baby*
Maribel Vasquez's *Entre Mamushkas*
Taika Waititi's *Two Cars, One Night*
Stefani Saintonge's *Seventh Grade*

Learn.

The live-action narrative short form is distinguished by its attempts to imitate the complexities of life in a fictional, heightened, or reductive way. It is considered the beloved traditional short, forming the meat of the film industry. It is easily recognizable, accessible, and consumable by the masses.

The narrative fiction film is the stuff of dreams. It represents the crux of early American civilization in many ways, including its portrayal of hopes, dreams, and possibilities.

A live-action narrative short will typically run less than 40 minutes although more commonly it will reach between five and fifteen minutes. These shorts are defined by the introduction of a set of characters who will navigate a setting or world in pursuit of an objective.

This approach requires thinking about your script in a linear way, considering a concrete beginning, middle, and end. These elements must all be demonstrated through evolving narrative devices like character, world, and plot. This is the crux of the Western storytelling, founded on principles established by the likes of Aristotle, Gustav Freytag, and Lajos Egri.

Memorable narrative shorts often center around intriguing or unusual characters, or empowering, persistent characters in seemingly mundane or unexpected spaces who get dropped into difficult circumstances. The most resonant shorts are the ones that are overflowing with emotion and personal details.

See.

Narrative shorts are regularly shown at film festivals, but in this postmodern, post-internet world, narrative shorts can also be found on streaming services, social media platforms, media archives, and various websites and articles.

Brainstorm.

A good place to start is thinking about characters or people who have captivated you. When considering making a narrative short, start with the basic elements: characters, world, and plot. Then, consider genre, structure, and style. Next, add in tension, tone, mood, perspective, and other literary elements. Finally, you need to know the theme, lesson, or premise. You want to tell a story with some linearity, whether it is fiction, a true story, or a hybrid of the two. You can choose to follow a traditional recipe or mix things up; this will largely depend on your story.

The challenge of a short is considering your story as a moment in the timeline of this character's life journey. In telling this story, whether it is a feature or a short, you must make decisions about when, why, and where your story begins and ends. These decisions are based around the conflicts and problems, core emotional ideas, and themes of the story.

This vital component of theme in a narrative film ties the arc of the story to a value or lesson. This trajectory includes some kind of shift in theme, illustrated through an arc. These shifts in thematic content follow the characters on their journey and reflect in their development. As you approach the final pages in your story, the end should convey the evolution of themes within storytelling elements, such as character, place, time, and emotion. This helps "the end" feel satisfying, different, and feel conclusive, regardless of our opinions on this ending.

All of the shorts listed in this section are character-driven, as I would assert is often the case with narrative shorts. As human beings on a continual search for connection, this isn't surprising. While higher budget films tend to emphasize spectacle and may place more focus on plot and location, character-driven films can blossom under budget constraints. These character-driven films listed above span various genres, showcasing the versatility of short form. For example, *Hair Wolf* is horror comedy featuring a distressed beauty shop customer plagued by a different kind of monster, while *Do No Harm* is a more serious action horror following a doctor who uses unexpected skills when some unexpected visitors show up for her patient. *The Baby* and *Seventh Grade* are each distinct coming-of-age dramas, each led by young women pushing the boundaries of their gender and cultural norms. One revolves around a seventh grader struggling to understand puberty, intimacy, and sex, while the other focuses on a college student who must find a safe space for her child. *Entre Mamushkas* is fantasy comedy that follows a young doll who yearns for a life beyond her nest, and *Two Cars, One Night* is a bittersweet part-drama, part-rom-com about kids making the most of a night while their parents drink in a pub.

Write.

The writing process of a narrative follows a traditional format defined by the Academy of Motion Pictures Arts and Sciences. This format secures the commercialization and industrialization of the art form so that it may be executed consistently and in mass quantities. It dictates that one page of script equates to one minute of screen time, and governs elements such as font type and size, margins, and the rules for capitalization and indentation. While these formats continue to change and evolve, the intention remains the same: to create a literary document serving as a blueprint for the execution of the work's final form—a motion picture.

Narrative writing follows a traditional structure that leads us toward a determined end. This conclusion resolves the various subplots and plots.

Just as we perceive life as unfolding with structure and resolution, we expect narrative stories to do the same. The writer must measure and sift the beginning and end of the narrative, ensuring that ingredients added in the first act effectively contribute to a fully baked reconciliation of said conflict.

Plan.

Filmmakers typically make narrative short films as a stepping stone toward a career in filmmaking.

Shorts can often be used as calling cards for new writer-directors. The narrative short demonstrates to an executive or industry representative that you have a grasp on storytelling and know how to wield cinematic tools. It tells your audience that you have something to say, and this is how you want to say it. Your narrative short establishes your individual voice as a filmmaker through its style. It serves as an introduction, inviting others to experience the world you inhabit and welcoming them to your perspective.

While new writers can benefit from the narrative short, there is a greater emphasis in the industry on the "produced writer." Your script cannot sit on a shelf. If you aspire to have a writing career, producers and executives will expect to see your short work produced in addition to seeing longer-form work. In one studio development meeting that I had attended, my short script opened the door for the executive to request that I write the pilot.

Narrative shorts also serve as a playground for artist development. Creative labs will scout, invite and potentially fund, a short narrative from a promising new talent. Here, we can watch a new filmmaker grow and develop their vision and craft. While some filmmakers launch their feature or commercial careers on just a short or two, other new filmmakers will fall in love with the short format and find themselves making five, eight, or ten! In this way, the short is a great vehicle for preparing for the next level. They can also lay the groundwork for a feature or television project—more on proof of concepts later in this chapter.

Strategies.

In a narrative short, it's easy to fixate on mechanics and forget the core of filmmaking—emotions. Many short narrative films replicate overused plots without adding unique perspective, insight, or emotional connection. The field of narrative filmmaking is vast, and most storylines have already been explored, including themes like the first date, the growing pains coming of age, the sibling rivalries, the cop action film, detective noir, warring factions, new world fantasy redux, the sci fi virus/zombie take over, the rape revenge thriller, the musical, the identity, and more. To compete with other narrative films, you must innovate an already existing framework. Roberta Marie Munroe's book *How Not to Make Short* discusses common pitfalls that new filmmakers encounter when pursuing a "cool" market-driven idea. The downfall of market ideas is that the market they attempt to court is always changing! You must consider other ways to distinguish your story. Think about specificity of detail, potency of emotion, richness of imagery, uniqueness of structure, and innovation.

In this age, diversity movements, from Black Lives Matter to #MeToo, are demonstrating that one way to innovate is by changing perspective. You can also innovate by changing the world. What if an entire love story took place in a bathroom or in a laundromat, like Barry Jenkins' *My Josephine*?

The Experimental Short
Jenn Nkiru's *Rebirth is Necessary*
Maya Deren's *Meshes in the Afternoon*
Christopher Harris's *Reckless Eyeballing*
David Lynch's *Six Men Getting Sick*
Cauleen Smith's *Sojourner*
Allison Schulnik's *Mound*

Learn.

The experimental short is distinguished by its commitment to nonconformity. It evades the comfort and convention of the linear narrative.

While some experimental shorts may have linear aspects, other experimental shorts will contain little to none. Therefore, defining an experimental film can be tricky; however, experimental films generally tend to be shorter than narrative and documentary shorts due to their departure from predisposed structure, often addressing core ideas in a seemingly less organized way.

Experimental shorts films often have novel structures, unusual approaches, or a mixture of mediums, utilizing abstracting techniques like animating, scratching, or painting film to convey their central ideas. Some may emphasize theory over application, appearing to require minimal effort to produce. Both approaches fit into the realm of experimental filmmaking precisely because of the lack of boundaries defining it.

In contrast to narrative films, which are commonly used for entertainment, experimental shorts often voice social commentary. However, this commentary tends to be more personal and obscure. The experimentalist's palette is broad, but it often seeks to provoke or to challenge. While the authors of narrative films strive to meet their audience's expectations by the film's conclusion, in experimental films, the author might want the audience to explain things to them!

Experimental media is also characterized by a more independent and individual artist approach. While narrative films tend to encourage industry-wide group collaboration, many experimental filmmakers work alone or in small groups. The undertaking of the work can depend heavily on the artist and their access to resources. Interestingly, this limitation has allowed the experimental film to find a home in more esteemed institutions.

See.

The experimental film is often regarded as a highly artistic form by media makers pursuing careers in the field. It is seen as a highbrow art form, which is why many experimental filmmakers receive invitations to museums, exhibitions, and art galleries rather than theaters and other traditional screening spaces. While the experimental film often finds its audience questioning its departure from narrative expectations, it is precisely this space of limitless possibility that makes experimental film so great.

Brainstorm.

The experimentalist might engage in a writing process, but oftentimes, they do not. Again, the limitless boundaries of the experimental form make even the tradition of a writing process optional. More narrative-like experimental films tend to include a script similar to that of a narrative short film, but may challenge other elements of the traditional form, especially structure.

The experimental films above encompass a range of experimental media. Jenn Nkiru's revolutionary *Rebirth is Necessary* rhythmically combines documentary and composed imagery, forwarding concepts of black identity, while Maya Deren's impressionable *Meshes of the Afternoon* explores the realms of the interior and subconscious of the individual. Allison Schulnik's stop motion and claymation *Mound* and David Lynch's *Six Men. . .* are both animated meditations on existence and illness. Christopher Harris' provocative *Reckless Eyeballing* sweeps through a series of abstracting techniques, text, and repetition, asking questions about desire, identity, and perception, while Cauleen Smith's *Sojourner* caresses a live-action collage of images, people, and places, exploring ideas of radical generosity and bringing forth community of impossibility.

Write, Draw or Capture.

While some experimentalists might decide to create a baseline for the film by creating a script, other filmmakers might decide to use some other form of documenting the process. Storyboards, sketches, previsualization photos, notes, or a treatment—a prose summary of the film—might be utilized. Like a script, this treatment serves as a blueprint for the project, but unlike the script, there is no conventional format. The treatment can be as sparse or detailed as the media maker would like and can take any form that supports the experimentalist's vision. It's worth noting that if the experimentalist seeks funding through outside resources, like a foundation, a treatment would be required.

Plan.

The fantastic nature of the experimental film lies in its ability to leave previous boundaries and strictures behind, creating something original and new. It can demand more from the artist because of its singular request to unlock their imagination. Unlike narrative films, which attract redundancy and false repetition due to their linear format, the experimental shakes the new filmmaker out of these habits, urging them to think outside of the box! This is where true artistry flourishes.

Many socially conscious and marginalized media makers have utilized the experimental form to convey political or social commentary that often gets drowned out by commercialism. However, the artist who has worked in both media forms will undoubtedly find their artistry strengthened by building this muscle.

Therefore, I suggest that every new filmmaker try making something experimental. Doing so not only opens your mind to new forms, ideas, and structures but also makes you a better filmmaker, regardless of your preferred format.

Strategies.

The experimental film is challenged by its singular and most appealing strength: its novelty. As mentioned above, experimental films tend to be harder for audiences to consume because they ask viewers to think and reflect more, and even to act from a space of discomfort. This takes us away from what many consumers desire in their media viewing experience—escapism, entertainment, and effortless transportation away from the concerns of our reality.

Additionally, experimental films, lacking any structural norms in time, are more difficult to program for commercial outlets. Consequently, experimental films commonly have more limited exposure. Some of the more popular experimental films can be found on social platforms, often uploaded without permission. That said, numerous experimental visual artists have made careers in visual media or launched commercial careers from their artwork, including David Lynch, Arthur Jafa, and Steve McQueen, to name a few.

The Documentary Short

Kathryn Everett's *Girl Section*
Cecil Emeke's *The Ancestor's Came*
Ja'Tovia Gary's *The Giverny Document*
Sophia Nahli Allison's *A Love Song for Latasha*
Kamran Shirdel's *Women's Quarter*
Matthew Harmer's *Immoral Code*

Learn.

The documentary is distinguished by its relationship to investigating, examining, and/or documenting a subject, issue, or circumstance.

The live-action documentary can utilize many different techniques but is commonly characterized by shots with talking heads or a question-and-answer technique that mimics the experience of a news report or interview. Documentaries typically include factual representations demonstrated through title cards, created charts, or articles. In this way, documentaries tend to utilize mixed media, and live action might be interwoven with other modes of content presentation, like animation. Many documentaries have also expanded beyond this idea, and the documentary short has grown to include animation, as well as augmented and virtual reality films.

The short documentary is still growing and finding a place in the new media space in the US, but is more prevalent overseas, where access to advanced technologies is sometimes more limited. While festivals love the ten-to-fifteen documentary for programming purposes, most short documentaries tend to run on the longer side, which makes them more attractive as television pieces. More recently, the short documentary has become attractive to the festival world as more documentary-centered festivals have blossomed. Its approach is often still grounded in linear reality, but the storytelling journey may be unique in how we come to know the subject.

One significant difference with the documentary film is its educational emphasis. The educational slant of the documentary usually requires slower pacing than a genre film where spectacle is more paramount than comprehension, and emotion is more urgent than fact, although many personal documentaries have been tenderly effective in accomplishing both.

Documentary is often seen as a medium more grounded in realism (or *verité*) and truth than the experimental or narrative short. However, like other forms of media making, it is ultimately shaped by the filmmaker's suppositions and explorations. I've also fallen in love with documentarians who have utilized the form with experimental media where the documentary is almost unrecognizable: Ja'Tovia Gary's *Giverny Document* and Cecile Emeke's *The Ancestors Came* are great examples of this. You will also see these categories of the documentary: essayist and poetic, expository and observational, or more participatory or performance-focused.

There is a tacit understanding that the documentary, a more fact-based form of filmmaking, garners more respect than narrative films. This has led to documentaries attracting financial support from foundations and other grant-making organizations for their perceived intrinsic academic value. However, in recent years, the field of documentary has expanded to include mock documentaries and docudramas, fictional re-enactments that cross boundaries of fiction and drama. That successful cross-pollinating has continued in a variety of ways.

Brainstorm.

Documentaries often ask questions about real people, issues, or events, requiring strategies of research and investigation. Filmmakers must also be familiar with navigating spaces like libraries, archives, and databases to verify, challenge, and support assertions. This process may also involve engaging directly with the subject or community, although approaches will vary. Some documentaries adopt the tension and drama of a narrative, serving to indict its subjects or subject matter for crimes or injustices. Other documentaries might honor a subject and highlight aspects of their life, like a memoir.

The short documentaries above span a range from traditional to experimental: Kathryn Everett's *Girl Section* challenges the rights of young girls to go to school, and Kamran Shirdel's *Women's Quarter* humanizes the lives of sex workers in 1960s Iran. Ja'Tovia Gary's *The Giverny Document* includes impromptu interviews on the streets in New York City next to archival footage of black female activists and recently shot footage of her in Giverny's garden; and Cecile Emeke's observational *The Ancestors Came* highlights artist and activist Faith Ringgold and the children going to visit her alongside disorienting shots of a New York landscape; The poetic documentary, *A Love Song for Latasha*, celebrates the lost life of Latasha Harlins; her death became an unexpected precursor to the 1992 Los Angeles riots. Matthew Harmer's *Immoral Code* takes a more traditional approach, combining interviews with media to issue warnings about the encroaching artificial intelligence and its potential to perpetuate racist attitudes.

In recent years, there has also been a movement towards documentaries that are less than five minutes in length, like Christine Turner's *Betye Saar: Taking Care of Business* or Andrew Norton's *In Decision*. These micro-documentaries take a snapshot view of a subject of interest, showcasing what is possible to capture in these brief, intensely focused moments.

See.

For these reasons, documentaries often find homes in educational spaces rather than commercial ones, with local public television stations and libraries commonly finding space to host short documentaries. However, this dynamic is changing in the post-internet era, as niche audiences demand more space for documentaries to thrive on streaming platforms, which offer diverse viewing options. Streaming services available through libraries and institutions also embrace documentaries, both short and long-form, for educational purposes and beyond.

While many short documentaries are featured at film festivals, on streaming platforms, and in media archives, their academic and investigative nature tends to limits their potential on social media platforms, where frivolity and shock value thrive.

Write, Sketch, Note.

Documentarians, like experimentalists, are not limited to the confines of a specific writing format. They use varied approaches, which may or may not contain some organized written form. Those who work alone or in small groups may lean toward a more improvisational process, where personal notes may be used. However, like a narrative film, larger projects with more subjects or more crew may require a shared document to communicate the core question or assertion of the story. In this circumstance, a treatment would be created.

As with the experimental film, a documentary treatment acts as a blueprint, helping investigators articulate and share the purpose and vision of their story. It may include sections addressing history and background, intent and question, process and execution, as well as visual style and structure. Documentary elements could include interviews, statistics, visual media, animated charts or graphics, and even fictionalized scenes.

In the case of hybrid films that combine structures, the filmmaker must decide which elements drive the narrative—the fiction or the facts—to determine the best way to format and deliver the blueprint of their film. It would not be uncommon to include elements of both treatment and script in such cases. Some documentary treatments have adopted the format of commercial treatments, where a two-sided chart divides visual and text - one side shows the visuals and the other side, the text.

Plan.

The documentary is grounded in non-fiction, the realm of factual events and reporting, where investigation takes time. Documentarians are highly invested in research and long journeys, siphoning out the "truth." They are undaunted by the amount of time, material, and detail required to create a documentary. At the same time, documentarians often carry the coveted ability to connect with, and sometimes confront, real people to capture their stories. Learning how to shape mountains of detail into story in a developed way is a great skill for filmmakers.

Documentaries are striking in their ability to capture raw truths and honest engagement. Documentarians must uncover drama and conflict within their stories and present content in a compelling manner. Unlike narrative films, documentaries rely less on visual bells and whistles to maintain audience interest; instead, the material itself must captivate viewers, prompting filmmakers to carefully structure their narratives.

Documentary filmmaking also teaches creators how to capture their audience's attention through other media tools like sound, animation, diagrams, and titling. Narrative filmmakers can commonly get lost in the action of their films and forget to nurture the substance behind it. The quiet nature of documentaries encourages a focus on storytelling and effective communication of ideas through a variety of techniques.

Similar to narrative shorts, documentary shorts serve as valuable jumping-off points for expanding into larger documentary projects. They allow filmmakers to explore one particular facet of a subject. Short documentaries are commonly used to garner support for further development of longer-form versions.

Strategies.

New documentarians can find themselves lost in the process of creating their work, either by being too rigid or too flexible in their investigative approach. Rigidity might confine the depth and breadth of the narrative, while excessive flexibility can cause the narrative to lose purpose and focus easily.

Documentaries can get overwhelmed by the sheer amount of information that gets uncovered. It's easy to get lost in the research phase and have difficulty digging your way out into the story. Starting out with a strong idea or premise becomes vitally important.

On the other hand, the documentary can begin with a question or an idea that can tunnel the vision of the story. Sometimes documentaries will lead filmmakers down unexpected rabbit holes of discovery if enough ground hasn't been covered in early research. At that point, filmmakers often must reflect on how prepared are they to accept that their original thesis may be wrong or that they need to go much deeper or in a different direction than they expected. These discoveries can alter the landscape of the film they intended to make, and sometimes, lead to grand conclusions.

Unlike with a narrative film, the documentarian cannot build in a vacuum toward a preconceived conclusion. There must be room to adapt, reshape, and learn. Doing all of this in the short form can be challenging but fruitful.

The Animated Short
Brandon Lake's *Tin*
Alisi Telengut's *The Fourfold*
Renata Gasiorowska's *Cipka (Pussy)*
Bruce Smith, Everett Downing, and Matthew Cherry's *Hair Love*
Niles Atallah, Joaquin Cocina, and Cristobal Leon's *Lucia*
Kara Walker's *8 Possible Beginnings: or The Creation of the African America*

Learn.

Animated shorts are commonly distinguished by the presence of animated characters or environments and are typically narrative and/or experimental in nature. Animation sequences also often appear in documentaries.

The boundlessness of animated films makes them a favorite for those interested in more experimental explorations. Animated shorts tend to be brief in nature because of the high production that is involved. While you will find animated shorts in the ten-to-fifteen-minute category, you will also frequently find animated shorts that are five minutes or less in length.

For a long time, animation has widely been considered a medium for children and young people, but animation has come into its own with the explosion of gaming and the success of animation-driven production companies and studios. While animation shorts are still largely targeted toward young audiences, animation has become a tool for many independent filmmakers, whether used throughout or in short segments or sequences within a film.

The field of animation is large and includes traditional 2D and 3D animation, stop motion, claymation, motion capture, collage, and more. Animation techniques continue to be widely used in many commercial tentpole films, but the animation short still holds its own as a unique tool, whether it explores themes for children or adults.

Brainstorm.

Illustrators and designers are widely drawn to the field of animation. However, because animation is a costly and time-consuming skill, some media makers choose to develop and learn the skill on their own, while others prefer to hire animators to complete their shorts. Whether you choose to animate on your own or find support, animation has stretched into all categories of genre in recent years expanding its reach far beyond the children's realm.

The films featured above remind us of the breadth of animation in terms of medium, themes and genre.

In *The Fourfold,* Alisi Telengut uses animation to explore our relationship with the environment by animating layers of actual plants and oil pastels. Renata Gasiorowska's *Cipka* tells an unexpected story of pleasure personified using drawn animation. Niles Atallah, Joaquin Cocina, and Cristobal Leon's *Lucia* tells a memorable dark tale with its stop-motion imagery created using charcoal, dead flowers, and dirt, while Brandon Lake's *Tin* mixes clay and 2D animation in an electric, jazzy love story set between fire escapes. Kara Walker's *8 Possible Beginnings* renders early silhouette animation with puppeteer's strings in a provocative social commentary on race.

See.

The animated short is an exciting space because it has the ability to navigate both narrative and experimental arenas. It can adhere to the lengths and traditions of the narrative short film, or it can break the boundaries of live-action films, like experimental shorts. For this reason, animated shorts are widely accepted at film festivals and museums at varying lengths. They have also been recognized in traditional spaces like television, especially when appealing to parents and their children for educational value. Animation is also easily found on various social media platforms, whether as still images or action-packed shorts.

Draw, Write, Capture.

Animation, as one of the earliest forms of visual storytelling, has its origins in drawing or capturing movement between shifts in figures. Similar to experimental filmmaking, animation does not always require a written document, although longer shorts may necessitate it for collaborative reasons akin to narrative shorts. In such cases, a treatment or script will be desired.

An animation script does not have any particular nuances in format that distinguish it from a live-action script. The same storytelling structures applicable to narrative or experimental films may be used; a script can be employed for a more narrative-based film, while a treatment or notes may suit a more experimental one.

However, the writer should consider how the animated script leverages animation as a form to bring the story alive. The limitless potential of the animated short demands a script that clearly calls for animation to enrich the narrative. Looking at the films above, each goes beyond the limits of a live action film.

The animating writer will want to push the boundaries of live-action filmmaking in aspects like world-building, character development, and even elements such as props and set design. They should be more conscientious in crafting the details of a new world due to the endless possibilities afforded by animation. This becomes particularly important if a team of animators undertake the responsibility of constructing the film. While this scenario is more common in long-form animation than in short-form, the type, style, and length of the animation will determine the necessary team to complete the project.

Plan.

Like experimental shorts, animated shorts are a fantastic way to open up your mind and consider how to bend and break conventional rules of the live-action world. Making an animated short is similar to making an experimental film, in that the boundaries are limited only by your imagination! If you can illustrate it, you can create it.

Animated shorts can also be very brief. It is not unusual for animated shorts to be as short as one or two minutes because of the amount of work involved. Animation is a skill that calls for fastidious attention to detail. The tediousness of creating the animation short has earned it the right to break out of traditional lengths of the ten or fifteen-minute film.

If you are interested in gaming, anime, or animation as a career, making an animated short can serve as a wonderful introduction to this world. Careers in animation tend to pay well because it is such a specific skill set. While the jobs may be rare, and therefore highly competitive, they are great jobs, if you can get in the door.

Strategies.

Although animated shorts have continued to grow their audiences and are respected as a highly skilled craft, they still struggle to be seen as an equal to prestigious live-action films, despite long, persistent efforts to combat these ideas. The 2022 Collider article, "Phil Lord & Chris Miller Comment on the Oscars' Dissing Animated Movies," reveals the ongoing challenge animated shorts face in wanting to be more recognized by award-nominating organizations when compared to live-action shorts.

However, within the industry, animation has undoubtedly found success as a popular form of entertainment. Animation feature films bring in solid box office sales, but actors rarely receive recognition for their portrayals. Also, although animation has received critical acclaim and expanded across many genres, from drama to comedy to horror, it still carries with it the stigma of being "for kids.[2]"

Creating an animated short can be an expensive endeavor, both in terms of cost and time, especially for those who are not expert illustrators. The numerous drawings required to create the illusion of movement demand meticulous attention to detail and a significant time commitment. However, the recent growth of animation has led to the emergence of many electronic tools for novice illustrators who prefer working with software over hand-drawn animation.

The Web Series
Issa Rae's *Awkward Black Girl*
Bea Cordelia and Daniel Kyri's *The T*
Tony Zhou's and Taylor Ramos's *Every Frame A Painting*
Christiaan Van Vuuren and Adele Vuko's *Over and Out*
Kim William's *The Unwritten Rules*
Sameer Saxena's *ImMATURE*

Learn.

The web series is distinguished by its serial nature and its initial release onto the internet, whether they are standalone units like episodes or a larger serialized story that has been broken up into smaller bites to be delivered over an extended period. Web series also encompass a range of genres but tend to lean toward the documentary or narrative form, either live action or animation.

---

[2] "Phil Lord & Chris Miller Comment on the Oscars' Dissing Animated Movies" by Erick Massoto, *Collider*, April 6, 2022

Similar to television programs, web series tell the story of a group of characters over several installments called webisodes. Web series often fall into the comedy or drama genres, though intriguing cross-genres are emerging, influencing their length. Comedies are typically shorter, often lasting five minutes or less, while dramas tend to run longer, closer to fifteen or twenty minutes. Due to their short length, web series usually feature limited characters, settings, and plotlines compared to their television counterparts.

Webisodes have marked some of the greatest strides of the short form in how they have made their mark in the digital space and ultimately demanded their own platforms and showcases. The expansion of member qualifying criteria by industry award-granting organizations and guilds to include and recognize web series in "short form" categories is one way that webisodes have made their indelible mark.

WRITE, WRITE, AND WRITE ONE MORE.

The writing process for a webisode is unique in that it shares aspects with both a television episode and a short film. Webisodes are typically narrative, documentary or reality-based like tv talk shows; however,

unlike television episodes, web series formats do not adhere to constraints such as single-camera or multiple-camera setups, broadcast, cable, or streaming platforms, or, usually, the phenomenon of "commercial breaks." Typically, web series formats resemble those of short films, perhaps because of the limited budgets of shorts, which often use one camera. Even with single camera, web series will apply different approaches to the serialization or episodic nature of the series.

Like a serialized television episode, webisodes may contain an extended arc that will occur over several episodes in a season, instead of only one. In a short film, we commonly see one arc (or climax) that comes to completion over the length of the film, but in a webisode, there may be narrative cliffhangers that keep the audience coming back to see what will happen in the next installment.

On the other hand, if the web series is episodic in nature, the arc may focus on the individual episodes. Comedy webisodes are often more episodic, while dramatic webisodes tend to be more serialized. Many television shows use a combination of serial and episodic elements across seasons, or even over the length of the entire series. Achieving this balance is harder to do with the time constraints of a web series pilot, but if you do it well, it may lead you to television waters.

The web series pilot, similar to the television pilot, typically carries the weight of the project's success. It is expected to lay the foundation for future webisodes by developing subplots, characters, and other key elements. The strength of the pilot episode is crucial as it can determine the project's trajectory, and in many cases, web series pilots serve as proof of concepts for potential long-form television adaptations.

However, because web series are so short, it's not uncommon for writers to plan and arrange a full season's worth of content at once. Seasons typically range from four to ten episodes. This strategy has been a successful approach for those who have kept budgets low, and has helped launch both television shows and careers.

See.

Web series are primarily designed for release on the internet, frequently appearing on social media channels that host video content. However, recently, webisodes have begun carving out greater spaces at festivals, with some festivals welcoming web series into an episodic or "new media" section, and other festivals focusing exclusively on web series. These festivals often function as markets, serving as strong launch pads for networks looking for their next new breakout series. The web series festival market was an effective vehicle for securing meetings with production companies and networks for my own projects because it allowed me to bypass traditional gatekeepers like agents and managers.

While a few successful web series may secure placement on paid streaming platforms, they are more commonly found on open platforms and the web itself. These platforms allow web series to reach audiences without financial barriers, facilitating audience-building and engagement.

Brainstorm.

This abbreviated version of television that lives on the web has the chance to capture our hearts in the way one-stop-shop shorts can never do. Any series offers the potential to know someone like you would a friend, classmate, or family member. The invitation we extend to any series to share our living room or bedroom should not be diminished. The series has always felt so vital to me, and it also explains to me why I suspect horror does not perform as well in the series realm, although there have been some recent modern exceptions especially when creative innovations are applied.

Above I've featured a few web series that have successfully cross-pollinated genres, like the hilarious zombie sci fi comedy *Over and Out*, which sees parents trying to raise their child in an apocalyptic world, bouncing between family, sci fi and horror. *ImMature* is a fun rom-com at a boys' school that includes some fun video game animation sequences, while *The T* looks at intersectional LGBTQIA+ relationships under a dramedy lens. *The Unwritten Rules* uses a comedic form of talk show inner monologuing, talking to the camera between sketches, and plays with social justice satire, similar to the scintillatingly satirical *Revenge of the Black Best Friend* by Amanda Parris. Most of all, *Every Frame A Painting* stands out from these as a video essay docuseries, which is a part-documentary, part-educational tool for filmmakers.

Finally, Issa Rae's *Awkward Black Girl* serves as the best example of a comedic web series that got welcomed into our hearts so much so that studios took a closer look—leading to the immensely popular *Insecure!* Like this success story, there are plenty of others that let their web series become steppingstones for their careers, including Quinta Brunson's *Broke*.

Plan.

Web series are a wonderful platform for presenting stories we rarely get to see from voices we rarely get to hear. If you treat it as a low-budget enterprise that allows good writing to shine, you can begin planning your journey to the small screen on your own terms.

The webisode stands apart from the other short forms due to its potential to be a launchpad for a television show. Many web series are thrown out onto the web like fishing lines to see if they will catch an audience's attention before a company decides to invest in them. If the web series gains traction, it becomes attractive to networks.

Webisodes tend to prioritize story over visual aspects. You will less frequently find genre web series with the spectacle of sci-fi, action, or adventure due to the high budget requirements. However, web series are usually made with an eye toward television, which itself was born out of the "talkies" era of radio. You'll find that most webisodes tend to focus on dialogue, like a television show, although some will draw upon more cinematic aspects of the short film. Webisodes are a great space to develop your comedic skills and attention to dialogue. For this reason, sketches fit well into the web series format.

Strategies.

While web series typically don't have a life beyond the web and only last a few seasons, they serve as a wonderful showcase for aspiring writers and actors, aching to break in to the industry through untraditional channels. Producing-minded web series writers will aim to develop their content into long-form series on larger platforms. Web series often act as a pivot or advancing step for the writer who may have considered the traditional paths of entering screenwriting, such as winning script competitions or building credits in a writer's room. They also do this for the actor by offering an alternative to auditions by allowing them opportunities to perform on the small screen.

However, the greatest challenge of the web series is holding audience attention after its release onto the web! In the boundless internet, attracting and retaining viewership is hard to do. Strong storytelling is essential, but even with compelling writing, it still takes a lot of persistence, determination, and commitment to sustain a series. Keeping production costs low will aid you with consistently laying the tracks for the train of your series, because once your audience is hooked, you become obligated to meet their demands for more content.

The Commercial

Spike Jonze's *Ikea Lamp*
Dee Rees's *Walmart The Box*
Spike Lee's *Be Like Mike Nike Commercial*
Wong Kar Wai's *Déjà Vu Chivas Regal*
Erica Eng's *Panda Express*
Nadia Hallgren's *LinkedIn*

Learn.

A commercial is differentiated by its intent to extol the positive aspects of a product for purchase. A commercial is an advertisement.

Commercials have typically been short segments that interrupt or introduce long form media. Commercials are one of the shortest forms of media content, typically running from thirty seconds to a minute. However, with shifts in marketing and branding, we have seen commercials expand to the length of full short films as they've changed from product promotion to lifestyle promotion.

Commercials have traditionally been used to financially support other types of media, such as radio, television, theatrical films, and now, streaming. They usually appear as breaks between listening or watching a show. These short intervals have defined the brief time segments of the commercial form.

With the digital age encouraging crossover between television and film, commercials have also benefited from this trend. Many commercials have taken to creating long form narratives that elevate the idea of branding to an entirely new level. In these newest renditions, commercials run in longer form from ten to even twenty-minute films where the promotion takes a subtle backseat to story.

See.

Commercials can be found between shows or events, typically showing up between or bookending films, television shows, and other series. They also often precede major events like the Super Bowl or movie theater screenings. In today's social media-driven world, great commercials can have a longer lifespan on social media platforms as they are repeatedly uploaded and shared on various platforms. Industry events and awards shows also showcase some of the best commercials, highlighting those that have undeniably risen above their basic function to sell products.

Brainstorm.

Writing a commercial is a fantastic way to exercise a different creative muscle, requiring you to build story intended to promote an object or event. The goal here is to sell. . . not unlike your film.

Filmmakers often forget the business side of the industry. However, if you decide to pursue a career in the industry, having this understanding will aid you as a working storyteller. It will help you appreciate and communicate better with those involved in decision-making roles. Knowing how to add elements in your story that will attract certain audiences is an attractive skill, and the most successful filmmakers recognize that.

Advertising companies are well aware of the influence of popular culture and entertainment and have hired established film directors or talent to help create brand recognition for their products. Many established filmmakers have nurtured careers in commercials alongside their feature work.

Of the commercials mentioned here, I wonder which ones you may have already seen. Spike Jonze's personified IKEA lamp ad was such an effective commercial that it led to a sequel! Spike Lee's 1991 *Be Like Mike* commercial for Nike with Michael Jordan and Dee Rees' Walmart Box commercial featuring Mary J Blige were both films that deftly married the voice of the filmmaker to the promotion of the brand. Wong Kar Wai's *Déjà Vu Chivas Regal* does the same as a highly stylized web series masquerading as a luminous commercial wrapped in poetry. On the other end, we see Erica Eng's heartwarming Panda Express commercial highlighting Chinese culture and traditions for families and communities; and Nadia Hallgren's LinkedIn commercial supporting the concerns of subscriber's social issues.

Write, Column, Build.

Similar to television scripts, there is a specific format that is used for creating the traditional commercial break script, where two columns side-by-side are utilized to separate audio (dialogue or voiceover) and visual elements (onscreen). It reads much less as a literary document than the short script. The writing on these pages is sparse and brief and allows for a lot of flexibility for the commercial director.

For longer form scripts that have more narrative or experimental elements, you will tend to see formats similar to treatments or narrative scripts. Commercials also commonly build concept art, such as look books and storyboards, to help illustrate the ideas for the commercial. These require minimal writing, and the concepts will be more visually driven.

However, the most elusive element to writing the commercial is writing a concept to capture your audience in mere seconds. Unlike these other forms, the commercial is focused on the commodifying of values. Branding is designed to grab the audience's attention in a tiny span of time, and a time when they will likely be at their most distracted! In this way, writing a commercial is a practice of impact and efficiency.

Plan.

Although it might initially appear as if approaching a commercial is not storytelling, it is absolutely a story-delivering venture. To approach the commercial is to begin with a product you love and create a story that revolves around that idea. Once you've established a product, identifying the themes that will reach the targeted consumer will dictate that story.

Themes will shift depending on the focus group or audience that the company wants to attract. In earlier, simpler decades, wide audiences were up for grabs; in this distraction-heavy era, niche lifestyles and desires can really activate a core group.

Creating a good advertisement can be a sophisticated undertaking. In the past, commercials were easily recognized by obvious promotion of a product; however, that has changed in some recent years as commercials have taken to creating higher-end and stylish forays into narrative. Now, commercials tend to be more subtle in attracting their audiences; they've turned to focusing more on lifestyles and experiences than product. Instead of a clunky logo brandishing the product, audiences are more likely to see a commercial reflecting a lifestyle their audience identifies with or wants to appear to have. Cars, computers, and fashion designers have developed stylish worlds and narratives with prominent directors and actors for their commercials; the trusted face of an icon selling a product in a far more impressionable way to attract audiences than commercials of yesteryear.

Strategies.

Most filmmakers know very little about marketing, and this can be a drawback for those who are aspiring to retain control over their film as a producer. The advertising industry works differently than the independent filmmaking industry, but like the other media industries, there is some overlap. A big secret in the industry is that commercials can help you sustain a career in filmmaking.

The commercial industry is a lucrative industry. Some of the most successful directors in the industry are those who do not depend solely on their craft to pay their bills. Making commercials alongside industry or independent films is a great side-gig and also creates more opportunities for them to make the films they want on their own terms.

One thing to note is that it's easier for narrative directors to become commercial directors than the vice versa. For those who begin in commercials, breaking into the narrative world is a significant shift. Commercial writers are considered more marketers than storytellers, although they undoubtedly wield the tools of storytelling in their work. Consequently, commercials are seen as a less prestigious form of content. Nonetheless, major film directors have come out of commercials and music videos, so don't let that deter you. Ridley Scott, Guillermo del Toro, and Wes Anderson all made commercials early in their careers. A good strategy in your marketing work might be developing more recognizable storylines within your commercials so that shift is easier for executives to imagine.

The Music Video
Beyonce's *Formation*
Fat Boy Slim's *Weapon of Choice*
Childish Gambino's *This is America*
LMFAO ft. Lauren Bennett, GoonRock's *Party Rock Anthem*
PSY's *Gangnam Style*
Luis Fonsi's *Despacito*
Blondie's *Rapture*

Learn.

The music video is differentiated by its focus on song and music. Collected images, sequences, or storylines are captured to add a visual experience to listening to music.

The earliest music videos can be recognized as films that depict a focus on the playing or performance of music, such as singing, dancing, or concert presentation. However, the digital revolution expanded music videos into the narrative realm in various ways.

Some music videos feature a performance segment alongside a narrative storyline, while others commit to a narrative plot with singing elements or narrative plotlines that lead us into performance. Many music videos lavish the digital space with extravagant set pieces that serve as repeating backdrops. Others might be completely experimental in their approach. The beauty of the music video is that it holds few boundaries, outside of following the lyrics or song, much like an experimental film.

Music videos tend to be three to six minutes, usually encompassing the length of a song or piece of music. However, some music videos have stretched visual content to expand beyond the length of the song itself.

In their early years, music videos were a breeding ground for independent and underground artists and voices. Interestingly, in recent decades, they have become a platform for political expression. Some artists have used music videos as platforms to challenge oppression and prejudice, making the music video noteworthy as a medium for radical and innovative expression.

See.

While the concept of music video appeared in early films as segments, it truly began to develop as centerpieces on shows and longer-form movies with the popular groups like Beatles and the Jackson 5. However, the MTV years allowed the music video to flourish on television in an entirely independent way. Now, we get to see how the music video has continued to evolve to come into its own, inundating social media channels and demanding space on television networks and streaming stations. Now, even a music tour can fill the space of a feature film on cable and streaming stations as prestige content, and some savvy musicians have even managed to bring their tours to theaters.

Brainstorm.

Music is such a powerful, emotional art form, like film, and encourages you to open up artistically in a unique way. Music and sound are such potent gifts in filmmaking, but they often take a backseat to picture for new filmmakers. This is not the case with music videos, where music is king.

Writing a music video treatment will introduce you to the idea of adaptation. Making a film from an already existing form, a song, article, or event, is an important part of learning how to mold and reshape story across different mediums, genres, and forms. Crafting a story from a song is such a great exercise for learning how to adapt lyrics or music into film. Adapting music, poetry, fables, or folktales gets your mind maneuvering ideas in a different way. Interestingly—my first scriptwriting gig was adapting a lyric poem! You look for ways to expand story, whereas with fiction adaptations, you look to condense. Music can take you to so many places!

In the music videos above, we see a wide range, from the overt racial and cultural political statements of Beyonce's *Formation* and Childish Gambino's *This is America*, which reference Hurricane Katrina, police brutality, and mass shootings, to the narrative leanings of LMFAO's *Party Rock Anthem*, a zombie flick featuring GoonRock and Lauren Bennett. Fat Boy Slim's Christopher Walken solo dance-a-thon *Weapon of Choice*, set in an empty hotel, is a fantastical journey that's a joy to watch, while PSY's *Gangnam Style* outrageous flair ignited the international dance craze. The latter moves between Korean and English, showing us several set pieces as we move through the music. Luis Fonsi's *Despacito* highlights local set pieces that showcase Puerto Rico's La Perla as a colorful, vibrant neighborhood. Blondie's iconic *Rapture*, one of the first videos to air on then newcomer MTV, blends rock and rap as she highlights hip hop and underground artists like Basquiat, Lee Quinones, and Fab Five Freddy. This video features voodoo dancers and a goat, all set in a styling NY house party basement apartment.

Listen, Write, Draw.

The style of the music video will determine the appropriate format for its creation. While many music videos use treatments, pitch decks, and concept art, narrative scripts may also be used. However, the most significant aspect to writing a music video is that the writing follows the music.

The writing process for a music video is shaped alongside movements in the music; the music becomes the centerpiece for composing the media project. The writing may be demarcated by song, lyrics, or turns in the structure of the music itself. This same structure may be used to organize the treatment by using terms such as first verse, second verse, etc. if lyrics do not naturally delineate sections of the script.

Narratives in a music video may either follow the story within the song or develop from specific themes touched upon in the lyrics. At times, the narrative may unfold seemingly independent of the song's lyrical content.

Some music video treatments incorporate pictures, either as storyboards for framing or as thematic content. It's worth noting that some treatments have evolved into visual or concept decks resembling director's look books or pitch decks for film, where images are displayed alongside the lyrics. If the initial document for the music video is a longer treatment, an additional step of creating a shooting script may be necessary.

Plan.

Writing a music video starts first with identifying the music that you love, and researching the band and their values, style, and, of course, songs. What do they write about? What has meaning for them? Then, write something that represents the core themes of the song. One of my early students found a song that he loved, hunted down the singer, and made his pitch. Now, he has a full-fledged career as a music video director.

What I've also loved about music videos is the universality of music. It doesn't take an understanding of the lyrics for listeners and audiences to fall in love with a song; this allows for the internationalization of music videos in a way that films, long and short, cannot do. Music videos tend to elevate spectacle more than story; rhythm and dance often overtake any dependency on narrative. This makes them easy to consume and easy for them to capture our attention, although you will definitely find dramatic ones as well.

Many film schools ask their students to create a music video in the process of learning filmmaking. It's a useful tool in helping filmmakers to develop skills as visual storytellers because music videos don't typically include spoken dialogue. So, there is a focus on developing story purely through the visuals while the lyrics may be used, directly or indirectly, to guide the visuals.

Strategies.

The music video has helped to launch the careers of many established film and television directors: David Fincher, Antoine Fuqua, Jonathan Glazer, Michel Gondry, Mike Mills, Sanaa Hamri, and of course, Melina Matsoukas, who directed *Formation*. Additionally, the crisscross of artists working between fields as writers, actors, directors, and producers is not uncommon.

Even though there is overlap, the music video world is distinct from the film industry, and there are many aspects that come under the umbrella of the music industry, which has its own rules, regulations, and standards, which are driven by the demands for licensing and live performance.

Developing a career in the music industry can help you move into the film industry, but it may take reaching the higher levels of the music video industry, another highly competitive industry, to get there. Focusing on developing story narratives within the music video, as opposed to only on performance, will aid you in making the connections to cross over.

The Educational Film
Kate Messner's *How to Build A Fictional World*
Katrina Bryan's *Nina and the Neurons*
David McCall's *Schoolhouse Rock*
Hannah and Eliza Reilly's *Sheilas*
The Hollingsworth Family's *Gracie's Corner*
Vicki Wong and Michael C. Murphy's *The Octonauts*

Learn.

The educational film is differentiated by its purpose to educate its audience about a specific topic or subject.

Educational films can vary in topic, length, and format because they carry a goal of spreading knowledge. Perhaps because of that, educational films have emerged in so many different media spheres, appearing as short films, television programs, and content for teaching institutions and public access stations. Educational films can be live action, animated, or documentary style in their approach. There is no conventional format for the educational film, but the style will help to dictate any written form.

Despite being one of the earliest forms of film, educational films don't get quite enough credit in the filmmaking world, even though they often have overlap with the documentary. However, educational films have helped many of us learn about the world, whether it is learning how to count or learning how to build our own computer at home.

In early years, educational films tended to be live action when intended for adults or animated when catered to children. Many live-action films presented information that was clear and straightforward, but often dry in their approach; the animated film, especially those for children, offered more in creativity or style. Since then, we have certainly seen educational films evolve with elements of both to serve either, and sometimes, both groups.

However, it's quite a challenge making a good educational film that can educate while also holding the attention of its audience *and* bringing them back. While we may think of many educational films as being simplistic or only for children (who are very sophisticated about what they watch!), the internet's DIY generation has posted a number of educational films that have appealed to adult audiences and found or created a space for themselves there.

See.

Educational films have always been nimble in their placement and have thrived in many avenues beyond the theatrical realm. Television carved out a space for long and short form educational films with shows for kids in the sixties, seventies, and eighties; and networks, studios, and streamers have capitalized on that trend. On television, you may find educational shorts between shows or educational shows that have combined shorts to create a series of skits or sketches, filling the length of a TV show.

However, we can also find educational films in libraries, institutions, and archives. Still, educational film have continued to evolve, finding new ways to attract audiences. In recent decades, educational short films have rebranded themselves as a new kind of media that often combines popular culture with educational strategies. Like commercials, educational films have also taken advantage of narrative constructs to engage their audiences. Some educational films have set the stage for returning audiences by developing their stories as web series.

This shift has made social media a comfortable home for educational films, offering opportunities to learn anything from child-rearing to computer-building. The digital revolution has enabled anyone with access to a camera phone the ability to shoot a movie that teaches a skill. Educational films can be found in many spaces on social media platforms, especially those that showcase video content.

Brainstorm.

Like experimental films, educational films encompass a wide and ever-expanding field. With education as the primary goal, the possibilities are limitless. Educational filmmaking allows for exploration in any direction. Writing films for learning is a valuable exercise for any new storyteller because it requires building upon narrative knowledge to keep the audience engaged and connected throughout the process.

While this might seem like a simple goal, effectively teaching a skill that also engages the viewer, particularly younger audiences, is no simple task. Consider the amount of time it takes for a teacher to convey a lesson, with media serving as only one tool in the process.

Similar to commercials, educational films must also consider their audience actively. Success hinges on the filmmaker's ability to engage, enrich, and enlighten the audience. It's fascinating to observe how various educational films gain traction, often for unexpected reasons. The simplest lessons may go viral, as well as the most complex ones. I'm continually amazed by the diversity of educational films that appeal to adults, children, and both demographics. Some adult educational films have adopted an irreverent approach while remaining fundamentally committed to educating their audience, such as the women-centered *Sheilas* or Derek Walter and Jeremy Konner's *Drunk History*, which developed into a half-hour series.

I also want to acknowledge the educational films that have become pillars of our society. I grew up with *Schoolhouse Rock*, which aired regularly on Saturday mornings, seamlessly blending between commercials and episodes. Even today, I vividly recall the videos explaining how a bill becomes a law and the catchy multiplication songs, which played a significant role in shaping my childhood. Additionally, shows like *Sesame Street* and *The Electric Company* masterfully combined animation, live action, and puppetry in skits and sketches that captivated audiences during television blocks.

Currently, I love using Kate Messner's animated *How To Build A Fictional World* in my classes, and you'll remember it from the world-building chapter. Katrina Bryan's *Nina and the Neurons* is a part-live-action, part-animation show that teaches kids different topics around science. Even though the episodes are short, it functions as a regular television show with a live audience. What I love about the show is that it is a live audience of kids, so anything could happen, and that's a testament to Katrina Bryan and her work. Starting in the pandemic, *Gracie's Corner* is a delightful animated series notable for adding sing-alongs and dance-alongs to their episodes that teach educational topics but also self-love to kids of diverse backgrounds. Then there's Vicki Wong and Michael C. Murphy's animated adventurer's exploration of the deep-sea universe, *The Octonauts*, which is a series developed from a book that eventually became a movie and a longer series, before receiving its own subsequent spinoff series! When you have a great story, a lot can happen!

Write, Sketch, Outline.

The writing process for an educational film will depend on its style and approach, whether it's documentary, narrative, or experimental. Experimental or documentary styles will lend themselves more to a treatment or outline. More narrative and longer projects will demand a script.

However, many DIY educational films may require minimal or no writing at all if the steps can be worked out mentally. For lessons taught with just one person, one camera, and one setup, this may be all that's needed.

Overall, there is no standard format for educational films, and approaches and structures can vary widely, making the educational film an exciting space to explore.

Plan.

When considering an educational film, start with something that you know better than others. Do you want to teach a technical skill like knitting, or convey something more knowledge-based that will stretch comprehension, like how did knitting come about? Next, you want to think about how you want to deliver this information: will it be something more straightforward and direct, or something tied to a larger story? Interestingly, I can't say that the level of the task, whether it's a complex endeavor or a simple one, determines its potential for virality and views on social media. Likewise, its potential for virality and views doesn't determine the effectiveness of the educational outcome in your segment.

Instead, reflect on what you want to achieve and break down that process into steps that your audience can later *apply*. If you can find a small audience that catches on and shares it, you will have achieved more than a modicum level of success. Most importantly, like any of the films we've explored previously, a personal connection will always elevate the project to the next level.

Strategies.

The educational film is beloved by families and homemakers and well-respected in the educational industries; however, it has less influence in the commercial movie world. That said, streaming content platforms are overrun with educational videos that teach everything and anything you can imagine. Particularly for the internet generations, these DIY videos are consumer junk food and can help a media maker build up a substantial online presence. Many of these online teachers have become vibrant and powerful influencers that have led to the development of a variety of reality shows.

For those who desire to cross over into the commercial or independent film industries with an educational film, it might take a little convincing. Having the foresight to produce educational films that can borrow aspects of other styles, whether they are experimental, documentary or narrative, may help to give the film a home beyond education film outlets and social media.

However, if making educational films is a decisive career choice, high-quality educational films, especially those for children, are in high demand. As the media ideasphere continues to expand, more and more adults look to the digital arena as an additional source of teaching and learning for their children, and studios and media companies want to get in on the action.

SPECIALTY FILMS:

The Trailer vs The Proof of Concept Film
Kasi Lemmon's *Dr. Hugo*
Ethan and Joel Coen's *Blood Simple*
Robert Rodriguez's *The Customer is Always Right*
Neill Blomkamp's *Alive on Joburg*
Jennifer Phang's *Advantageous*
Jennifer Kent's *Monster*

Learn.

The trailer or proof of concept film is defined by its purpose to promote or showcase a longer form of media.

Trailers can introduce content for shows, tours, experiences, or films, which may be narrative, documentary, or experimental, featuring live action or animation. For short films, trailers or proof of concept (POC) tend to range from 30 seconds to a minute; for longer forms such as television pilots or feature films, they could be anywhere from one minute to five minutes. Some short films serve as proof of concept films, running longer, anywhere from five to twenty minutes.

Proof of concept films are created to provide "proof" of what a longer form film will look like. Typically made in advance of the longer form film, these abbreviated forms often concentrate on the film's concept to communicate to the audience what the larger story will entail. They might focus on the main conflict in the larger story or delve into a study of the main character.

There are two common types of trailers, each serving a different purpose and engaging the audience at different stages of the film's development:

Teaser trailers: These trailers are created to promote a longer film before it is complete. They are usually limited in range and budget, focusing on highlighting marketable aspects of the film. Teaser trailers are made for investors, executives, or producers early in the process to attract support or enthusiasm for the film. Teaser trailers are also sometimes called funding trailers because they are largely used to solicit funds from investors or donors to the project.

Movie trailers: These trailers are created to promote the film's release and are usually completed after the film has been finalized, but before release. These are the trailers you typically see in a movie theater. They are used to garner interest from movie goers and to increase sales. These trailers tend to suggest the story of the full movie or highlight sequences that will lure the audiences into buying a ticket to watch the full movie. For studio movies, they often release several trailers as they try to stretch the time to market the film. In these cases, the further they get into editing the movie, the longer or more developed the trailers become.

See.

While movie trailers are crafted to thrive in various media outlets such as television, theaters, and social media, the proof of concept serves a slightly different purpose. Proof of concept films often don't make it to film festivals because they are primarily created for funding purposes. They can typically be found on crowdfunding platforms or personal or hosted websites. Occasionally, they may appear at film festivals (proof of concept categories and festivals are still emerging), but this depends on how well the proof of concept stands alone as a compelling piece of work. Some proof of concept films, like Robert Rodriguez's *The Customer is Always Right*, geniusly transition into longer films as part of the creative process.

Brainstorm.

Writing a condensed form of your short or long-form film is a great exercise in understanding the core concepts of the story. This process encourages you to think about your characters and plot in a simple and focused manner. Additionally, crafting a proof of concept for a character can serve as a valuable introduction to revealing their desires, flaws, and talents, ultimately enriching the longer-form narrative.

Several established filmmakers have utilized proof of concept films as stepping stones to their feature projects. Kasi Lemmon's *Dr. Hugo* served as the precursor to her first feature film, *Eve's Bayou*, a mystical and hypnotic film about a young girl coming of age amidst a mysterious and fascinating family, set in Louisiana. Similarly, Ethan and Joel Coen's *Blood Simple* laid the groundwork for their noir western of the same name, famous for its haunting imagery. Robert Rodriguez's pulpy black and white noir, *The Customer is Always Right*, became the opening sequence for *Sin City*, based on Frank Miller's comic series. Neil Blomkamp's fantastic and convincing alien mockumentary, *Alive on Joburg*, catapulted him into completing *District 9*. Likewise, Jennifer Kent's terrifying mother-son horror short, *Monster*, paved the way for her acclaimed mother-son horror feature film, *The Babadook*. Lastly, Jennifer Phang's tender and intimate sci-fi episode, *Advantageous*, from the PBS *FutureStates* series, led to the creation of a feature film with the same title that showcased the power of parent-child dynamics in a racially and youth-biased futuristic setting.

Write, Edit, Sketch.

Proof of concept short films typically require a document to mirror or bridge the longer-form project, whether it be narrative, documentary, or experimental. Therefore, they may follow in the steps of a script or a treatment. Proof of concepts may take some planning, as the short must stands on its own while also serving as a preview for the future project. This makes the use of a written document essential.

If the proof of concept is a standalone short film, it should follow the rules of a script or treatment. A teaser trailer might follow this same approach. In some cases, the filmmaker might only choose a scene from the already existing short film to use as their proof of concept without writing anything new.

On the other hand, movie trailers do not always require a written document. Sometimes, a trailer may be pieced together using specific scenes from the completed film. Written notes, a treatment, or an outline may guide the editing process to determine the trailer's content and structure.

Plan.

Trailers and proof of concepts can also serve as excellent calling cards for new filmmakers, providing a platform to showcase their artistic vision. A strong project can propel a filmmaker's career forward, garnering attention and opportunities.

If you have an interest in editing, making trailers is also a good way to develop this skill. Trailer editing requires a deep understanding of storytelling, rhythm, and pacing, as trailers often rely on narration, music, or sound elements to engage audiences effectively.

Additionally, trailers may be created in response to challenges with the footage or production. This happened with one of my projects. Missing scenes and damaged footage might create an incomplete narrative. If reshooting is not feasible due to budget constraints or other limitations, the filmmaker may turn their short into a teaser trailer. However, it's important to ensure that the teaser trailer is compelling and effective on its own, as it may not have a lifespan beyond the making of the larger film.

Strategies.

It's important to determine the purpose of your trailer or proof of concept early on. As I shared, trailers, whether teasers or movie trailers, often do not have much life outside of the promotion of the longer film. They are considered a marketing tool more than their own category of film form.

With only a few exceptions, trailers are not typically recognized by film festivals or other film competitions. So, your trailer, if it is a teaser, must excel in showcasing the filmmaker's talent as a writer and director and presenting a story that captivates investors or producers. Movie trailers, on the other hand, should highlight the most compelling moments of the film while conveying its storyline. Failure to achieve these goals may result in limited opportunities for the trailer's distribution. There are few other routes for the trailer except for landing on your personal website page, or on a paid private or public streaming content service where they might get lost in the shuffle. That said, remarkable content tends to rise to the top in this gargantuan content metaverse.

Proof of concepts films, however, can live longer if the proof of concept can stand on its own and exist as a complete film. In this case, the film can have a life of its own going the route of a short film. This allows for more eyes to reach it, increasing the opportunities for the larger project to get produced. Still, the success of these promotion projects is based on the quality of the work and the stalwartness of the idea. Story is story. Good and steady planning early on will help to ensure that your trailer or proof of concepts achieves its mission of delivering the larger form project to your target audience.

The Anthology Short
Tim Miller and David Fincher's *Love Death + Robots*
Peter Huang's *5 Films on Technology*
Neil Blomkamp's *Oats Studios*
Akira Kurosawa's *Dreams*
Netflix's *Homemade*
V/H/S 94

Learn.

The anthology film differentiates itself by being a part of a collection of separate short films that are connected through a common theme, genre, or topic.

There are several types of anthologies. Anthology shorts can be mini-shorts within a short, episodes within a series, or a collection of shorts that altogether make up the time length of a feature film.

The anthology is defined by its relationship to other shorts sharing a common idea, which may be loosely or tightly connected through storytelling elements such as characters, settings, or themes. While the anthology short can exist alone, they are typically part of a group of films. Anthology shorts can be narrative, documentary, or experimental, as well as animated, live action, or a hybrid of both forms.

Anthology films have been around for a long time and were popularly used in horror films in the 1940s and 50s before gaining traction in the 70s and 80s. Examples include *Tales from the Crypt*, based on Al Feldstein's comic series, Mario Bava's *Black Sabbath*, and Stephen King's *Creepshow*. They were a fun way of covering multiple stories in a single segment, often on a constrained budget.

WRITE, WRITE WITH OTHERS, OR WRITE ALL OF THEM.

There is no specific writing process for writing anthologized shorts. The approach varies depending on factors such as whether it is live-action or animated, narrative, experimental, or documentary. However, there will be differences based on whether you are writing anthologized sequences from the perspective of one author, or if you are contributing one short to an anthology alongside other writers.

If you are writing all the sequences of a short anthology, you should consider how these segments connect and how the order helps tell the story. If you are writing with a group of people, you should understand how your short will fit in with the others, and within the anthology's theme, to maintain cohesion while avoiding redundancy.

See.

Anthology shorts in feature films can be found in streaming and theatrical releases, as well as in festivals and experimental venues. Anthology shorts in a series are commonly found on television and streaming platforms. For shorter anthologies like Peter Huang's satirical *5 Films on Technology*, you may encounter them in spaces such as film festivals and social media platforms. As mentioned previously, Huang's short was eventually picked up and expanded into a longer series for television!

Brainstorm.

Writing according to a shared theme is an important exercise for working writers. As a professional writer, you may often be asked to craft stories that may not initially resonate with you personally. This is simply part of the job, rather than purely an art form; it's the reality of a career in filmmaking. However, you can still look for ways to infuse your work with personal touches. This skill is valuable to develop, as many working directors have kick-started or advanced their careers by seizing opportunities to contribute to anthology features.

For some feature directors, short anthologies offer collaborative opportunities. *V/H/S 94* (94 is the fourth installment!) is a horror anthology that brought together Jennifer Reeder, Timo Tjahjanto, Steven Kostanski, Ryan Prows, and Chloe Okuno, all working directors in the feature horror genre. Similarly, *Homemade* was a project that brought together directors during the pandemic to share how they kept creating in their individual quarantined spaces.

The phenomenal worlds in Neil Blomkamp's *Oats Studios* are jaw-droppingly intense, immersing viewers in apocalyptic settings with seamless transitions between segments. Although all related, each segment is distinct. Akira Kurosawa's *Dreams* is memorable for exploring the personal reflections of an iconic feature director in his later years, delving into the whimsy and terrors of childhood. Lastly, *Love Death + Robots* is an animated sci-fi anthology series that traverses various animation styles and genres across its episodes.

Plan.

The anthology film provides so many rich opportunities: to write according to theme, to write with others as a part of a collection, to write a series anthology exploring various elements such as time period or reality. By maintaining a consistent thread, whether it's theme, character, or setting, you can anthologize diverse story elements in myriad ways. If you recognize a theme in your childhood recurring into adolescence and adulthood, these are glimpses that can be depicted through a sort of anthologist approach. This approach is also a useful tool in telling stories that may contain varied realities.

For new filmmakers with limited budgets, the anthology format is popular for achieving recognition through a feature release. Three or four (or more) filmmakers can come together to make one feature film, as seen in the horror anthology *Southbound*.

Strategies.

When contributing to an anthology series or feature, you're tasked with telling a story in a condensed space alongside other filmmakers, where the connections may or may not be clearly defined. Some anthologies are weakened by a lack of cohesion, while others suffer from a range of quality. Evaluations of anthologies typically focus on standout segments, but, in the event of a strong anthology, the overall strength of the film will work in your favor. However, if the collection varies in strength, this disparity could raise questions about your ability to tell a full, more developed story. However, crafting a series anthology with interconnected parts, akin to *Dreams*, can address these concerns by demonstrating a cohesive storytelling vision. In the industry, executives may want to see that you can demonstrate proficiency in both short and long forms. Writing an anthology that connects the shorts in a larger way will demonstrate that you have a good and versatile understanding of story structure for both forms! Knowing how to execute both either way will advantage you.

THE TERRAIN OF NEW MEDIA AND NEWLY EXPLORED TERRITORIES

Wasfia Nazreen and National Geographic's *A Woman's Epic Journey to Climb 7 Mountains*
David Darg and Bryn Mooser's *The Painter of Jalouzi* featuring Duval Pierre
Park Chan-wook and Park Chan-kyong's *Night Fishing*
Jason Van Genderen's *Mankind is No Island*
Victoria Mapplebeck's *160 Characters*
Michel Gondry's *Detour*

THE CAMERA PHONE FILM

Learn.

The camera phone film is differentiated by its mode of production, where the entire or majority of the production is shot on a camera phone. As such, camera phone films can encompass various forms and lengths. After a few mobile phone players shifted focus to developing more photographer and filmmaker-friendly phones, the camera phone film was born. The low budget requirement and versatility of the camera phone have provided ample opportunities for emerging filmmakers, leading to a significant expansion of the camera phone film genre.

See.

Surprisingly, there are dedicated camera phone film festivals, and occasionally, traditional film festivals include categories for camera phone films. However, due to the growing advancement and versatility of camera phone films across various forms such as narrative, documentary, experimental, animation, and web series, they often find their place alongside traditionally shot films without any particular recognition. Consequently, the writing process for camera phone films is similarly influenced by the chosen form and structure of the project.

Brainstorm.

If you want to witness the incredible range of camera phone films, check out Park Chan-wook and Park Chan-kyong's *Night Fishing*, a dark, fantastical descent into another world—a blend of music video, fantasy, and horror.

Or, explore Michel Gondry's whimsical fairy tale short, *Detour*, which follows the adventures of a tricycle and its owner after they become separated on a family trip. For a more contemplative experience, watch Wasfia Nazreen's documentary *A Woman's Epic Journey. . .*, which chronicles her ascent of 7 mountains with poetic and meditative storytelling. There's also Victoria Mapplebeck's *160 Characters*, which offers a unique perspective on a love story told through text messages, while Jason Van Genderen's *Mankind is No Island* presents a thought-provoking, dialogue-free portrayal of a city. Finally, David Darg and Bryn Mooser's *The Painter of Jalouzi* provides simple yet impactful emotional storytelling about Haiti's Jalouzi, its art, and its children.

Strategies.

The camera phone film serves as our biggest reminder that making a film isn't about having the most expensive camera, equipment, or tools. It's about your vision and craft. While shorts introduced us to the possibilities of the camera phone film, many independent directors helped us recognize the verisimilitude, intimate utility, and budgetary flexibility of camera phones through feature films, series, and more shot entirely on camera phones. The work of established directors like Steven Soderbergh and Sean Baker has pulled the camera phone film into the mainstream and validated the digital camera phone, not simply as a stepping stone, but as a form unto itself.

Sophia Stephen's *Quarantine Quarrels: Connecting in Quarantine*
Vincent Renee Lortie and Brittney Canda's
Owen Pallett—A Bloody Morning
Alisha Bhowmik's *Disaster Panties*
Jesse Hunt's *Meet Me At The Stairs*
Jono Freedrix's *Cupid-19*
Vesyee's *Lockdown 28*

THE QUARANTINE FILM

Learn.

The quarantine film is distinguished by the mode of production, similar to the camera phone film. Quarantine filmmaking required productions to separate technicians and cast members from each other during the filmmaking process. Indie filmmakers determined to create work when it seemed much of the world was standing still in fear and grief. They were driven by a profound desire for communication and connection, as people around the world found ways to still tell stories with whatever resources and emotions surrounded them. Like the camera phone film, the quarantine film encompasses any of the aforementioned forms of filmmaking, from narrative and experimental to documentary and more.

See.

Some film platforms and festivals created quarantine film categories, but like the camera phone film, the production mode often did not affect the placement of the film, and you will often find a quarantine film in categories according to their specified form.

Brainstorm.

Quarantine films were a powerful statement that no matter what is happening in the world, you can't keep a passionate filmmaker down. In an effort to protect crew and cast from high-risk infections in the pandemic, productions were forced to enact measures that might (or might not) reflect images of separation and protection or carry themes of isolation, disconnectedness, or frustration. While many feature films attempted to shoot during the pandemic and fought to reduce the presence of the pandemic, many short films embraced the idea. This resulted in more introspective works. Some focused on solitary characters, while others explored themes of frustration and disconnection. For independent filmmakers, these films became urgent expressions of struggle during chaotic times. They adapted by shooting within their circles, creating smaller, more intimate, and creatively driven productions.

Alisha Bhowmik's *Disaster Panties* is a great example of this, dealing with issues of female sexuality with a smartly placed computer screen and a Zoom camera. Jesse Hunt's heart-tugging documentary *Meet Me At The Stairs* similarly takes a natural boundary and uses it to accentuate an emotional distance with a visual one. Vesyee's *Lockdown 28* took the idea of isolation and created a sci-fi horror short that would actually require a quarantine. Jono Freedrix's 2-minute *Cupid-19* expressed the humorous frustrations of continuing to date in a quarantine world. Sophia Stephen's in-home therapy meditations in her bathroom lighten our spirits and do so much with so little, while Vincent Renee Lortie and Brittney Canda's part-dance film, part-music video for Owen Palette's *A Bloody Morning* crafts a moving collage of windows, hallways, and dance against city landscapes, delivering beauty and anguish to us. I found these quarantine films particularly inspiring and full of hope.

Strategies.

During a time of great obstacles and fear, creativity flourished in many of these projects, and some of these productions returned independent filmmakers to their roots of shooting with tiny crews, focusing on performance or simplistic pleasures, and reflecting inward instead of outward in their machinations. The result was a new category of film that marked a new path in this strange, new era; a film genre marked by richer stories built against new obstacles and with resources like visual communication platforms, mobile phones, and sometimes, simple physical obstacles like staircases and windows. What the quarantine film showed us is that we have many filmmaking tools at our disposal, when we don't take them for granted.

Geography of Robot's *Norco*
Tracy Fullerton's and USC Game's *Walden, A Game*
Courtney Cogburn and Stanford University's *Virtual Human Interaction 1000 Cut Journey*
Maddy Thorson and Maddy Makes Games' *Celeste*
Giant Sparrow's *What Remains of Edith Finch*
Studio Pixel *Punk's Unsighted*

NARRATIVE VIDEO GAMES AND GAME APPS

Learn.

The narrative video game and game app are distinguished by the development of a narrative alongside digital entertainment gaming principles and concepts. Digital games and mobile apps usually lead players through stages or levels, presenting challenges that culminate in a story-driven conclusion. Spurred by the electronic revolution of computer and mobile design capabilities, the first electronic game actually paved the way for the computer! The electronic video gaming industry has expanded significantly with the growth of social media. This expansion includes more gaming conventions, conferences, and fandom events celebrating digital games, as well as comic books, and the widening intersection of technology, media, and storytelling. Concurrently, with the rise of tentpole movies targeting young audiences through redeveloping existing material, video games have increasingly intersected with filmmaking in recent decades. The desire for more realistic and authentic gameplay experiences has driven narrative gaming into fields where new tools like virtual reality are not only enhancing gameplay but also are telling stories from cultures in remote corners of the world.

See.

Completed and released video games are typically available on consoles, such as PlayStations, and platforms that offer controls and switches for enhanced gameplay interaction. Video game apps, on the other hand, are accessible through mobile phones. These games may also be available on operating computer systems, such as Mac or PC, using a web browser or interface. Distribution storefronts like Steam and GOG (formerly Good Old Games) are common places to find games. During early development phases, particularly with educational and independently developed video games, they may be found in institutional spaces on the web, such as schools and libraries, as well as gaming competitions and festivals, depending on their purpose and intent. More commercial video games can be accessed through consoles and consumer brand gaming platforms.

Brainstorm.

Like indigenous oral storytelling traditions, games have served as an integral part of human societies since ancient times, with storytelling intertwining aspects of values with gameplay and culture. However, what is remarkable is how modern storytelling tools are leading us back to the foundational concepts of gaming, using games to shape society, culture, and learning through narrative. They serve as a means to explore the human condition, reflect on identity, and contemplate our place in the world. What does your game convey about the world through its narrative?

Tracy Fullerton's *Walden, A Game,* Courtney Cogburn's *1000 Cut Journey,* and Geography of Robot's *Norco* are all video games dealing with social concerns. *Walden* immerses players in the principles of nature and transcendentalism, drawing from the experiences of Henry David Thoreau. *1000 Cut Journey* tackles themes of race, prejudice, and perspective using virtual reality technology, while *Norco*, inspired by a multimedia documentary, explores the environmental impact of corporate negligence in the city of Norco, Louisiana.

On the other hand, games are also becoming more reflective of the individual experience. Maddy Thorson's *Celeste* deals with a character, Celeste, as she grapples with anxiety and depression while attempting to traverse a treacherous mountain. Studio Pixel's *Unsighted* sees their main character, Alma, awakened and trying to traverse a war-torn city before she withers away. Finally, *What Remains of Edith Finch* is an intriguing horror and magical realism game that sees a woman returning to her ancestral home to investigate her family's past. Presented in an anthology format, this game allows players to explore a house to discover what happened to Edith's family and why she is the only one alive. Narrative video games are becoming very sophisticated ways of telling story and addressing urgent societal topics.

Conceptualize, Diagram, Write.

The writing process for video games differs significantly from traditional screenwriting. While a good handle on storytelling is still essential, the narrative in video games revolves around the objectives, outcomes, engines, and interfaces unique to gaming. Unlike other forms, the story is shaped by gameplay, unless a pre-existing narrative has already been established. In my experience developing a game app, I had to take a few steps back to mesh my original narrative with that of the game's. The hierarchy here is grounded around the player's experience during gameplay. Therefore, an early consideration is determining the type of game that aligns with your goals and the objectives of gameplay. Conceptualizing the game's mechanics and how the story will progress is crucial. Diagramming levels, turns, and choices can aid in this process. Once the plot is outlined, attention shifts to world-building and character development. Themes play a significant role: is the game centered around competition, community, heroism, identity, or self-discovery? As the narrative takes shape, scriptwriting for scenes becomes essential. While writing dialogue and action typically occurs in later development stages, marrying principles and themes has to be determined early in game development.

Strategies:

In a narrative game, the experience of playing the game is paramount, but the gameplay is still subservient to story concept. While many feature-length movies are adapted from successful games, we also see games developed from original stories. The most effective strategy involves developing a story concept alongside gameplay. Focusing on character development, world-building, and the player's experience connects these approaches, which is why many games are based on existing material. This writing departs from the traditional screenwriter formats and responsibilities, prioritizing the purest form of storytelling: interactive participation.

Social Media Storytelling and The Less than a Minute Short Film

Tik Tok and the Stories
Facebook Stories
Instagram Stories
Snapchat Stories
YouTube Stories

Learn.

Social media storytelling is distinguished by its ability to effectively deliver stories through the resources of a social media platform, emphasizing and promoting social engagement and interaction with content. Early introductions to the social media format began challenging users to connect more using visual media. Now, the internet generations craft stories in three minutes, a minute, thirty seconds, or less! They achieve this through various methods, utilizing whatever tools the social media platform offers, leading to immense cross-pollination in the process. What's remarkable about these social media shorts is that users have learned how to wield storytelling tools within significant limitations. Stories lacking background, character, or plot find ways to compensate with what they have. If there's no compelling backdrop, attention may shift to costumes; without costumes, focus may turn to expression. In cases of minimal plot, text, dialogue, action, or behavior is utilized. Social media content creators maximize the tools available to them, often showcasing adaptability by navigating across platforms and utilizing different tools. This evolution prompts platforms to keep pace and transform accordingly.

Brainstorm.

While Facebook, Twitter (now called X), and YouTube originally pioneered content-bearing platforms, other social media platforms have followed suit and found ways to develop visual stories using video, photos, text, and unique design elements: Instagram, Snapchat, TikTok have emerged as leaders in social media storytelling. New platforms like Spill are also emerging, particularly after Twitter's catastrophic transition to X. Now, there are Snapchat stories, stories told with pictures and texts that last for only 24 hours, along with similar features on Facebook, YouTube, and even LinkedIn. While LinkedIn and Instagram have cultivated audiences for brands and businesses, what has truly helped social media stories thrive is their embrace of the ordinary realities of our lives: "a day in the life," relationship ups and downs, and behind-the-scenes looks are all popular themes.

Conceive, Capture, Shoot.

Scripts and treatments are documents that could be utilized, but may not be necessary in these extremely short-form formats. This doesn't mean that there isn't some prep involved in coming up with the original idea. It doesn't mean that it's easy; it just means the preparation may look different.

Strategies.

The most intriguing thing about the explosion of social media stories is how little content it takes to tell a story. The most important thing you need is the idea. Your limitations will fundamentally dictate the structure of what you can do, and then you go from there.

PRACTICE AND PLAY

1. Write your short script idea as a one-sentence logline for your project as a narrative, documentary, and experimental film.//
2. Choose a song or poem that you love and adapt it into a short film, narrative, animation, or experimental.
3. Write a story for release as a TikTok (<1 pg), a game app (<3 pg), and a webisode pilot (<5 pg). Consider the main character and what they want in each version.
4. Write a 5-7 episode season of a web series based on your childhood experiences growing up. Decide the thematic thrust of the season and then use 3 sentences to summarize each episode.
5. Write your own educational film about something small and personal that you do very well. Then write it as a commercial for you as the maker. What do you recognize as your personal voice?
6. Draw or capture your own version of animation by drawing a picture of an object you place near a window and capturing it every day from different angles for 10 days. Place them into a chart and line them up alongside each other. You can find the 1878 *The Galloping Horse* online as your guide.
7. Take a story from your childhood, write it as prose and then adapt it into a narrative or experimental film using Academy of Motion Pictures Arts & Sciences script standards.
8. Write a commercial for a product you love, text and visuals. Tell a story around this product based on how this produce makes you feel; identify what theme you want to convey behind the emotion.
9. Research reddit or a newspaper for an article that captures your attention, seems wild, but is true. Write five inquiring questions that come to mind. Then take a few minutes to research answering these questions. Write a one or two-page summary about what you might expect to find and how that makes you feel.
10. What is your quarantine story? Using your camera phone, create a short 3-5-episode anthology short. Structure it using your emotion as a guide and consider the steps from where you were then to where you are now.

11. Take your idea and make it into a game, developing objectives, obstacles, levels, and rewards.
12. Hybrids are all the rave now. Combine two forms to make a new one. I suggest a music video-commercial-game!

NOTES ON DIRECTING:
THE DIRECTORS' TOOL

The Director
—*A person who supervises the production of a show (as for stage or screen) usually with responsibility for action, lighting, music, and rehearsals*

THE DIRECTOR'S TOOL

Krzysztof Kieślowski's film *Blue,* part of a feature trilogy that explored the themes of the French flag through three colors, was one of my favorite films when I was exploring becoming a director. I was riveted by Juliette Binoche's character's infinite sorrow and her journey back to living. As I read different interviews and essays on him, I was shocked to learn that although Kieślowski was Polish, the entire film was in French—and he didn't speak French. He collaborated with a translator. This boggled my mind (as did the fact that Akira Kurosawa directed when he was blind) as I struggled to understand what tool or technique allowed a director to direct in these circumstances. How did they do it? What stayed with me was his observation that everyone on the set has a tool that they work with: cinematographers have cameras, costumers have clothes, production designers have props and set dressing. However, the director doesn't have a tool. It took me a long time to realize that the director's tool is themselves, along with to what they give their attention.

THE EASIEST JOB ON THE PLANET

Directing looks like an easy job. The person sitting in the chair marked "Director," telling everyone what to do appears to have it all. What you don't get to see, is everything they did to prepare to make things "look" as if they were easy. From connecting and choosing shots, to directing and guiding actors, to approving bedspreads and overalls, directing always seems to give the idea that that person in the center of the room is doing extraordinarily little when, in fact, they are doing everything.

Directing is one of the most challenging careers out there, and only a grateful small few get to pursue it sustainably, whether directing a multi-million-dollar film or a low-budget indie project. Establishing and executing a clear vision demands such persistent energy, emotional resilience, and unwavering focus that it steals so much of you. This is also why, besides budget constraints, many directors helm only a handful of projects throughout their careers. Interestingly, I've found that directing is also one of the most elusive crafts to teach.

My first experiences as a student director in film school were troubling endeavors, marked by common traits of film school: competitiveness, jealousy, and a lack of commitment. We were all thrown together and asked to create something remarkable with limited time and resources, each, in the moment, feeling the pressure to succeed in a way that felt like it could make or break our futures in the industry. So it's not surprising that conflicts and challenges arose amidst these circumstances. I don't think I truly understood what directing was about until much, much later in my years.

THE DIRECTING FACILITATOR

When I started teaching filmmaking, I learned that teaching directing often involved creating foundational documents: things like shot lists, overheads, director's notes, camera angles, and aspect ratios, similar to producing, which is so much about organizational paperwork (more on producing in the notes on producing chapter). However, directing is not about paperwork at all. It's not to say that these tools don't have relevance because they absolutely do. They are concrete structures that help convey specific techniques and demystify some of the technique of shooting a film. But directing is a mysterious process, and in many ways, accepting that will get you closer to the truth. Because directing is not only about the concrete; it is about the metaphysical, about accessing intuition, and about the highest art, personal expression.

When you are directing, think of yourself as a guide leading your group on an exciting adventure. You will guide your team through pathways and roads towards an intriguing destination. Along the way, there may be some who wander off, others who make wrong turns, and some who try to confront you or alternately run away out of frustration or fear. As the director, you will bring them back, encourage them, and make them feel that the end is in sight and when we reach this destination, it will all be worth it. As you lead your team down these paths, you will face adversities and challenges that you will be asked to surmount. Friction will divide members of the team, but prayerful reconciliation will bring them back together. At times, you will be deeply tested, but you will persevere. To accomplish these tasks, you will often need to help your team manage and wield different tools and abilities. Some will have a lot of experience, others not so much. All will depend on you. You will help them because you see the destination even if you have not been to it. Only you know what it looks like, and you are clear and determined in getting there. You know that once you reach the destination, there will be joy and celebration, and you will feel you made a small difference in the world.

For me, when I was finally directing, it seemed like my brain had been wired up to some sort of voltage unit, and when I was directing, I felt that I was accessing parts of the brain that I didn't know existed. I felt like there were parts of me that had been dormant, and suddenly they were turned on. And not on low either, on high! My senses were all amplified, and I was more present than I'd ever been, making decisions. I could feel all my synapses firing off all at once—perhaps lots of oxytocin exploding. I felt electric, and truly, there were times I felt like I was flying! Yet in the center of it all, even when things were at their worst, I felt an inner calmness that was ethereal. I had a core foundation that made me feel cemented. I had a guide and a knowing. I knew my story, I knew who I was in the story, and I knew in my deepest soul why I was telling the story.

When I reflect on that feeling today, I believe this core had to do with one thing: your attention.

THE MASTER OF ATTENTION

Above, I explain that the director's tool is themselves. I want to expand upon that idea and say that as the tool, how and to what they give their attention will shape how the film comes together. What I mean by this is that what you believe is important will help to mold how the film comes together. I've shared how writers and artists are unique because people are unique, and that inevitably will impact the film. So, as you look at some of the filmmakers we have visited in the book, you'll realize that they are all so incredibly different as are their films! Some of those differences get expressed through focus. For some directors, a focus on dialogue might be urgent to them, for others it might be design, for others it might be camera. This doesn't mean that they believe that the other aspects are unimportant; but we all have elements that we are drawn to and that we are particularly good at! So, our attention might contribute more to one element than another at times, and this is perfectly normal. It is impossible for every director to have the same approach to every aspect of the directing. What we give our attention to, along with our personal themes and premises, will aid in the creative process of constructing the film.

The Director's Attention

Attention is about listening with all your senses, perhaps even all the cells of your body. In my earliest directing experiences, this concept of fully immersing myself in any experience was new to me. However, I suspect that it must be similar for many athletes when performing in sports. You can get the feeling that you are fully "in" it. Mostly though, the metaphor I think most of when I consider directing is war.

I was surprised in my later years to learn that many directors of the 50s and 60s were men who had been in the military, and that much of the organization of a set mirrors the structure of battalions and other military designations. I don't think that film has to be that way, and I believe other structures can redefine approaches. But I often feel like I am fighting. Not the crew or the cast, if I have chosen well, because they should be your team. The biggest enemy is time.

On a set, you are always being pulled in a hundred directions and making decisions a mile a minute. A false step could plummet the production down a rabbit hole of cutting scenes and losing your movie. Or cutting shots and losing your movie. Or cutting locations and losing your movie. Any step in these situations has a domino effect because sets tend to be high-intensity situations full of long hours, high demands, and not enough resources.

Therefore, you always have to be ultra-prepared. Not somewhat prepared or a little prepared, but over-prepared, meaning that there is nothing significant left for you to do except show up on set because your tool is you; and you are ready. You will never know what will happen next, but for sure, something you don't expect will absolutely happen, and you want to be ready to find an answer when none is provided.

In the midst of all this, as the director "general," you must be the one to keep your cool and make everything appear effortless. A false step of panic can send morale spiraling, and the crew may head toward desertion. The phrase "I don't know" is probably the riskiest phrase on a film set because you are expected to know, and if you don't, you'd best find out within a hundred seconds. Everyone looks to you, and you are asked to carry all of that.

So, in the confluence of crisis, balance, and forward movement, the one thing that you must possess in vast quantities to lead your team through battle is your attention.

The attention on set is not like the attention you give your friends or your parents while you cook pasta on the stove and text your brother. It is highly concentrated like a laser. This doesn't mean that you are huddled in a corner with a deeply furrowed brow either. Your attention must be open to receive what's coming and give whatever is needed.

Good attention is also about being present. Meditation can help if you know how to meditate properly, and of course, this needs to be done before you're on set. If you're fully present, you will not reside in your head, asking inner questions and dialoguing with yourself about whether what you said was right or wrong. Any self-talk, even positive self-talk, will cause you to retreat into your head instead of being present in the moment. If you are not present, you will not hear what the crew is saying, see how the actor is not engaged in the scene, or notice that the sound team is missing their cues.

Being present will allow you to see clearly what is happening in front of you. When there is a lot of excitement, that is incredibly hard to do, but sets are always full of excitement. So much is happening, yet you must find a space of openness, inner peace, and readiness to move, focus, and execute; it's like a state of alert tranquility.

Alert Tranquility

This state of alert tranquility will enable you to recognize poor performance. It opens access to your intuition when your costumer asks for red, yellow, or blue curtains, and it outlines a clear path forward when time is dwindling, morale is thinning, and the central shot has not yet been accomplished. The clock is always ticking, and productions can rarely go overtime because the norm on a set is usually already twelve-hour days. The director must make a choice—whether it is right or wrong, we might find out later, maybe never—however, in that moment, right or wrong doesn't matter; what matters is that the choice feels like a good and informed one. This state of alert tranquility allows you to seize this moment, consider stakes, weigh outcomes, and make a decision that doesn't linger in your gut and prevent you from moving forward.

> *"But the funny thing is and I've said this before, of course, but when you're directing, it doesn't matter who wrote the script. You are trying to make the script work."*
> —DAVID CRONENBERG

THE DIRECTOR AS STORYTELLER

It's useful to note that when you are writing, directing, and producing, each of these tasks requires different skill sets, although there will be some overlap. You might find this advantageous if you're making an independent short, because odds are you might be all of the above. However, there are disadvantages to this as well. They all have to deal with where you place your attention at different cycles of the story. So, I make this suggestion: wear each hat on a different day. It is exceedingly difficult to be all these things at once, but you can get a lot done if you focus on each role separately.

Sometimes, my students ask about writing the script while developing the budget, or they'll be worried about producing a stunt while they're in the midst of writing. Then there is directing and deciding to halt production to go back and rewrite the script. These are the kinds of examples that will harm your short, because you are trying to do too much at the same time. Wearing too many hats simultaneously will not benefit the film. Instead, I encourage you to think about your script and each task as a role, a role to be accomplished by a single person.

When you're wearing the producer's hat, you can select a story that is low budget before you start writing. You can make choices about where it takes place and start building a story around the resources that you have. Once you have a skeleton, then you take off the producer cap and put on the writing one. Now, you stop thinking about costs because you have instituted boundaries that will aid you in keeping costs low. This enables you to write freely and turn your attention fully to the story. After writing is done, some ten, fifteen, or twenty drafts later, now you can start to think about how to accomplish the stunt, perhaps in an even better way than you first envisioned! This is my favorite part about shorts because I find that often the constraints lead to really innovative solutions.

Whether you have written the script, selected it, or been assigned it, wearing the director's hat makes you the storyteller for this final phase of the story's life. Grounded in your vision, you will utilize tools that will come directly from you to execute the film.

THE DIRECTOR AS PROBLEM SOLVER

One of the biggest aspects to directing is problem-solving. As mentioned above, no matter how much you prepare, unexpected issues will arise. You prepare for the expected, but you also prepare to predict the unexpected; good preparation will render you ready to take on new tasks. Like a long-distance runner or swimmer, you are preparing for many things, most of which you will have very little control over. If you are well prepared, you can have or find answers at the ready.

The director, in their preparation alone and with their crew, can also use their intuition as insight into what might happen and how to handle some of these circumstances should they arise. Much of this will happen when there is good attention paid to the script, not simply as a literary document but also as a blueprint.

Remembering that the script, when in production, becomes a document of somewhat scientific study is a solid starting point. Every key technician working on the set is going to refer first to the script and then to the director to find out how to approach their task. That script will be scrutinized more times than you can count, especially on large, expensive productions. Even on shorts, it will be the touchstone for everyone. That means that you, as the director, will need to know that script backwards and forwards. You will also need to know the curve of the story and how it needs to be cemented in the themes of the story. Ultimately, on the set, the film takes on a new life when the production starts, and the script takes a backseat to the actual footage.

Anticipation and expectation often collide with the unforeseen and uncertain. Sometimes, remarkably innovative solutions emerge; other times, chaos ensues. One way a director can mitigate some of the chaos is by considering options. Whether it involves performance adjustments, unexpected arrivals of extras, or dealing with electrical panel malfunctions, everyone on set appreciates having alternatives, and it's the director's responsibility to brainstorm them and make decisions.

Early in my career, while watching *Inside the Actor's Studio*, I recall host James Lipton frequently asking actors, 'What word turns you off?' Surprisingly often, the answer was 'no.' While there's nothing inherently wrong with the word 'no' and it can sometimes be a powerful statement, what I learned is that once a film starts production, it's like a moving train. It rarely stops unless for emergencies related to safety, finances, or health. No one on set enjoys hearing 'no,' even though it may occasionally be necessary. Instead, everyone prefers hearing about options. If one approach doesn't work, what about another? If we can't achieve this, can we pursue that instead? If we lose one element, can we still salvage another?"

A DIRECTOR PREPARES

Good preparation is essential for directing a short film, but understanding how to prepare can sometimes be challenging due to the dual nature of directing as both a technical task and an experiential art form. Technical tasks that a director should prepare for include conducting rehearsals, creating shot lists, meeting with production heads, storyboarding, script analysis, location scouting, designing sets, and charting blocking diagrams. Many directing instructors emphasize the creation of lookbooks, which condense these exercises into a succinct format.

However, the meat of directing lies in the experiential aspect, which involves opening up your mind, sharing a part of your soul, accessing your inner self, and tapping into intuition. If you focus solely on technical tasks without delving into this experiential realm, you'll find yourself lacking a unifying theme or purpose. Therefore, it's crucial to start by exploring yourself first. This allows you to infuse your tasks with a personal vision that resonates with both the cast and crew, fostering an emotional connection necessary for the story to transition from paper to screen and evoke genuine emotions in the audience.

TECHNIQUE AND TOOLS

Finding Your Connection

If you've written the script, this doesn't automatically mean that you've found your connection. You will take off your writing cap and put on the directing one so you can start to investigate what you actually know from what you think you know. In the theme chapter, I discussed how identifying the overarching theme that ties everything together can deepen the emotional impact of your story. This is what you seek when you take off your writing cap.

This begins with a process of script analysis. While the writer might think that they know all that there is to know about the script they've written, they don't. There are lots of things that will appear from the subconscious. Some of these elements enhance the story, while others may lead it astray and need to be trimmed.

Script analysis involves approaching the story anew, and excavating language and poetic devices beyond their surface meanings. Effective analysis aims to establish purpose and forge a personal connection to the story, characters, and material. You have a good foundation if you wrote the script, but that is the beginning of your process. Judith Weston's *25th Anniversary Directing Actors* has a wonderful chapter on script analysis which I often use.

Delving into the deep-seated themes of the film means you must examine the themes in each scene as well. You'll explore how to infuse each scene with pertinent themes through performance direction, design, location, editing, and camera work.

Yes, camera.

Herein lies some of the surprise in directing when I speak to new writer-directors. Few recognize that directing relates to intuition; most often, I find that new directors think it's all about technical production. Everyone wants to handle cameras, C-stands, and lights. Sure, fancy software that sets up overheads and shot lists are helpful. However, this means little if your film lacks a central theme. As the director, you should evaluate every technical tool in terms of the story's theme, calling upon your intuition at every turn.

How can shots, lighting, angles, pacing, rhythm, as well as more obvious tasks like location, design, costuming, and performance, contribute to tying together the threads of theme so that they all lead to the same place? Pretty pictures alone will not make a good film. Formulating a connection with the material, establishing a relationship with it, is the very first step. Determining the central theme and how it supports your premise will pave the way toward achieving your vision.

When you establish this connection to the material, you will witness your imagination opening up with possibilities and opportunities. It will guide you during times that you may feel stuck or uncertain.

A COHERENCE OF VISION

Style is one of those elements that is difficult to identify because it is so individual. However, style is how your vision is expressed, specifically how you see the world. When you watch a Spike Lee film, a Wes Anderson film, or a Kathryn Bigelow film, it is easy to differentiate them and recognize some staples of each of their styles. This vision ultimately grows out of the themes and premises that you establish. Your vision should reflect how it is distinct from others' perceptions, and the more specific you are in your vision, the easier this becomes. This vision is powerful. This is the part when you have to say "no" to conformity, trends, and tradition, and say "yes" to your unique imaginings.

Going against the trend can be terrifying to new writers, and there's no guarantee that this time is the right time. Cult classic films like *Heathers*, *Blade Runner*, *Willy Wonka and the Chocolate Factory*, and even *Citizen Kane* did poorly in their initial releases. Many auteurs and artists were ahead of their time, and the world had to catch up. Bending as a pliable tool to meet audience demand has its own risks. Even if it helps you in the short term, it won't lead you to a lasting or fulfilling career.

Barry Jenkins' *Re-Migration*

Having a coherent vision also allows you to make intuitive decisions in the midst of your shoot. In a PBS interview on his short *Re-Migration*, a speculative piece commenting on gentrification in San Francisco, Jenkins speaks about the spontaneous decision to include real-life families who had left the city because of gentrification. In speaking with some of his background actors, he discovered an emotional core within his film. This decision, he described as "a gut thing." Yet, this decision was only possible because he had a clear vision of what the story was about emotionally. Don't forget also that he had to convince the actors and the crew to also support this significant change that deviated from the script and schedule. Jenkins made decisions that elevated a story that he knew deeply and that made the film more impactful.

Your style, your vision, is your most urgent tool. It speaks for you. It goes before you. Your film should say something about you: what's important to you. Films that fail often do so because they lack a coherence of vision. One of the most difficult tasks when directing is to adhere to your style because there will come circumstances when someone suggests that you do something else. You must have a firm grasp on why this way and not that. This might come from a key crew member or it could come from a producer. If it's a key crew member, one way to circumvent some of this challenge is to ensure that your vision has been discussed and clarified in multiple ways. This is about getting the crew and cast on the same page and making the same movie.

A simple way to measure the success of your translation is to ask one of your crew members, perhaps your production designer, to sketch a pre-shoot document—in this case let's say some *mise en scene* elements for one of the scenes ahead of the shoot. This simple device will give you clues for how effective you have been at conveying your vision. Pre-documents, whether they are storyboards, costume sketches, or designer sketches, will help to ensure that you are all in alignment; and that the crew member has something new to contribute.

Being on the same page is one of the most under-recognized struggles of making a film. It can cause the complete downfall of the film if the director has hired crew who think one way about the film and the director thinks another. Being on the same page means that everyone who is involved in the process has a clear understanding and commitment to the vision of the director. At base, this is about expressing a strong theme, but if these divergences are not resolved, they can present as conflicts in style and approach when looking at the film. When a film doesn't work, it is often said that "everyone is not making the same film." Early and good communication through meetings and conversation about the project can help to avoid this; but it is important to not presume that simply because someone says they "get it," means that they do.

SHOWING THE WAY

What does leadership look like? It depends on your background and perspective. For some, leadership looks like a large man screaming at the top of his voice telling others what to do. For others, it's the elderly woman in the middle of the room who speaks in a soft, low voice and tells a story. Leadership is very much shaped by what you have seen and witnessed. Ultimately, leadership revolves around how successful a person is in leading a group through a task; sometimes this is done through demonstrating or showing the way forward. To do this involves many different skills and attention to many matters.

In a battle, we think of leadership as a means to an end, an end that we often think of as winning. However, leadership is also about the skill of getting people to do what you ask them to do, convincing people to listen and trust what you say, and providing confidence that what you say and model can be achieved. Do not make the mistake of thinking that simply because you've been given the reins to direct, automatically means people will do what you say. Leadership needs to be earned, and if you do not earn it, people will walk away.

As a director, leadership comes into play in how you lead your crew and cast, your team through the completion of the film. In some cases, you will have a crew or cast members that you will be assigned to work with. In a short, there is more likelihood that you will hold some power in the decisions of who you get to work with. An aspect of leadership that often gets left behind is how you select your crew. However, this is one of the most important parts of getting your film done. Your crew can make or break you. Yet, sometimes I have seen new writer-directors choose crew cavalierly, and that is not good leadership.

Choosing a crew member requires evaluating many aspects. From connecting energies to having aligning value systems to effective communication. Do you feel energized when speaking with the candidate? Are you on the same page about the main themes of the film? Do they know how to clearly communicate their ideas? All of these answers will weigh on the director-crew member relationship. Yet, here are some places where selecting a solid crew member can get tricky. Choosing friends seems like a great idea for your shoot; sometimes it is, other times it isn't. A good reference point for collaborating with friends is checking in with yourself about past experiences working together. How did that go? When disagreements came up, what happened? A red flag is if you've never argued. Disagreeing is healthy. If disagreement hasn't happened before in your friendship, letting your set be the first place it occurs may not be a good idea. You want to know what happens when someone's ideas differ from your own. In good circumstances, disagreement can lead to great things! It can lead to new ideas!

The exchange of ideas is one of the most wonderful things about the collaborative experience of filmmaking, and this exchange happens because people have different ideas. When looking toward new crew, something that always excites me is when a crew member has something new to add to the short production. I always want crew to add something to the production whether it is an idea, a vehicle, or a borrowed mirror. Those who are open to hearing new ideas can become respected collaborative directors. However, first, you must hire crew who feel that their ideas are welcomed and accepted; yet they should also feel comfortable realizing that their ideas may be tossed away for the good of the film.

Once you have the crew aboard, it becomes about energizing them. Depending on which form of leadership you are accustomed to will determine how you choose to do that. Some directors work through fear; others

I've seen work from a place of arrogance where they expect everyone to be at their beck and call. Yet, I encourage you to work from a place of support, invitation, and openness. You can energize crew through gestures, words of appreciation and validation, through generosity and acknowledgments more so than fear and punishment. Some prominent directors (and actors) are well known for the fact that they converse with every crew member. It's not something that has to be done, but it's a lovely gesture that says "I see you." That kind of leadership might allow the crew to stay a little later on a shoot even if they don't get paid more.

Even though no one really talks about it, leadership is also about safety and care. How do you provide for cast and crew, and ensure that they have what they need to perform their tasks, not only in a basic way, but at their very best level? That means making sure that food and beverages are available for everyone whatever their diet. No one likes to get caught doing crafty on shoots, but on short films, crafty is all there is when people aren't getting paid union wages. Never skimp on crafty.

Never, never, ever skimp on safety. The recent accidents in the news have detailed just how dangerous a film set can be when people are taking shortcuts. Making a film should not be a life risking endeavor; it should be a life-enriching one. Good leaders make decisions that protect the cast and crew, and they surround themselves with those who share the same values. Life is a value whether it is your life, your crew's life, or the life of an ant—a wonderful anecdote from a friend who is a producer who had to explain to a new director that killing hundreds of ants for the sake of a shot was not alright.

THE TRUTH OF THE DECISION

Directors are always wrapped up in a cocoon of decision-making from the start of pre-production to final delivery. How in the world do you make good decisions? Accessing our intuition is one of our strongest tools in directing. Our intuition is the thing that guides us above all things: advice, information, even past experience. While these elements can prove entirely helpful and sometimes even needed in a high-intensity decision-making situation, our intuition gives us permission to reach for something higher. With our intuition, we can reach into the unknown and find direction, clarity, purpose. Our intuition in many ways goes back to our personal themes and values.

Our intuition knows a lot; I might even say that our intuition knows more about ourselves than we do because it's operating on a subconscious level. Our intuition is embedded in these core values that go beyond not just what we have learned or absorbed, but the emotional crux of who we are. It sets up boundaries and pathways for us as we grow, and I suspect that if we channel a clear path to it, it can help us a great deal. The trouble is some of us are very good at sensing our intuition; but for others, we have to work a little harder to find it.

We can recognize our intuition at work in situations when the facts and present information seem to say "go right," but our intuition says "go left." Intuition might also be something we use in a gambling situation when we look to our insides to tell us this one or that. But intuition is also that thing that tells you to visit your grandmother two days before she passes. Intuition can present itself in many ways, through how we think, what we feel, our bodily reactions. Importantly, intuition is the thing that we draw from the most when we are making a film.

Questions on a set are like an avalanche. There are so many, and the director will decide concerns so rapidly; strong directors make it look easy and effortless but that's only because they've streamlined accessing their intuition. As the director, you can't leave set. You cannot disappear because everyone is looking at you and looking to you for guidance. Your presence is the guide and the rudder of the ship. While it's possible that perhaps a decision can be put off until "later," you can't do that for every decision and most need to be made in the now and will impact production immediately. I can't think of any production I've been on that didn't require me to make a decision based solely on my intuition. The raw thing about these decisions when you make them, is not so much that they are right or wrong, but that you are true to yourself and prepared to bear the results whatever the consequences.

The scariest decisions I've made on set have always been made through intuition. Intuition gives you the courage to walk tightropes without nets. Taking on a fight when I knew I had everything to lose, opposing the fact-supported guidance of a crew member when it went against my moral code, making a decision around needed funding when I knew I didn't have it. I learned that these were all the correct choices, but you don't know that in the heat of the moment. You have to trust your intuition; when you do, it will allow you to walk through the fire, even if you have no idea if you will get to the other side. However, that doesn't mean that you will be unscathed. There will always be consequences. It simply means you have made the right decision for you at that moment.

The main issue with intuition is that sometimes we don't hear it or don't listen to it. This might happen for a few reasons. Perhaps we don't trust our intuition. Somewhere in your life, it was suggested to you that listening to yourself is the very worst idea. Coming back from that may be hard, but definitely possible. Another reason might be that you have other self-sabotaging voices that talk you out of trusting your intuition. If you've been made to feel that your choices or circumstances are bad, this might move you away from trusting yourself. It could also be that you haven't taken time to cultivate your intuition so you can't hear the voices when they're guiding you. There are many books, classes, rituals out there that can teach you how to cultivate your intuition more; exercises that practice being present are also related and great activities. Developing strong intuition is such an urgent tool to shaping your short, but also is especially vital when it comes to recognizing strong performance.

Your intuition will be the central tool you use for delineating a good performance from a poor one. Everyone thinks they can recognize good performance because many of us watch content hundreds of hours every week. Some poor performances appear problematic in more obvious ways. But if you're working with a decent actor or even a very good actor, the differences will be more subtle. Some actors might even test a director to see if they can recognize good performance. Remember when I mentioned Akira Kurosawa directing blind—yes, that is intuition! In these situations, your intuition is really the only tool you have to assist you. On the film set, performance is also the one task that is entirely yours. No one else is required to do this or should do this. This task defines if you're up to snuff as a director. Performance is about truth and honesty and if you can't find your own truth, how can you recognize it in someone else?

TALKING THE TALK, PERFORMING THE WALK

Most of my communication and performance techniques were developed through the guidance of my mentor and directing teacher. My thoughts here really only touch the surface of what she shares in her three books on directing performance. However, the most urgent thought I have about performance is to listen to your actors and engage them as team members and partners. Build a relationship with them based on trust, freedom, compassion, appreciation, love, and respect. This may be the single most important relationship you will have on set. Conflict with your actors, and especially your lead, is the one disagreement that will likely sink the ship; even if you may not see it on set, you will see it in the rushes.

In my early years as a director, I attended a directing lab consisting of workshops for actors and directors. Through these workshops, I really came to understand what it means to have a relationship with an actor. When I work with new writer-directors, they rarely have this approach. One notable exception is the student director who married her actor! I took for granted how powerful and affirming these workshops were until they were gone. They taught me about the powerful bond that directors and actors can create and how devoted we can be to each other, taking performance to an entirely new level.

In every workshop, there were new people, faces, scripts, and opportunities to stretch as a director. Only once in a while would I work with the same actors. When I left each session, I always felt bonded to my actors. Not every actor will become your best friend; however, the actor-director relationship bond can be uniquely intimate. Look at the amazing pairs grew out of them, such as Zhang Yimou and Gong Li, Akira Kurosawa and Toshiro Mifune, Alfred Hitchcock and James Stewart, Guillermo Del Toro and Doug Jones, Kelly Reichardt and Michelle Williams, Dee Rees and Mary J. Blige, and Michael B. Jordan and Ryan Coogler. However, this can only happen in an atmosphere of trust, care, and safety, sometimes reaching into something much deeper like soul mates.

These are the connections I want to encourage you to seek with your actors. Do not think of them simply as tools to getting your script made or even icons that you will swoon over. It's important to get to know your actors, establish a connection, because this connection is where deep performance lies. A good actor who trusts their director can move emotional mountains, reach heights they never expected. Once you've established this bond, show up for each other, be prepared, respect their time, be open about what a scene means to you, your fears, or limitations for the scene. Your actor can be your colleague, and sometimes your most trusted collaborator.

As a director, you'll have opportunities to embed values of trust, care, and safety in your project. There are three key spaces where you'll interact with your actors: the audition, the rehearsal, and the set. In the audition, ensure you create a private environment where the actor feels safe. Make the location easy to find and provide clear instructions on how to prepare. Have sides and water available for them, and reserve enough time for them to showcase their skills. Give them your full attention during their performance, and thank them afterward. Follow up promptly to inform actors of their role status. Never leave an actor hanging. That is unprofessional.

During rehearsals, allow actors to present their own ideas first. It's common for directors to impose their ideas, but this may discourage less confident actors. Here's a big note: actors can never be wrong about their ideas. If there's a difference in ideas between you and the actor, it can create conflicts in performance. It's your job to align director and actor ideas. If your idea is not accepted, find a way to reconcile both ideas or the actor may not fully commit, and that will result in a weak performance. Be clear about the rehearsal's purpose and keep to the allotted time. Come overprepared and be open. Most of all be ready to play.

On the set, make actors feel important, because they are. Remember the pointless pretty pictures? Your film and your career ride on actor performances, especially in your early years. If you can, pay actors for their time; if you can't pay them, compensate them in other ways. Maybe that's paying for mileage or driving them to set. That might be providing makeup, costumes, and clothing to pamper them. Give them a private changing room and protect them on set. Schedule shoots according to their calendar. Make the production fun and enable actors to do their best work in a supportive environment. Listen to what their personal needs are and address them. Honor their time, communicate with them honestly, and keep your word.

FORAGING TIME

When making a film, you are always aware that time is an irreplaceable resource that is always diminishing. Relationships might get healed, and there's always a chance that money can be gathered from somewhere unexpected, but unlike in the movies, you cannot turn the clock back and get back time. So, it's helpful to think about how to use your time wisely. More than anything else, a director needs stamina to finish a movie, and it wanes with time. Try to save your stamina for the production and find ways to manage your time so that production is more fruitful.

Production meetings are often required on a larger set or on longer short projects, even though gathering everyone at the same time can be difficult. On smaller sets and shorts, calling meetings is easier, but can feel unnecessary. However, the more time you put into pre-production, the smoother your shoot days will go, even when there are hiccups along the way. Regardless of how ready you feel, calling a small meeting over lunch or dinner will help to elucidate questions that crew members might have about the script.

Cast meetings over coffees and dinners make spaces of delightful connection! While prominent cast may not be available to meet with the director on larger projects, I still suspect that most actors would love a chance to meet the director and see with whom they will work. The actor-director relationship is a special connection where sometimes great, long-lasting professional friendships are built when trust is established. It's a wonderful way to clear the air and get a sense of each other.

Location meetings may not always be possible, but it's very helpful to visit the location in advance and spend time there—a lot of time there, with or without your crew! Locations are always a function of time, so getting to know the ins and outs of your locations is exceedingly helpful. This will give you ample knowledge of what can be done in the space, saving you time that might be lost figuring out what goes where. Committed actors and crew can also surprise you with what they can create in a space, which is why you should try to rehearse or prep in the space if possible. I've seen great student directors create rain machines, train interiors, and fantastical new worlds. Early investigations and previsualizations of the space will help you achieve this.

Equipment checkouts are a frequent time vacuum for both students and independent projects, and in professional settings, they often take an extra paid day. A simple solution might be to practice the checkout process early with your cinematographer or visit the checkout center before the scheduled checkout to ensure that you understand what is needed, how it works, and where issues might arise (broken lights, missing batteries, or scratched lens). Asking the vendor about the best time to check out (and check in) is also a good way to avoid long lines and delays.

THE PLAY OF THE FERTILE IMAGINATION

Good directors possess fertile imaginations. That doesn't mean that they can visualize the exact version of the movie that plays in their head. In fact, it often means the opposite: what plays in the mind is open to sudden evolutions and changes. Strong directors can create options and possibilities as problems arise, thanks to their vivid imaginations. So, how do you exercise that? Remember the values from the premise chapter? Well, one value that is often forgotten in the adult and professional world is play. Yet, play is vital to artists, performers, writers, and inventors.

Even though as adults, play seems to drift further and further away from our daily lives, many still exhibit, participate in, and require play in their lives for its revitalizing properties. Playing, like singing, laughing, and dancing, can reinvigorate a rigid mind, keeping it flexible.

So, what does play look like? For different people, play takes different forms. There is physical play (on playgrounds or in parks), (video or board) game play, or simply engaging with children or family in playful ways. There is also playing with numbers (mathematicians and statisticians), with facts (reporters and newscasters), with words (poets and comedians), pictures (photographers and painters), imagery (media makers, designers, and visual artists), and more. To play is to release yourself from demands and boundaries, to explore and enjoy.

When I've lost my ability to play, I've seen how the world devolves into a reality of problems without choices, obstacles without exceptions, impasses without possibility. Or worse, it becomes a cassette tape of monotony where everything appears to always be the same. The truth is that life is never the same, and there are always new choices to be made, regardless of how our perspective might try to convince us otherwise. When a problem arises, it is this practice of play that will encourage the director to stay loose and keep moving forward; or to surrender to a mistake that transforms into a blessing.

THE SHOOTABLE SCRIPT

There's a turning point that will occur with the writer-director when they transform from writer to director. This important transitional moment happens when they start to look at the script through the lens of actually shooting it.

We think of the story as something occurring in our minds, where the imagination can often feel limitless. However, as writers, we may not consider the practical aspects of execution, even if we have strong visuals in our minds. This is OK when you are writing, but not when it comes to shooting.

As a director, you think about the practical aspects of telling the story on the screen. This is when you shift to considering the shootable script. You start to think about how to execute things for the actors, stunt performers, and crew. You think more about efficiency and how the camera can execute what's on paper in an interesting or novel way. You put yourself in the perspective of the audience—this is a significant shift in approaching your script. This is the moment your script stops being the story in your mind, and it becomes its own living creation.

But Wait, What About the Section on Camera?

When I began teaching film classes, I learned that new writer-directors often assume that everything starts with a great camera. However, the camera is simply another tool in the process. There are many types of cameras available: fancy digital cameras, reliable film cameras, versatile camera phones, budget-friendly cameras, cameras for a special look, and prestige cameras. There are, and will continue to be, many cameras offered in this visually influenced and technology-impacted world. Whether it is your camera phone or your six-figure prestige camera, your project will always come down to vision and performance. Many new filmmakers wonder "How can the story exercise my cool camera so I get the best bang for my buck?" The real question is how can your camera deepen your story when instead many new filmmakers will allow camera gadgets and whistles to overcome the story? It's always about the story first. Your potential to shoot a film with a $100 budget will entice executives to provide you with larger budgets. Build your shootable script first; then use whatever camera you have access to in the most unexpected, innovative, creative way that heightens story. With that foundation you can then explore what different cameras can offer and add to your storytelling. This will lead you to a grand future in directing.

DEFINE YOUR WORKFLOW

In my most recent show, I realized that the changes in the industry, due to the pandemic and the guild strikes, had also affected the workflow. As a director, you have to figure out the workflow that works best for you. A good production meeting can establish it, but if that doesn't happen, it means the crew will have different workflows in their minds, different expectations, and assumptions. Working with supportive producers, I was often asked this question and found it novel to rediscover these fluid boundaries of process. New filmmakers are great at creating boundaries and systems when they haven't been taught, but for those who went to film school, you might begin with your instructor's direction.

Workflow is a very fluid thing. It's a function of time and medium, whether you shoot on film or digital, of the camera—its boundaries of cartridges and batteries, a function of the size of the crew, and the depth of the setups of the shots. It's whether your shoot is fully permitted, involves children, and elderly actors; it's whether your set is community engaged and connected or a set of discreetly stealing shots. It's also about how and when you say action, cut, and print—with a video village or without. The workflow is about defining the steps toward how you will reach the end product, your movie.

This workflow begins in preproduction by setting transparent and clear assignments of duties and responsibilities and then establishing accountability for each production team member. Constant communication and check-ins to keep the team on track will set a good foundation. Sometimes things will change, and you need to adjust. When I can, I try to do small things to strengthen morale and build a culture of appreciation and grace. I love sets where people are happy in their positions; that was the culture of the first set I worked on, and I suppose I have never forgotten that. But a tier of tasks, structural goalposts and steady movement forward are needed to build confidence in the production and keep it from falling apart.

Whether you decide to follow the traditions of an old Hollywood set or a contemporary one, or you establish a new way that befits the tools of your production, defining the stages of process becomes necessary. Simply talking through or mapping out your process of completing the film on set (a micro vision) and through delivery (a macros vision) is an important start because everyone needs to comprehend the workflow. You or a strong producer will need to lead that discussion or your film will run away from you. The changing of dates, procedures, formats, or crew members is a space that will be particularly vulnerable to production but still may occur. Regardless, you have to determine what works best for your film.

YOUR CHOICE HAS MEANING

I've seen how, sometimes in this world, it is very easy to fall into a resigned attitude of "nothing really matters." I've glimpsed it in my students when they become overwhelmed by it all, and it feels familiar when I reflect on the current of apathy and futility moving through our everyday world. I also recall the war on my television in my dorm as a student and thinking, "How could I go on? How could I just go to school when people are dying?" I wondered, when these things happen, does the world just stop and do something about it? Often it doesn't, or at least it can appear that way. For some, clinging to normality in the clutches of chaos is all we can do. Even when it is a convenient pretense, a falsehood, a lie. That lie can be much more comforting than any truth. When terrible things are happening, politics are dismal, and people are sick, it's easy for us to check out and believe that nothing we do has meaning or effect. This couldn't be further from the truth.

Our choices have meaning, consequences, and impact.

Our individual choices carry meaning: the big ones and the small ones too; sometimes I think that the small choices mean that much *more*. What you do, what you think has meaning; your work in cinema has an effect whether it's touching one person or a million. Just consider who that one person could be. As a director, when you make a film, every choice you make in that film has the potential to be seen by a mere one million people when you send it out to the web. Tiny choices as well as big ones. The words on the screen, the colors of a dress, the presence of a character that says "I exist" in the film. It means something, and it says something, and you want to acknowledge and be aware of what you're saying.

As a director, the study of film can seem like a faraway planet from making films; but film criticism helps us to recognize what statements we're making about society through cinema; while film history allows us to witness the evolution of change as well as the horrifying failures of the present. Film history and criticism introduced me to the terrifying simplicity of films that paved the way for the Holocaust, and the gross acceptance of misogyny globally. They also showed me the LA Rebellion and allowed me to recognize a space for me as a maker. It was film criticism that led me to watching movies beyond the leisure of entertainment; and film history that bridged the relationships between maker, viewer, and viewed to help me comprehend the impact of cinema and how vital the role of film critics and historians are to championing what we see and do not see through the hands of distributors.

> *The more we know our history,*
> *the more we know ourselves.*

Film history shows us the pasts of our nation and a global view of our societies. Film history tells us where we were, where we are going, and where we could have gone; but it also shows us how far we have come and, sadly at times, how little progress we have made. Film history is the undervalued path to our future. With the help of film history, we can understand cycles we repeat, and perhaps change them for better outcomes. While many film students are bypassing the study of film for the making of film, the two are intertwined. Understanding the statements of your film and its context within our past and present is the responsibility of the director and cannot be understated. How can you know what you're making without knowledge?

PRACTICE AND PLAY

1. Revisit your personal themes exercise and identify a favorite film director. Research the history of this director through their film histories by watching as much of their work, both shorts and features, as possible. Try to find ten interviews. Write about this director's evolution as you see it.
2. Sketch or map out the workflow of your film from development., preproduction, production, post-production to delivery. For a bonus add in marketing and distribution.
3. Think about your favorite tv show or movie and see if you can find the script online. Choose a favorite scene from this and rewrite it in your personal vision. Then shoot it expressing your vision of how this scene could occur.

4. Build a *mise en scene* that tells the story of a scene through three shots. Do not change the camera angle or lens, only change the stage and scenic elements.
5. Visit a favorite private place that reminds you of one of the scenes in your story. Using all of your senses, find five things each to see, hear, smell, touch, and taste. Write down these five things for each; then rewrite the scene based on what you heard and saw.
6. Take a favorite film from earlier in your youth. Search for a film critic's article on the film that is longer than three pages and read it. What new insights does it reveal about the movie?
7. Choose a scene for rehearsal and take the scene and create an improvisation for your actors that deals with the same feelings and emotions you want to convey in the scene. Try it with your actors by giving them different objectives that are unknown to each other. Remember to tell them to continue the scene until you end it.
8. Over a coffee, interview your actor about the character before you begin to rehearse it. Take notes and figure out ways to align the actor's vision of the character with your own before your rehearsal. Do the same for a prospective crew member interviewing them instead about what they think the role should encompass.
9. Choose a good dialogue scene from your script that has special significance to you. Create a conference call rehearsal where you give both actors direction to play out the scene past where it currently ends. Text them different objectives and then allow the scene to roll out as improvisation and end only at your request. (This is also a great exercise for pre-scenes.)
10. Play your favorite game for an hour, the more physical the better! Then revisit a scene that you've been struggling with. Consider the lessons you learned in the game, and how they might help you resolve issues in your script.
11. Go through the script and see if you can find some representation of the main theme in every scene. Rewrite the script ensuring that your vision of the premise shows up in every scene either directly or indirectly.
12. Once you've started active pre-production, keep a daily journal. In this journal, write five big decisions that you anticipate will significantly impact production and then brainstorm the best- and worst-case scenarios and how you will approach them.

XI. NOTES ON PRODUCING:
GUARDIANS OF THE CINEMATIC UNIVERSE

The Producer
—A person who supervises or finances a work for exhibition or dissemination to the public

THE GUARDIANS OF THE CINEMATIC UNIVERSE

Producers are guardians. When I reflect on producing, I think about how the film needs to be protected and ushered through all the stages of the process until it is ready to go out into the world. The producer will handle much of the business of filmmaking; the numbers and data side of the filmmaking, but also the connecting and managing personalities sides. The producer's main role is to oversee every aspect of the project, protecting both the film and the numerous parties involved. Like a good parent, the producer is there to ensure that the film is surrounded by a healthy network of people who are dedicated to its successful completion and delivery.

Which Producer Are You?

Unlike the director, who is typically alone in their role (unless the project is being co-directed), there are commonly many producers on a set, especially if the project is larger or more complex. The more complex the shoot, the more producers that may come aboard. On a short, you will often have one producer, but if it is a longer shoot, it is not uncommon to see more than one name under the title "producer." It is also not uncommon to see competition around who gets credit (especially in the feature world) and how that shows up on screen, which has probably led to the expanding of titles in the role of producer. There may be the creative producer, the line producer, the executive producer; there may also be associate producers, co-producers, and assistant producers. The production manager (also called UPM for unit production manager) might also be a producer on your project. These different titles signal how and to what extent a producer is involved. As a new filmmaker, you may end up being the writer-director-producer, a role I often have held on my films. However, this doesn't mean that I don't have other producers involved in the project along the way. I've often hired producers, line producers, co-producers, and associate producers to help ensure that when I take off my producer's cap and focus on directing, there are others there to take up that role so I can fully concentrate on direction.

What do some of the roles mean? How do you separate them? How do you know which ones you'll need? As the writer-director-producer, you will inevitably have your fingers in every aspect of the short. That is a good thing since you are the film's guardian; you want to have knowledge of every aspect of the film's development process—when you do not, decisions will be made about the project without your consultation. This might lead to problems later in the completion of the project. However, it can be a difficult thing to do because, as I mentioned earlier, doubling up (or tripling up in this case!) on roles can spread responsibilities too much and thin out over their individual performance. So enlisting the aid of other producers so that you are not tasked with every responsibility but have knowledge of the process can be useful.

You also want to understand that trust becomes very important at this stage because you will not make every decision even in the best circumstances. So, ensuring that you surround the project with those who are in alignment with your vision as the writer-director-producer will be important. Communication becomes an ever-urgent skill at this level of producing.

Above, I mentioned a few of the various titles that explain the different jobs of the producer. On occasion, you will find a very good producer will handle all of these tasks on a short; but many times you will divide roles and responsibilities because of the way a gig economy works. The primary roles you will recognize in the shorts world will typically be the producer known as the creative producer who oversees every aspect of the short—as the writer-director-producer (this could likely be you); the line producer who will break the script down to executable price points—this role will commonly double with UPM or production manager (this should not be you); and the executive producer who provides the funding and talent attachments for the project (often this will also be you if you put up your own money). Because the UPM or PM will manage the day-to-day duties (parking, food, equipment) on set, the writer-director-producer should at the very least hire a producer to production manage the set. There are other titles for the producer but these are the most common to the set of a short film.

So, can one producer handle your production? Which ones will you need? Answering this question will depend on your individual short's needs. If it's a short that takes several days, with a lot of FWAKS that require intensive production (More on FWAKS below!), extras and many locations, you may need more than one. However, I've also seen a writer-director-producer miraculously get it all done... but I do think in most cases, there's a cost to that: in quality, time, perhaps attention because you've surrendered a resource. Know that adding producers will tend to increase your budget as a person to compensate and to feed; it may also decrease your control over the project; but maybe that provides more efficiency of time, focused attention, or better quality for the project. It's a trade. You have to decide what your priorities are. Choosing the right producer(s) will always be a balance of resources and needs, which is what guardians do best.

BEHIND THE SCENES FINISHING

So, what exactly does a producer do? When watching the movie, it is not very apparent. Different from the work of the artistic teams like the hair stylist, costumer, or the set decorator, you don't get to see or recognize the work of the producer. However, it's akin to seeing the child of two parents. You may not easily recognize the value systems or even the inherited traits of the child unless you get to spend some time with parents and child altogether. The film is the "finished" work, the sum of these many parts. I place "finished" in quotation marks because, like a child who becomes an adult, the human being is never really a finished work; they are an evolutionary work. In the same way, a film even when it is "finished," it can also become an evolutionary work as settings, time periods, circumstances cause its continual shifting in meaning. Director-producers will often go back to their films for re-editing, preserving, transferring, et al. However, the producer is always working behind the scenes: doing the work of engagement to put the film on the screen. Perhaps that is the best way to think about the task of the producer. If the director's ultimate tool is their attention, I would say that the producer's primary tool is translating.

The Lost & Found of Film Translation

The producer's most urgent task is translating ideas into tangible realities. What that means is that the producer seeks to execute transplanting the idea in their mind into something that will be funded in development, prepared for in preproduction, captured in production, organized in postproduction, advertised in marketing, and delivered for distribution. In a feature film, this might involve the work of hundreds of people. In a short, this will involve the work of a small but mighty and committed crew. This gargantuan effort will be led by the vision of the director under the guardianship of the producer.

During this process, the producer will not only have to work to translate the intangible to the tangible but also to translate information between multiple bodies and groups involved in the filmmaking process: they will communicate concerns between funders and directors, between lawyers and companies, and between guilds, cast and crew. They will establish and execute the plan to secure the funds, identify the crew, attach the cast as well as present the strategies for marketing the film, distributing the film, and engaging the audience.

The Practical Magic of Reserves

The producer's role is one of the most difficult, and because of that, their work often starts at the very beginning. They will often build from ground zero. Imagine the work of a producer who starts with only an idea! This is also why so many producers resist coming aboard other projects that haven't yet left the station. They have the awareness and knowledge of where so many of the obstacles lie. They get to see all of that, and so like the director who must so often act on faith and intuition; the producer will draw from facts, figures, and circumstances—the practical possibilities of what can be done with the resources that are provided.

I do believe that producers still wield these magical tools of intuition and faith albeit in a different way than the director. But they often must be the parent who says no when the other parent says yes; although I think the best producers present issues more diplomatically: "well, we can't do that, but perhaps we can do this." I believe the best producers are those who know how to find and manage resources that others can't uncover. Great producers will uncover amazing loopholes that lead to magical ways to reserve money, reserve time, or reserve crew or cast energy. They must look at the film as a project of reserves and figure out how best to serve the project within these limitations. Of course, that is the boundary of creativity—when you create something with limited resources.

The Movie Anthropologist

The producer's job is commonly misunderstood to be a position that is all science: numbers, data, organization; but what's important to consider is that film, this great connector, is a social construct, and in that way, the producer is also a social scientist. So like the anthropologist studies the human body and its cultural histories, so does the producer study the film. This study examines not only the materials and assets of the film itself but its relationships with other bodies over time: the industry, the culture, and the society. The producer will also analyze the film within the context of current and past marketplace, platform, and presentation so they can foretell its future. The producer will extrapolate the life of the film based on this deep excavation that uncovers its relationship to the world, the industry, and society, thereby determining the monies of its future (which varies widely depending on the form).

What is Producing?

Kalyanee Mam's *Lost World*

As a natural-born event planner, producing has always come easy to me. I've always found taking a task and breaking it down into executable segments to be fun. In my earliest positions pulling together an event or program, I discovered one of my hidden gifts. First, it was programs, then parties, then events. These skills of organization, analysis, and segmentation have always stayed close to my fingertips. It also made me a great resource for other producers who could rely on my tight organizational skills to ensure that tasks were completed.

The film producer is really producing an event, but an event that has several stages, multiple segments, and numerous participants and suppliers. To be a good producer, you must have a grasp on the entire process and understand that the completion of the film's journey, a process that may take years, even for a short, is your ultimate goal. The producer must be steadfast and determined; they must also be flexible and fearless and be ready to step into a room and capture the attention of those they hope to work with and keep it there. I can imagine the events of coordinating all of the locations, permits, travel, and shoots of Kalyanee Mam's *Lost World*, which took us from the sands of Cambodia to the waters of Singapore, to reflect on the depleting mangrove forests in Cambodia. Watching this film from a producing perspective, you start to count the days, the hours, along with the miles, and the shots of what needed to be accomplished to tell this story of the women and families who are affected by the sand mining of their homeland.

Producing is equal parts art, science, and grit because a producer must be willing to "handle it," whatever "it" may be: rolling up their sleeves, defending the production and crew, making demands, or simply acquiescing, if that's what best suits the production's life. A well-produced film is like an event, a seamless immersive experience; but it is only possible through the guardianship of strong producing connecting people, things, and places every minute. Producers are guardians, and guarding the production is never a simple thing.

The HR Manager

The producer is also the one who manages the hiring of all crew positions, whether this is you or someone you bring aboard. A good producer often has a team they like to work with and will present this team to the director, hoping for a good match; if a match is made, the producer will process the paperwork for the hire—this will include shuttling through any contracts, whether they are union or non-union. Completing the tasks of union paperwork is a good reason to bring aboard another producer because many unions have literally reams of papers that you need to use. However, if you go non-union, I would still resist the urge to go paperless.

As a manager, the producer's job is also to negotiate and make deals, and this requires clear communication. This means that the producer may post job ads, conduct interviews, and secure crew. In hiring crew for various projects, I've learned that verbal words are never the same as written words. Writing out clearly expectations for the position is a good way to avoid confusion and conflict later on in the shoot.

The producer is also the person who needs to be well-versed in the laws and customs of the area. What is appropriate for the shoot in this area and what is not? Is shooting in Los Angeles the same as shooting in Birmingham or Anchorage? There are film offices in each of these states, but the resources available are very different. So the producer will also have to know some legalese. Should the authorities come on set for any reason, the producer (or the AD) is the one who will address them.

In Between the Lines: The Story in the Budget

One of the things I geek out about as a writer-director-producer is the story hidden in the budget. Line producers will understand this innately. The budget tells its own story about how the project was conceived, where challenges and difficulties arose, where mistakes were made, and what can be learned from those mistakes. Topsheets will act as a summary of the story, but the flesh and detail, the nuance of the story, is hidden in the details section of the budget. It tells you about where the film's attention and priorities were focused and about the director's focus as costs were incurred.

In the header of a budget, some essential budgetary issues get established: how many days, the dates of the shoot, the unions involved, the location, the camera being used, and the date. Each of these will have a direct impact on the cost of the project. In the body of the film, you might have a topsheet if you are using a budgeting software program; or if you choose to go old school, you might simply have the basic budget that is constructed through a spreadsheet or writing format. Whether you go old school or decide to utilize a software program, you want to understand how the budget works and how each line of the budget impacts the other.

In my first significant short film, I worked with a line producer who prepared a budget based on my basic ideas. Your budget will give some hints about what kind of project it is: drama, action, sci-fi, but it will also tell a lot about you as a filmmaker. Your budget will typically be broken down into categories that describe how and when the money will be spent. Within this group, you see items broken down into categories that include cast, key crew, locations, equipment, insurance, meals, design and makeup, safety, and travel. How you divide your resources in this area will tell you where your priorities are; it will also tell you where you are the most vulnerable. In my classes, sometimes I share a copy of one of my early budgets as an exercise in analyzing the story of the shoot. With it, you can see where we made mistakes and how we paid much more for them in the long run. For my project, a minimal sound budget in production led to a sizable amount of work in post-production when we had to fly the actor out to re-record his lines.

Some of the common downfalls and stereotypes for a "student film" from a producing standpoint are projects that lack design, strong acting, and good sound. I cannot emphasize enough that taking a look at your budget and examining where you put your resources and attention tells you a lot about how your film will turn out. There will always be unexpected occurrences during your shoot, and being prepared to pivot with a contingency plan (and funds) still remains my best advice on any production.

Resources at the Ready

When asked about obstacles that stand in the way of making a film, the resource that you hear most often from independent filmmakers is money. However, money isn't the only resource that you can wield when making your short film. A good producer will know this and carry a deck of resources at their disposal, knowing how to play their best hand at the best time. Time and relationships are urgent currencies that filmmakers must also contend with, but people often forget about barriers of access that can pop up and augment this common pyramid of resources. However, there are also resources of skills that are invaluable to the producer.

Fighting for time is a constant battle when making a film. On a film set, time becomes the silent antagonist we wage war against in trying to complete our film. Now, that said, when money is in short supply, turning time into your ally is a great way to get your film done. Many a film has been accomplished by lengthening the time. For young people who have access to friends and equipment, time can become a saving grace if you can be flexible about how to use it. Some feature films have been shot over several weeks or even months if shot on the weekends or nights. Factors like the size of the crew and the setting will affect the potential for this to occur; however, for a short film, the short length can become an advantage. A strong producer can glimpse these kinds of untraditional routes to getting a film complete, especially if the producer has a great network of connections.

Relationships require strong skills of communication, negotiation, and listening, but also values of loyalty, humility, and collaboration. More than money, relationships are the merry-go-round of the industry. Everything is about who you know, but also what they think of you. When producers consider taking on a new client, they evaluate the person's character on a lot of levels: can they take a note, hold up under intense pressure, are they trustworthy? These seem like simple qualities in a creative relationship, but many people lack these qualities, and an easy red flag is discovering that no one wants to work with that person again. Since the earlier years of film, the "old boys" network has characterized the relationship side of the industry with its legacy and nepotistic leanings, but even in the shadow of the #MeToo movement, I assert that relationships continue to prevail as the number one predictive factor of success within the industry. Sure, you might have a lucky go on one successful project, but it's the relationships that enable you to keep working beyond the success of a lucky draw. These relationships really begin on your earliest projects, whether it's at film school or shooting projects with friends. Your character and your reputation will always precede you in these circumstances, and when you need someone to work longer than you promised, do more than you proposed, or bend the rule of some union contract, they will do it because of the relationship, not the money, and not the time.

Money is the most sought-after resource in the industry, but—and I'm going to say something very controversial here—money is not everything. I'll agree that it's important for people to not feel that they are losing money when they come aboard a production (i.e., gas, meals, software, etc.), but I've listened to many of my teaching colleagues say just the opposite of what I tell my students, which is: 'money won't make your film'. The end of that statement goes back to relationships because I believe relationships to be the core resource in making a piece of art that is commonly a collaboration. Why do I say this? Because I don't believe that when you're making a small indie short and paying people to work on your film, the dollars that you compensate them do not address everything they have to give to you and the production. You can, and certainly I recommend, that you compensate someone for working on your film, whether it is money or some other exchange. But that money doesn't pay for their spirit. It doesn't pay for their joy or their soul that they bring to the table if they are excited about the project. It doesn't pay for the innumerable hours your film takes up in their mind trying to figure out the best way to do things. It doesn't pay for their passion in wanting to bring a new idea to the table that might change everything for the better. Money is a tool, and like many tools, it is a supplement to something bigger and more important and that something is feeling valued. Honor, appreciation, and respect will take you much further with your cast and crew than a rosy paycheck, because you will never be able to pay someone enough for the invaluable assets of time, energy, and passion. In the indie world, a minimum wage paycheck only goes so far. When people make independent films, and especially shorts, they make them out of love or passion.

Access is the resource that has really only come to the forefront in the last few years as conversations about inclusivity and diversity have become center stage. The early Hollywood days limited knowledge about filmmaking to only a few; but this is a much different world today where knowledge and education are the most important resources of any endeavor. Coming from that approach, access is fundamentally about understanding that we all have access to some resources, but first, we must recognize what we have to use them.

The biggest myth of resources in my past was the thought that I didn't have access to what I needed to make a new short film. It was something nestled so deep inside me, I didn't even realize that it existed. You must realize what you have and what you don't have to approach this idea. Too often, new filmmakers focus on what they don't have instead of what they do. Sure, I may not have had a camera, money, a location, or a crew. What I did have was a vast community of filmmakers living in Los Angeles, a story that people loved, the passion and perseverance required to get it done, communication, marketing, and networking skills, and friends. I HAD FRIENDS. And guess what: my friends had friends, and my community of filmmakers had friends.

Friends mean a lot in this industry if you can keep them.

Having access to resources is often a factor of relationships because when you can't purchase access through money, you can develop access through relationships; community, family, and extended family. That is what has helped me through my productions more times than I can recall.

However, I still want to acknowledge that access is also a privilege, one that Western civilization has coveted. Access is not the same for everyone in the West, and it is certainly not the same for everyone in the world. Access can sometimes be blocked, and access at times needs to be earned, both fairly and unfairly. Access may also look different in many diverse communities, so it's important to remain open because opportunities will always present themselves. You want to be ready when they do.

Making it Work

When teaching one of my favorite producing classes, I introduced a game that producers play every time they decide to come aboard a production. This game is about resources, your film, and how, when you prepare to shoot a film, something will inevitably go wrong. This is when producers handle things best and truly earn their spot on your team as the magic-wielding guardians of the universe.

In this game, let's say that you are shooting your short film, and the budget is $10,000. You have raised money the old-fashioned way: mom, dad or grandparents, or through online crowdfunding, savings, and secret stash, all totaling $5000. So, you are short $5,000.

This is the story of virtually every indie filmmaker I know.

What Do You Do?

The answer to the question will vary depending on the circumstances. How far are you into the shoot? What do you have to lose if you push off or cancel the shoot? What are your resources? Many filmmakers have a 'the show must go on' approach, where you should never postpone the shoot under any circumstances. There are many good reasons for this. Making a film is so much about momentum but also trust. If you are at the point where you have hired crew and cast, pushing off the shoot can cast a cloud of doubt for your crew, which could travel to the set and create an atmosphere of distrust and ultimately sabotage. Additionally, inevitably when you push a shoot, you risk losing someone—be it a cast member, crew member, or even a location. Sometimes this loss becomes a gift in disguise. Other times, you may end up eating your shirt because you lost more than you expected (but it doesn't matter because ultimately you must go on). However, if you do decide to postpone the shoot, you should do so after a good evaluative analysis of loss and benefits, and then go with your intuition.

The other important option is to go begging for money from someone else. Most filmmakers tend to exhaust their resources at the beginning, but that's a bad idea. The filmmaker must always have backup reserves—reserve bank accounts, well-to-do friends, supportive family members, or everything and the kitchen sink as 'other' reserves. If you haven't been cordial with friends or family, your journey will be much more difficult because filmmaking is, as I mentioned above, all about relationships, and you want your core team to be there for you. Lastly, I recommend consulting your core crew team members about this decision—who these people are will depend on your relationships with them. Who is your partner in the process? The other producer(s), the DP, the AD, the co-director, etc. Having good input will matter.

Then you decide and you stick to that decision.

In my class's case, I decided that we had exhausted all monetary resources. We couldn't postpone the shoot. The show had to go on. This is called "Making It Work." It's a common occurrence in the indie world, and sometimes the director's intuition helps in deciding the next steps. Sometimes, even the producer's intuition and resourcefulness might save you. These are some of the ideas we explored as potential options.

You are the Storyteller: one of the first and simplest (but not easy) things you can do is remember that you are the storyteller. Revisiting your script and identifying how it can be rewritten or repositioned to work with the money you currently have is a good first step. You are the storyteller, and only you have the idea of what can (or cannot) be changed to preserve the heart of the story. Perhaps it's reducing locations or changing the ages of the characters. Maybe it's transforming a night shoot into a day one. Shifting your period piece to a contemporary setting is a significant change but may be possible. Considering ways to adjust elements in the script is a great approach.

In the Land of Properties, Rentals, and Empty Halls. locations typically account for a significant portion of the budget, so finding ways to minimize the number of locations or company moves can help reduce costs. I am also a huge fan of the one-location short (more on that below). Setting your film in one location can greatly streamline the production process. Additionally, there are free locations available if you brainstorm and tap into community resources. You might be able to use a friend's guest house, yard, or farm, or even a church basement or choir hall. Consider unconventional options like your old high school during the summer when it's not in use. Finally, exploring locations outside the city can result in substantial cost savings. However, you'll need to weigh the benefits, especially if crew members live in the city and commuting is a concern. There may be solutions, such as renting a house where you can also shoot scenes.

Grandma's Spaghetti and Meatball. When money gets tight, leaning into family is a great resource, if they can help. Grandmothers, mothers, and great aunts or uncles can be wonderful support for feeding the crew. Asking family members to contribute a meal and/or snacks for the shoot is a great way to make them feel a part of the production but also save money on one of the significant costs of the production. Family members in early retirement might welcome the chance if they are not too busy with their own schedules, and given some time, they still might attempt to work you into their schedule. One caveat here is to still pay attention to diverse appetites and protein-rich foods (pasta is a hearty food, but typically does little to improve energy). No one on your set should go hungry.

Grocery Stores, Complexes, and Healthy Fast Food: Most students I know don't have the initiative or energy to ask commercial stores to donate, yet I've found that most stores I've asked are eager to support a new artist. It may not be a hundred dollars; however, they'll often toss you ten or twenty-dollar gift certificates. Just think, if you asked twenty stores, how much that could help. Many corporate places will toss out leftover or expiring food if they don't have a donation cycle in place. A nice letter and personal visit can do a lot to forward this. Never underestimate the cost of things like water, batteries, and napkins on a set. Asking Mom and Pop stores will depend on your relationship with them. If you've supported their store, they're more likely to want to do the same by you. However, how much they give will really depend on their own resources, and many stores coming out of peak COVID are still getting back to business.

Thrift stores, Garage Sales, and Free Rentals: Design tends to be an expendable element of many indie shorts, but it doesn't have to be. Resourceful design crew know thrift stores like the back of their hand. If they have time, they'll also know how to sift through newspapers for estate and garage sales that will have plenty to offer. On the other hand, some retail shops and designers might be open to lending their clothing and furniture items if they feel it will expose their film to a new audience. Occasionally, a costume shop might do this, but they are more likely to ask for a rental fee that they might reduce for you. Then there are family and friends who might be willing to allow you to borrow an outfit or table.

The Global World of Recycling: One of my favorite line producers talked about cost-saving items like avoiding separate water bottles and plates by using jugs and packaged meals. There's also plasticware and napkins. This is an excellent idea in pre-COVID times, and if done the right way, could still reduce costs, trash, and the large carbon imprint a movie production tends to make.

Safety, Safety, and Safety: The area of safety has really come under the magnifying glass with the entrance of not only COVID but also a casual system where crew members have died due to attempts to shortcut safety items and costs. Safety is not a cost-cutting item on any set. As a producer, your number one job is to make sure the crew and cast reach home safely and feel safe while they are on set. This means that stunt people, first aid kits, studio teachers, and the bundles of insurance that protect you from major costs should never be shortcut.

TOOLS AND TECHNIQUES
THE INSTRUMENTS OF MASS PRODUCTION

FWAKS, or Fire, Water, Animals, Kids, and Stunts

Oleksii Sobolev's *Breathless*

When my students come to me with projects that require heavy producing, I encourage them to think about what they really need to tell their story. In the US, any project that involves fire, water, animals, kids, or stunts like cars, guns, fighting, and running, particularly in Southern California, will require significant effort. I suggest they first explore the possibility of achieving the stunt through camera tricks. If that's not feasible, then we discuss how each of these elements will demand more producing. It's important to note some key aspects: cars in movies are rarely driven by actors; guns can be confusing and dangerous outside the set; fights are choreographed and often achieved with camera trickery; animals can behave unpredictably; and working with children requires special handling, including studio teachers and adherence to laws protecting minors, which can vary by state.

So again, I'll ask them, what do you really need to accomplish your short film? Certainly, we can inflate the budget with stunt people, officers, unions, and equipment to achieve what's in your mind, and some shorts will require some of these elements—but hopefully not all at once! However, the essence of making a short is the presumption that because you cannot acquire and exercise these resources of a larger budget, this ignites this space of magical thinking. It makes you think of alternate resources and typically more creative ways to tell your story. That might mean balancing the resources in an interesting way: fight sequences in one location; a car scene shot at night on an empty lot; shorter scenes to minimize the time with children.

When I saw Oleksii Sobolev's *Breathless*, I thought of all the FWAKS in this well-produced film. It tells almost an entire love story completely underwater and is a marvelous odyssey to behold! As I witnessed all of the professional synchronized swimmers, actors, and a world below and above the water, I couldn't help but start thinking about the mechanics of accomplishing this: the number of people underwater, for how long, how many days, what was the budget? So, I wasn't surprised to see three companies producing and then also two directors of photography—and one was a co-director! For this story, the core of the idea was the love story of a synchronized swimmer; but this idea required many resources, organization of schedules, attention to safety, and more. Once you acknowledge this, you have to decide what's possible with the budget you have.

Short scripts are about ideas, and you want to consider which ideas are urgent to your project, and how you can achieve them in an efficient and imaginative way. When I was thinking about shooting a short teaser for one of my longer projects that involved Hurricane Katrina, we came up with the resource of miniatures. That miniature shot was one of the best shots in the entire film, and it was an unforgettable experience to shoot. That is where good producing on a short can lead you—to something better than your original idea.

What's all the Scheduling Fuss About?

Determining your film's schedule is often the domain of the line producer. Breaking down your script schedule for a feature can be cumbersome and long; but for a short film, it can be a much easier task if there aren't many locations. Scheduling begins with breaking down the tangible structures of the film: how many days, how many nights, how many pages, how many places, how many people? You break these numbers down to determine the two elements that most impact the budget of your story: how many days or nights are needed to shoot your film and where.

Exterior locations, if they are contained like in a forest, can be great locations for low-budget shorts if they are during the daytime. Line producers dislike seeing projects shot exterior at night because it means high costs for shooting at night. Electricity, safety, food, and energy levels all become heightened resource concerns in an exterior night shoot. However, exterior locations also tend to be worrisome because, on small films, they often mean loss of control of external forces. Planes flying overhead, an unexpected noisy truck, or a group of people who suddenly show up can all disrupt the shoot. On one of my shoots, it was a group of monks who were chanting for the one week we decided to shoot. Gratefully, we learned early enough to move the shoot by having scouts check out the area in advance.

Interior locations tend to offer more control, but if you are not in a sound stage, the issues of control will still permeate the production if you are not using your own home. You will not know the issues using someone else's house, barn, or office until you get there, and most places are not prepared for the extensive demands that a shoot will require. However, an interior location will still provide more choices and offer more protection from the elements should new circumstances arise. Again, early scouts ahead of the shoot will help; as will communicating with the community earlier rather than later to prevent conflicts from arising.

The schedule will also tell you how long you need to work in each location by breaking down the lengths of each scene. The formulas of one minute to one page and counting scene lengths by eighths of the page are easy to find on the internet. In a short film, I find that most filmmakers don't have difficulties in generally estimating this aspect of production. Where line producers earn their keep is in the translation of the scene and understanding that one line may translate into the work of one day and how it can be executed with the typically insufficient amount of money that is available. A strong line producer will come up with ideas and engage with the director (and her team) to figure out the best way to accomplish said line.

Choosing Your Team: Do I Want to Work with You?

There are some wonderful sites for finding crew that you can explore by searching "film production jobs" or even searching for particular positions like "film director jobs." Other good places to search include film organizations, state or county film offices, and production hiring sites, but working within your community is always a great place to start. Communities act as an excellent network system, and if you are new to an area, finding someone who knows the area and community better than you will be important. Field producers, typically used on long-form series, are well known for that; line producers can also fulfill this role. These producers can assemble crew for you to evaluate and review. Sometimes the person they refer will work out, but other times it may not. You will still want to have some sort of evaluation process to help you make a good decision.

Steps to Crew

Post. If you are starting from scratch, building a strong post is an effective way of identifying crew that you want to work with. A hiring post represents you and the production so a loose or skimpy post with nominal information reflects a loose and disorganized production. A well-organized and well-written job ad speaks to an organized and well-thought out production. Including title of the project, details of the position, the date, locations, whether/how the project is paid, union or non-union are bare minimums. Adding loglines and synopsis, visuals, a website and a few descriptors of experience and what exactly the position requires is helpful. So, if you are seeking a costumer, explain what you expect them to do as the costumer: are they sewing, are they borrowing, are they using the actor's clothing? For how many people? Is it period or contemporary? Be specific. Be clear. This will save you time and heartache later. You will also gain bonus points if you share what you intend to do with the project and where its intended final home may be. Lastly, I ask for material: samples, letter, resume, and references. If they are a technical person like a gaffer or a grip, references will matter more, but if there are special circumstances for lighting or gripping, mentioning these and asking them to speak about their experiences will be helpful. Contrary to popular thought, everyone can't grip and gaff, and they are two of the most important jobs on a set.

Review. Understanding how to review a resume and cover letter is a simple but effective step. I've almost never hired anyone who didn't submit a cover letter. A cover letter is a letter of introduction, and as a writer, how could I work with someone with no introduction? It tells us something about the person, their priorities, and why they are interested in working on your shoot. No letter says to me that they didn't feel it was important enough to say anything. Resumes are also interesting documents that can reveal a lot. When I review a resume, I look for clarity around the work—if I am looking for an editor, how much work have they done in editing; I look for dates, the quality of the companies. Most importantly I look for consistency and how often they returned to work for the same people. This could mean a lot of things, but a resume that doesn't show longevity with any company or a position, signals inconsistency and potentially someone who does not work well with others. Finally, I will look at samples. I do this last because the quality of work is only one part of the hire and does not overshadow the other aspects. The ability to communicate, collaborate, comprehend and complete a project is just as urgent, and will tend to show up in the resume and not in the sample.

Interview. Conducting an interview may be the most obvious step here, but what I ask you to consider is discovering what you can uncover about this person. Whether it is over the phone or in person, the interview acts as your first sustained interaction with your possible colleague. Prepare questions and ask each candidate those questions to help ensure equity. Then really listen. Be attentive to body language. Try to hear your own body's response to being in a room with them. The things you want to look for in an interview are energy, disagreement, vision, and value.

Energy: Are they matching energies with you? Do they have a positive energy that surrounds them? If you're excited, are they also excited? Does their presence make you feel good or bad? Do you feel comfortable or tense during this conversation?

Disagreement. There will always be varying opinions; what matters is how the candidate handles disagreement. Do they walk away? Is their idea the only idea that works? Or are they open? Ask what happens when they have disagreed.

Vision. Is their vision for the project in alignment with yours? This doesn't mean that the ideas are the same, but they should have some understanding of where you want to go with the project. If there's no vision, that says something too.

Value. Most importantly, I look for someone who has something of value to add to the project. This could be something concrete like resources or something less tangible like great ideas or moral support. But I also look for an alignment of values. Do we think the same about money, safety, how we treat our team?

Meet. If the interview happened over the phone, then definitely meet with them in person. Even though social media will sometimes try to convince us that those interactions are real, they are not. Nothing replaces the experience of meeting someone in person, although visual chats have become regular options. Choosing a public place is always a good option for safety reasons. If you have access to an office space or a school classroom, great. Otherwise, I love to conduct interviews at coffee shops. Parks are also a good idea if they are quiet. I try to avoid interviews over drinks or at bars. Never do home interviews for your safety. Try to dress well for them, making them feel like both they and this project are important, but don't overdress. Neat and clean is a good way to go.

Reference. A lot of people don't have the energy or time to check references, but they are very helpful. A reference is not just about the position, it's about gaining a deeper understanding of this person in a more dimensional way. A good reference could share skills that the candidate has that you may not have known. Most references are done by phone, but some people will also provide references over email. A phone reference is more effective because you can ask specific questions and read between the lines. Legally, people cannot say bad things about someone, but sometimes, it's what they don't say that speaks volumes.

Hire. When you hire someone, make it a big deal! If you can, call them or tell the face-to-face—don't write it. Let them feel how thankful you are! Express your gratitude and excitement! It's an accomplishment! If you act like it doesn't matter, they will act like it doesn't matter, which can lead to mediocre or lackluster behavior, like showing up late to set. If you can, celebrate them when you introduce them to the rest of the team. They'll feel good about being a part of this special community. Everyone likes to feel appreciated, and this is the time that you want them to feel that most of all. The value part works both ways.

In the Fine Print

Producers sign on the dotted line. Legalities are one of the most complex elements of production. The fine print of any contract is where many decisions get made. My favorite absurd phrase in contracts is: "throughout the universe," and my second favorite phrase is "in perpetuity". Let me tell you those companies are not playing around. They are asking to become the absolute and undisputed owner of your film (or your image, words, every future rendition possible, etc.) forever and forever. Reading your contract and acquiring an understanding of what you surrender for what you will receive is one of the simplest but most helpful recommendations I can make to you. When contracts come to the table, your film stops living as an art form and transforms into a commodity. In this circumstance, I would say "nothing is free."

Established producers will often have a lawyer at the ready to assist them in negotiating contracts. Should your film reach the mountain-high tier of distribution or get picked up, I deeply advise you to have someone who speaks legalese review anything that you consider signing. "In the fine print" is a cautious reminder that contracts are not there to protect you; they are there to protect the entity striving to own and control the property of your idea. However, documents in writing allow you to also protect yourself when you take them seriously. These details about who owns the project, when and what rights you have surrendered, and whether you will ever see a penny of payment occur in the fine print.

The contracts will not bold, highlight, or underline the important aspects of your contract, and in many situations, if someone highlights particular areas, it is to intentionally take your attention away from the details that matter most. The common types of contracts you will encounter in the business aspects for your short will be releases (an agreement that releases liability), finders agreements (an agreement to enlist someone to find funders for your film), an NDA (an agreement that promises nondisclosure), option agreements (an agreement to shop your film to other companies for a select time), hiring contracts (an agreement of tasks and duties on the production), equipment contracts (an agreement of liability for the equipment), location contracts (an agreement to use a location property), union contracts (an agreement to abide by the standards of the union), partnership agreements (an agreement between multiple parties working on the project), and distribution agreements (an agreement of ownership in exchange for distribution). Many of these contracts may be given to you; many of these contracts you will want to supply to protect yourself.

Clearances, Rights, and Permissions

Just because you can, doesn't mean you should. I often find myself in the position of trying to explain to students what they can and can't use in their productions in terms of posters, labels, pictures, logos, etc. In large productions, there is an entire department that oversees and scrutinizes the project for potential lawsuits and elements in the film that the filmmaker doesn't own. As a writer-director-producer, you will often have to hire a producer or clearance advisor to supervise this specialized task.

I've seen that many young filmmakers don't know, haven't been told, or don't care too much about ripping off trademark information or other licensed content; but the issues really revolve around risk, responsibility, and liability. The likelihood that an obscure short might attract the attention of a big company is small, but the bigger the film becomes, the more that likelihood increases. If the trademark is used in a manner that demeans or diminishes that company, it may turn into a serious issue. Navigating the issues of public domain and rights is tricky business.

Projects that take place in exteriors or public spaces can make filming hard to maneuver, and issues of permission will arise. Filmmakers do not have automatic permission to use private information in their films just because they have a camera. Permission must be acquired. That's why trying to keep things small when you have a smaller budget is helpful. It allows the filmmaker to concentrate on the art and not the business of the film on the set. Too many issues may pull attention away from the creation of the work, but it will always depend on what the filmmaker wants to do. If getting permission is important, then the extra work will be required.

However, it's also a question of what you plan to do with the film in its life. Where do you want it to go? Or live? Distribution players won't touch your film if the risk is too high; or they will ask that you sign waiver or release forms that ensure that they will not be culpable. They might also ask you to retain insurance in the case that there is protection should an issue arise. Some film festivals will ask you questions about this as well. The important thing about contracts is that the moment that you are presented with a contract means that someone thinks you (or they) have something of value, and you want to ensure that you are protected.

The Big Secret of Funding

Online crowdfunding was very popular in the early 2000s and is now still fairly commonplace, but the idea of crowdfunding has always existed in other forms. The internet allowed us to reach more people around the world. Asking people to contribute to your endeavor has always been a type of fundraising, but what crowdfunding allowed you to do was not only broaden your audience but also share the experience of getting your project made. This novel idea made sense with the advent of the internet and the digital revolution, where access exploded for those with the means to the internet.

But there are other ways, too.

Good old-fashioned saving for a rainy day is a potential way to finance an inexpensive short. Setting this money aside from the money you need to live (because this money should never be spent on the film—see below!) might work. I knew one filmmaker who planned ahead so that she could receive a good refund from her taxes, and she planned for those funds to support her work. Her original plan was that she would receive a grant, but the grant didn't happen. This was her reserve plan, and this became the plan that got executed.

Then there are finding funders: donors, sponsors, investors. Donors make contributions typically toward a cause. Sponsors want to support in exchange for something valued. Investing is about money turning a profit. Investing happens less often with short content and in some ways is the antithesis of how I think of short filmmaking because it is a medium of freedom. When investors get involved, they are not donors. A donor is someone who typically provides funding without direct influence. But a sponsor or investor tends to look at the film as an investment property, and they will expect something in return. This could impact the vision of the film and happens often on longer-form projects.

Never start with your own money, because you will inevitably end up using it anyway. So, it's best at the beginning to keep your personal money out of the budget early on so that you have reserves later. Believe me, you will need it then.

The biggest secret of online crowdfunding is that it's an excellent way to find your audience. I've crowdfunded unsuccessfully more times than I have found success, but what I learned in the process was that the audience I expected my movie would appeal to was different from the audience it actually did. Studios have lost millions of dollars in poorly positioned marketing; in making your short, you will spend less, but its impact will be greater. Take the time to plan your marketing and distribution plan, and you will put yourself in a great position.

Marketing, Distribution, and Deals

Finding a home for your project is the final frontier for your short film. The good news is that the options are numerous. In my early years as a filmmaker, it seemed that the options were thin; your short was merely considered a stepping stone to other larger projects or ambitions. That has all changed with the digital revolution where there are seemingly innumerable amounts of content being made and distributed each day. Some shorts are still made for other content, and the intent and purpose of the short will guide its trajectory. Many times, the life of the short is tied to its impact, and in some cases sometimes the distinction of the short rises above its brand or successor.

In terms of marketing, there are still the tried-and-true methods of word of mouth, email, grassroots organizing, and posting in public spaces. Online, people use websites, blogs, and of course, the vast options of social media sites to promote their work. As I just said above, it's important to find your audience. Once you do that, you must ask yourself, "How do I shape my marketing plan to reach them?"

The big change I've witnessed in the marketing industry as I've grown older is how companies have learned that indirect marketing is a game changer. Watching the direct version of someone using a product that you're advertising is an old school way of doing things. Now, you watch a smart film where the product doesn't even show up until an end two-second title card! Instead, the film caters to class, gender, racial, and sexual identity by targeting societal and global desires and fears through story. Now, when I open a soap product, I read a story about how my recycling cardboard container will save the world, never mind how it will clean anything. Marketers learned that marketing is no longer only about effectiveness or even entertainment. Marketing can be about fear, desire, wish fulfillment, acceptance, image presentation, and what my students revealed to me: FOMO—*fear* of missing out.

However, distribution is where you get to witness the full imprint of the short. Social media has birthed distribution possibilities that are as vast as our oceans, and they continue to grow. No one yet knows how to control or efficiently monetize how social media works, and what are the formulas for reaching virality. Unlike features, shorts are creating their own domains, platforms, and statuses, and companies are having to find ways to keep up. Where can you distribute your short film? There are so many more options than when I was younger. Sure, there are film festivals, theaters, and local community venues. But now there are a plethora of spaces on the web, such as social media, hosted platforms, streaming, curation sites, networking channels, and funding organizations. Even crowdfunding sites are turning toward distribution to expand their reach. In my development of this book, I also learned that organizations focusing on sustainability and global unity like the UN and the World Health Organization are also creating spaces for short films. Many of these groups are also partnering with each other. For instance, curation sites are launching channels on social media; crowdfunding sites are adding streaming platforms. In the Short Film Filmography, you can get a sense of some of these spaces. Some are "free" and some are paid.

Notice that "free" is not really a true term; in the world of online distribution, nothing is truly free—in exchange for posting things for "free," you are paying by sharing your data with these companies. In this digitally influenced world, data is becoming the new money, and online companies are vying to get your information in every way possible to sell it to advertisers, banks, and credit card companies.

Finally, compensation for your short absolutely happens. Whether it's traditional deal-making buyouts through a channel, a streamer, or network; hosted platforms and websites that support content creators on a rental or downloads basis; social media revenue based on views, time, and stardom; or the hired hand way, that a brand comes to you and asks you to make a short form them, you can make money on your short. Some of the shorts in the Filmography acquire revenue through rentals but you can find other ways creators get paid for their work, like a formula of views that allows advertisers and platforms to pay creators for those they bring to the site. For any deal-making scenarios, if you are not working with a producer experienced with distribution, talk to a lawyer. Remember that section about the fine print? Now I will caution that making a full-time and consistent living wage entirely on shorts can be challenging but not impossible, especially if you can become an influencer. However, more often I see shorts made for other altruistic reasons: for freedom, for passion, for creativity, for social justice, for building portfolios, for the love of film.

ODE TO THE ONE-DAY, ONE-LOCATION, ONE-(OR TWO-) CHARACTER SHOOT

Sydney Freeland's *Hoverboard*

I'm a huge fan of the one-day, one-location, one-(or two-) character shoot. These are ideal for the short form! Why? They are ideal because the limitations in time and space have such potential to ask filmmakers to think deeply creatively. Instead of burning time and energy on resolving the many issues of production company moves, stopping and starting, reassembling crew, breaking down set multiple times, the filmmakers must turn their attention to the material. Digging into the material in this way is what the filmmaker's quest is about.

Sydney Freeland's *Hoverboard* is a charming film that takes place in a house with a backyard, blending childlike fantasy with innovative storytelling and some sparkly special effects. Set primarily between a living room and a yard space, this film demonstrates the creative utility of using small spaces and big ideas. Other great examples of this are David Lowery's *Pioneer*, which take place in a bedroom, Martin Scorsese's *The Big Shave*, which takes place in a bathroom, Naima Ramos Chapman's *And Nothing Happened*, which primarily takes place in and around her apartment, and Alisha Bhowmik's *Disaster Panties*, featuring characters in an apartment and a car, connected through a phone.

Acknowledging the Work

Never underestimate the power of acknowledging the work that your crew and cast has achieved and expressing appreciation for them. This goes for directors, but this goes doubly so for producers, because they will work with many more people outside of the set and after production. More than the director, the great producers are master translators, because they've not only learned the language of negotiation but also appreciation. Many great producers I know have a ton of relationships with vendors and other companies. This means that they are able to ask for a favor or two, which can translate to discounts, donated products and equipment, distribution meetings, and film reviews. It's all related and all interconnected.

At the end of the post-production, ensure that you take time to look deeply at the credits and make sure you have included everyone who needed to be recognized for their contribution to the film, big and small. As a producer, one of the first things you will learn is that the industry is very small, and people will talk. It will get around what kind of producer was on your project, and if anyone else wants to be a part of that community in the future. It is not an accident that some producers and directors work more than others. Look for ways to celebrate the work when it's completed:

a wrap party, a screening party, or premiere tickets to the film's opening. These will be the things that your crew remembers.

Preserving the Freedoms of Criticism & Distribution

Short film producers are usually not fully aware of how urgent the tools of distribution and criticism are in the film industry, as well as in cinema in general. The relationship between distributors and film critics is linked and influential to the world of cinema: Distributors control the access of what we see, and film critics highlight what we watch. Cinema has often been defined through the work of these bodies because if a film critic doesn't write about the film that is distributed, it doesn't exist. Conversely, a film may not get distributed if a film critic hasn't written about it, or its author so it also doesn't exist.

Film critics write about what they believe audiences want to see, and distributors also look for projects that they think audiences desire. However, there are instances where distributors and film critics can come together to shape what they want us to see in terms of box office success. This dynamic reveals that both bodies influence what we get to see, whether we want to see it or not, and whether we are even aware of its existence. The challenge of this is that these bodies are often come from a Western perspective which may unintentionally hinder new structures, forms and approaches. While streaming disrupted this initially, we've ultimately returned to this same space of access and control. In that way, distributors and film critics can be champions, but they can also be gatekeepers. The perspective and intent of these gatekeepers can limit and shape our understanding of what constitutes cinema, for better or for worse.

The film critic Jonathan Rosenbaum wrote largely about gatekeeping in his book *How Hollywood and the Media Conspire to Limit what Films We Can See*, while Roger Ebert was notable for creating more access to films with more diverse storytellers. High-profile celebrities like Brie Larson and Frances McDormand are using their platforms to make demands for more diversity in film criticism and other areas. There are also many current film critics who have taken up the mantle in various ways, including Ashlee Blackwell, Anya Stanley, Tambay Obenson, Justin Chang, Melissa Silverstein, Carla Renata, Tristan Ahtone, Inkoo Kang, Yolanda Machado, and Monica Castillo. Film historians and archivists like Jacqueline Stewart are doing the same by diversifying what gets included in our film histories and therefore what defines cinema.

So, when we think about shorts, we must celebrate them and value the fact that the US and only some countries abroad still have a largely open network of the web where the space is widely accessible, even if every platform, network, or channel is not. You get to see what you want to see, and everyone should have that same choice. Every time you post a short to social media, you are enabling others to have the chance to do the same. We must continue to embrace the freedom of the short film, which is freeing not only in its process of making it but also in sharing it, and we must be careful not to take this for granted.

The Gift of Shorts

My pathway to falling in love with shorts was made possible because I asked a few established filmmakers to share their short scripts with my classes, but that only happened because their shorts were online. The situation with many filmmakers is complicated when sharing their shorts. Many filmmakers want to find distribution for their films so they can get paid for their work. Then, there is wanting to protect the project because film festivals and distributors may not want to highlight or purchase something that is already free. However, there is also something to be said for openly sharing one or two short films freely.

This book is only possible because of the generosity of short filmmakers around the world, and as a producer, you can be one of them. By sharing your individual voice and vision, you are contributing to the universe of the short form and saying, "we exist." So, it's important that you not only continue to make films but also share them—share your films, other films you like, and why you love them. The exchange of ideas is necessary to ensure innovation, possibility, and change.

These are things all filmmakers want to preserve: the freedom of choice, vision, and imagination. If you admire the freedom of shorts, continue to protect it for future filmmakers by making shorts, helping others make shorts, and sharing and writing about shorts within and outside your communities, online and in the physical world.

PRACTICE AND PLAY

1. Make a list of all the locations in your film. Choose one of these locations that you think is most important. Rewrite the script in that single location.

2. After breaking down camera, equipment, and design elements, decide that you will only spend $100 on the shoot and "make it work". Identify all the resources that you can borrow. Then if you have anything remaining, determine external resources where you don't think you could borrow, but would ask them anyway.

3. After breaking down the schedule of your script, revisit it. Decide how you could shoot everything you need in one day, two days, and three days.

4. Reread your script and determine the core values of the story. Consider how many family members represent these values. Cast your film with only family members and close friends and ask to utilize their resources.

5. Research a few online crowdfunding campaigns that have similar elements to your film. Look at their donors to get a sense of their audience. Reflect on the audience for your film and draft a marketing plan for your film that includes crowdfunding, email, in-person. For a bonus, add interactive game elements.

6. Design a website for yourself that highlights you as a producer. Have a space for sample links or thumbnails and add a page for news and updates so people can follow your process.

7. Write the story of your budget and start with listing your top ten priorities. Explain why these are your priorities and ensure that your budget numbers reflect that. Let fifty percent be the most important and 1 percent the least.

8. Consider mobile phones. Is there a way to shoot your film entirely with camera phones? Write a plan that allows the actors, you, and the cinematographer to use camera phones to shoot each other.

9. Research one of the contracts mentioned here for your short film. After you review it, write what you think the signer will gain and lose in signing this contract.

10. Make an animated or motion graphics post for your crew based on the hiring crew section. Add in pictures or a logo for the project.
11. Find a scene in your film that has FWAKS in it and try to eliminate one or more of these elements by replacing it with a more fun or surprising solution.
12. Post your film and your distribution journey in a blog or on one of your social media sites. It will encourage others who also want to make a short film.

SHORT FILM FILMOGRAPHY

Organized by order of appearance

Ideas & Personal Investigations: The Filmmaker's Quest

Boneshaker, 2013, Nuotama Frances Bodomo; United States; Type: Narrative; Themes: Immigrant, Acceptance, Belonging; Last Published: Vimeo

Colors, 2013, Cid; Madagascar; Type: Animation; Themes: Discovery, Dystopia, Rebel; Last Published: Vimeo

Dear Mr. Shakespeare, 2016, Director: Shoola Amoo, Writer: Phoebe Boswell; United Kingdom; Type: Experimental; Themes: Race, Individuality; Last Published: Vimeo

Dol, 2011, Andrew Ahn; United States; Type: Narrative; Themes: LGBTQ, Cultural Identity, Family, Expectations; Last Published: Vimeo

Entre Mamushkas, 2020, Maribel Vásquez; Ecuador; Type: Narrative; Themes: Motherhood, Family Tradition; Last Published: FilmDoo

Flight, 2018, Kia Moses and Adrian McDonald; Jamaica; Type: Narrative; Themes: Dreams, Imagination, Adolescence; Last Published: Kweli TV

Kindah, 2016, Ephraim Asili; Jamaica and United States; Type: Experimental; Themes: Rebellion, Kinship, Community; Last Published: Criterion Channel

Love, Dad, 2021, Diana Cam Van Nguyen; Czechia (Czech Republic) and Slovakia; Type: Documentary and Animation; Themes: Family, Fatherhood, Loss; Last Published: YouTube

Maradona's Legs, 2019, Firas Khoury; Republic of Palestine and Germany; Type: Narrative; Themes: Sports, Children, Journey; Last Published: Netflix

Rose of Manila, 2020, Alex Westfall; Philippines; Type: Hybrid; Themes: Corruption, Beauty Pageants, Religion; Last Published: Criterion Channel

Small Deaths, 1966, Lynne Ramsay; United Kingdom; Type: Anthology; Themes: Coming-Of-Age, Death; Last Published: YouTube

Suicide by Sunlight, 2018, Nikyatu Jusu; United States; Type: Proof of Concept; Themes: Motherhood, Identity, Family, Race; Last Published: You Tube

The Big Shave, 1967, Martin Scorsese; United States; Type: Experimental; Themes: Death, Identity; Last Published: Criterion Channel

The Day I Died, 2006, Maryam Keshavarz; Argentina and United States; Type: Narrative; Themes: Coming-Of-Age, Love Triangle; Last Published: Vimeo

Vincent, 1982, Tim Burton; United States; Type: Animation; Themes: Adolescence, Maturity, Identity; Last Published: Vimeo

Storying Character: Emotional Building Blocks and Escapes

A Million Miles Away, 2013, Jennifer Reeder; United States; Type: Narrative; Themes: Girlhood, Adolescence, Healing; Last Published: Criterion Channel

Advantageous, 2011, Jennifer Phang; United States; Type: Narrative; Themes: Family, Renewal/Rebirth, Nature, Discovery/Transformation; Last Published: YouTube

Ala Kachuu—Take and Run, 2020, Maria Brendle; Kyrgyzstan and Switzerland; Type: Narrative; Themes: Marriage, Freedom, Gender Relations; Last Published: Criterion Channel

Chickens, 2018, Bryian Keith Montgomery; United States; Type: Narrative; Themes: Death, Darkness, Race, Identity, Community; Last Published: Vimeo

Coffee Colored Children, 1988, Ngozi Onwurah; United Kingdom; Type: Documentary; Themes: Race, Black Identity; Last Published: Women Make Movies

Cry Me A River, 2008, Jia Zhangke; China; Type: Narrative; Themes: Connection, Love, Family, Adolescence; Last Published: YouTube

El Bab, 2006, Yasmin Chouikh; Algeria; Type: Narrative; Themes: Daughters, Family Duties, Freedom; Last Published: Vimeo

Full Memory, 2021, Adolf El Assal; Luxembourg; Type: Narrative; Themes: Memory, History, Immigration / Emigration; Last Published: Vimeo

Guernica, 1978, Emir Kusturica; Czechoslovakia; Type: Narrative; Themes: War, Childhood, Family Ties, Jewish Identity; Last Published: Eastern European Movies

Happy Birthday, Marsha!, 2018, Tourmaline and Sasha Wortzel; United States; Type: Narrative; Themes: LGBTQ, Stonewall Riots; Last Published: Kanopy

In Her Boots, 2019, Kathrin Steinbacher; Austria & United Kingdom; Type: Animation; Themes: Landscapes; Last Published: Vimeo

Janine, 1990, Cheryl Dunye; United States; Type: Experimental Documentary; Themes: Identity, Sexuality, Adolescence; Last Published: Kanopy

Lights Out, 2013, David Sandberg; Sweden; Type: Narrative; Themes: adolescence, maturity, identity; Last Published: Vimeo

Made in Mauritius, 2009, David Constantin; Mauritius; Type: Narrative; Themes: Globalization, Class Differences; Last Published: Viddsee

Miu Miu Women's Tales #10—Tres Butons, 2015, Agnès Varda; France; Type: Commercial; Themes: Discovery / Transformation, Community, Adolescence, Non-Conformity; Last Published: YouTube

Pauline Alone, 2014, Janicza Bravo; United States; Type: Experimental; Themes: Insecurity, Odd One Out; Last Published: Vimeo

Save Ralph, 2021, Spencer Susser; United States; Type: Commercial; Themes: Animal Cruelty; Last Published: YouTube

The Changing Same, 2001, Cauleen Smith; United States; Type: Experimental; Themes: Alienation, Found Family, Kinship; Last Published: Criterion Channel

The Horse, 2009, Charles Burnett; United States; Type: Narrative; Themes: Love, Death, Connection, Loss/Grief; Last Published: Criterion Channel

Top Ten Key and Peele Sketches, 2023, Michael Keegan-Key and Jordan Peele; United States; Type: Narrative; Themes: Systemic Racism, Politics; Last Published: YouTube

Warsha, 2022, Dania Bdeir; Lebanon and France; Type: Narrative; Themes: LGBTQ, Muslim, Drag; Last Published: Criterion Channel

You and I and You, 2015, Terence Nance; United States; Type: Dance Film; Spirituality vs. Rationality, Imagination; Last Published: YouTube

Zori, Jack Niedenthal and Suzanne Chutaro; Marshall Islands; Type: Narrative; Themes: Adolescence, Environment; Last Published: YouTube

Sculpting A World:
What Are The Rules of Your World?

Auntie, 2013, Lisa Harewood; Barbados; Type: Narrative; Themes: Migration, Family; Last Published: YouTube

Dadli, 2018, Shabier Lee Kirchner; Antigua and Barbuda; Type: Documentary; Themes: Street Life, Adolescence; Last Published: Vimeo

Hair Love, 2019, Bruce Smith, Everett Downing, and Matthew Cherry; United States; Type: Animation; Themes: Family, Love, Race, Identity, Adolescence; Last Published: YouTube

How To Build a Fictional World, 2014, Kate Messner; United States; Type: Educational Film; Themes: Discovery/Transformation; Last Published: YouTube

Illusions, 1983, Julie Dash; United States; Type: Narrative; Themes: Race, Identity, Passing; Last Published: Kanopy

Leoforos Patision (Patision Ave), 2018, Thanasis Neofotistos; Greece; Type: Narrative; Themes: Violence, Motherhood; Last Published: Vimeo

Polygraph, 2020, Samira Saraya; Israel; Type: Narrative; Themes: Love, Politics, LGBTQ; Last Published: Criterion Channel

Pumzi, 2009, Wanuri Kahiu; Kenya and South Africa; Type: Narrative; Themes: Nature, Individuality, Discovery; Last Published: Vimeo

Re-Migration, 2011, Barry Jenkins; United States; Type: Narrative; Themes: Migration, Family, Nature, Future; Last Published: Vimeo

Seventh Grade, 2014, Stefani Saintonge; United States; Type: Narrative; Themes: Adolescence, Sexuality; Last Published: Vimeo

T, 2019, Keisha Rae Witherspoon; United States; Type: Hybrid; Themes: Time, Theory, Memory, Trauma; Last Published: Criterion Channel

The Phoenix, 2015, Noora Niasari; Iran; Type: Narrative; Themes: Theatre, Asylum Seekers; Last Published: YouTube

Xenogenesis, 1978, James Cameron; Canada and United States; Type: Experimental; Themes: Love, Justice, Race; Last Published: YouTube

Zapping, 2000, Cristian Mungiu; Romania; Type: Narrative; Themes: Fantasy, Absurdity; Last Published: YouTube

Developing a System: Finding Meaning in Structures

A Poem About Love, 2018, Nora Särak and Dominik Krutský; Estonia and Czech Republic; Type: Documentary; Themes: Yearning, Leaving Home; Last Published: Vimeo

Because Men in Silk Shirts on Lagos Night, 2018, Arie Esiri; Nigeria; Type: Commercial; Themes: Fashion, clothes; Last Published: YouTube

Cimpoiasca, 2021, Bara Hiralova; Czechia (Czech Republic); Type: Music Video; Themes: Folklore, Friendship, Women; Last Published: Vimeo

Favorite Heroes TikTok, Julian Bass; United States; Type: Social Media; Themes: Connection, Nostalgia, Heroes; Last Published: TikTok

Five Films About Technology, 2016, Peter Huang; Canada; Type: Anthology; Themes: Ordinary Life; Last Published: YouTube

Formation by Beyonce, 2016, Melina Matsoukas; United States; Type: Music Video; Themes: Love, Renewal/Rebirth, Race, Community, Justice, Identity; Last Published: YouTube

Hellion, 2013, Kat Candler; United States; Type: Narrative; Themes: Justice, Loss/Grief, Family; Last Published: Vimeo

Locks, 2008, Ryan Coogler; United States; Type: Narrative; Themes: Hair, Illness, Family; Last Published: Vimeo

Miu Miu Women's Tales #10—Tres Butons, 2015, Agnès Varda; France; Type: Commercial; Themes: Discovery / Transformation, Community, Adolescence, Non-Conformity; Last Published: YouTube

Morabeza, 2018, Amar Hernandez; Cabo Verde; Type: Experimental; Themes: Slavery, Freedom; Last Published: Vimeo

Passage, 2013, Kareem Mortimer; Bahamas; Type: Narrative; Themes: Refugees, Migration; Last Published: YouTube

Pioneer, 2011, David Lowery; United States; Type: Narrative; Themes: Love, Connection, Family; Last Published: Vimeo

Rebirth is Necessary, 2017, Jenn Nkiru; United Kingdom; Type: Experimental; Themes: Identity, Race, Connection, Community, Family, Love, Individuality; Last Published: YouTube

Red Apples, 2016, George Sikharulidze; Armenia, Georgia, and United States; Type: Narrative; Themes: Marriage, Relationships, Family; Last Published: Vimeo

Rehearsal, 2021, Michael Omonua; Nigeria; Type: Narrative; Themes: Miracle Healing, Faith, Religion; Last Published: Vimeo

Relic Quadrilogy, 2017, Larry Achiampong; United Kingdom; Type: Experimental Anthology; Themes: Afrofuturism, Colonialism; Last Published: Criterion Channel

Simpan, 1999, Park Chan-wook; South Korea; Type: Narrative; Themes: Family, Despair, Justice, Retribution/Revenge, Loss/Grief; Last Published: YouTube

Six Men Getting Sick, 1967, David Lynch; United States; Type: Experimental; Themes: Renewal/Rebirth, Despair, Non-Conformity; Last Published: Criterion Channel

The Force for Volkswagen, 2011, Lance Acord; United States; Type: Commercial; Themes: Dreams, Lifestyles, Family; Last Published: YouTube

Heartless, 2021, Haukur Bjorgvinsson; Iceland. Type: Narrative; Themes: Society, Love, Sacrifice: Responsibility; Last posted: YouTube

The Giverny Document, 2019, Ja'Tovia Gary; France and United States; Type: Documentary; Themes: Black Women, Safety, Integrity, Culture, History; Last Published: Vimeo

Tin, 2013, Brandon Lake; United States; Type: Animation; Themes: Connection, Loss/Grief; Last Published: YouTube

Trail of Hope, 2016 Mohamed Echkouna; Mauritania and United States; Type: Narrative; Themes: Women's Rights; Last Published: Vimeo

Two Distant Strangers, 2020, Travon Free and Martin Desmond Roe; United States; Type: Narrative; Themes: Time Loop, Police Brutality, Race; Last Published: Netflix

Under Bone, 2017, Dana Washington; United States; Type: Experimental; Themes: Loss/Grief, Family, Identity; Last Published: Amazon Prime

Wasp, 2003, Andrea Arnold; United Kingdom; Type: Narrative; Themes: Motherhood, Coming-Of-Age, Love; Last Published: YouTube

What Does Your Mother Do?, 1981, Eulalia Carrizosa; Colombia; Type: Experimental Narrative; Themes: Motherhood, Patriarchy, Labor; Last Published: YouTube

Women's Quarter, 1966, Kamran Shirdel; Iran; Type: Documentary; Themes: Loss/Grief, adolescence, sexuality, despair; Last Published: YouTube

You, the Choice of My Parents, 2019, Meli Tuqota; Fiji; Type: Animation; Themes: Indigenous, Arranged Marriage; Last Published: Vimeo

Tying Theme & Premise: Purpose and Intention

1000 Cut Journey, 2018, Courtney Cogburn, Elise Ogle, Jeremy Bailenson, Tobin Asher, Teff Nichols; United States; Type: Video Game Trailer; Themes: Race, Discovery; Last Published: Stanford VR

A Short Story, 2022, Bi Gan; China; Type: Narrative; Themes: Purpose, Meaning of Life; Last Published: Mubi

Amarrados, 2005, Amat Escalante; Mexico; Type: Narrative; Themes: Sexual Abuse, Loneliness; Last Published: YouTube

Boneshaker, 2013, Nuotama Frances Bodomo; United States; Type: Narrative; Themes: Immigrant, Acceptance, Belonging; Last Published: Vimeo

Childish Gambino's This is America, 2018, Hiro Murai; United States; Type: Music Video; Themes: Race, Identity, Justice, Passion, Death; Last Published: YouTube

Contrapelo, 2014, Directed/Written by Gareth Dunnet-Alcocer and Written by Liska Ostojic; United States; Type: Narrative; Themes: Forgiveness, Justice, Community, Retribution/Revenge; Last Published: Amazon Prime

Dr. Hugo, 1996, Kasi Lemmons; United States; Type: Proof of Concept; Themes: Relationships, Sexuality, Control, Women's Bodies; Last Published: DVD

La Voz Perdida, 2016, Marcelo Martinessi; Argentina, Cuba, Venezuela, Paraguay; Type: Documentary; Themes: History, Death, Memory; Last Published: Vimeo

Listen, 2014, Directed by Hamy Ramezon and Written by Rungano Nyoni; Denmark and Finland; Type: Narrative; Themes: Family, Despair, Justice; Last Published: YouTube

Small Deaths, 1966, Lynne Ramsay; United Kingdom; Type: Anthology; Themes: Death, Coming-Of-Age; Last Published: YouTube

Swallowed, 2016, Lily Baldwin; United States; Type: Experimental Narrative; Themes: Motherhood, Family; Last Published: Vimeo

Toward Tenderness, 2016, Alice Diop; France; Type: Documentary; Themes: Masculinity, Love, Desire; Last Published: YouTube

Wasp, 2003, Andrea Arnold; United Kingdom; Type: Narrative; Themes: Motherhood, Coming-Of-Age, Love; Last Published: YouTube

Language & Styling: Writing to Free the Imagination

A Mãe de Sangue, 2019, Vier Nev; Portugal; Type: Animation; Themes: Optical Illusions, Perception, Dreams; Last Published: YouTube

Behemoth: Or the Game of God, 2016, Lemohang Jeremiah Mosese; Lesotho and Germany; Type: Experimental; Themes: Religion; Last Published: Criterion Channel

Bint Werdan (J'ai le Cafard), 2020, Maysaa Almumin; Kuwait; Type: Narrative; Themes: Depression, Women; Last Published: YouTube

Diary of Cattle, 2019, David Darmadi and Lidia Afrilita; Indonesia; Type: Documentary; Themes: Environment, Animals; Last Published: Kanopy

Everybody Dies!, Nuotama Bodomo; United States; Type: Experimental Narrative; Themes: Death, Children, Black Culture; Last Published: Vimeo

Isle of Chair, 2020, Ivyy Chen; Taiwan; Type: Animation; Themes: Mental Health, Solace; Last Published: Vimeo

My Josephine, 2003, Barry Jenkins; United States; Type: Experimental; Themes: Hope, Family, Connection, Loss/Grief; Last Published: Vimeo

Real Man's Film, Nebojša Slijepčević; Croatia; Type: Documentary; Themes: Generation, War, Family; Last Published: Vimeo

Rew Day, 2012, Svilen Dimitrov; Bulgaria; Type: Animation; Themes: Rebirth, Life Cycle; Last Published: Vimeo

Snow in September, 2022, Lkhagvadulam Purev-Ochir; Mongolia and France; Type: Narrative; Themes: Youth, Relationships, Intimacy; Last Published: YouTube

The Discovery of Story:
Drafting and Revising

Moncler x Salehe Bembury, 2023, Hala Matar; United States; Type: Commercial; Themes: Fashion, Nature; Last Published: Vimeo

The Short Forms:
Short Landscapes of the Storyteller's Imagination

8 Possible Beginnings: or The Creation of the African-America, 2005, Kara Walker; United States; Type: Web Series; Themes: Race, Struggle, Oppression, History; Last Published: DVD

5 Films on Technology, 2021, Peter Huang; Canada; Type: Anthology Short; Themes: Technology, Family, Connection; Last Published: YouTube

160 Characters, 2015, Victoria Mapplebeck; United Kingdom; Type: Camera Phone Film; Themes: Connection, Family, Love, Loss/Grief, Discovery/Transformation; Last Published: Vimeo

A Bloody Morning, 2020, Vincent René Lortie, Brittney Canda, and Owen Palette; Canada; Type: Quarantine Film; Themes: Love, Connection, Family, Identity; Last Published: vincentrenelortie.com

A Love Song for Latasha, 2019, Sophia Nahli Allison; United States; Type: Documentary; Themes: Connection, Justice, Death; Last Published: Netflix

A Woman's Epic Journey to Climb 7 Mountains, 2016, Wasfia Nazreen and National Geographic; Bangladesh and United States; Type: Camera Phone Film; Themes: Dreams, Lifestyles, Struggle, Purpose; Last Published: National Geographic

Alive in Joburg, 2005, Neill Blomkamp; Canada; Type: Proof of Concept; Themes: Discovery/Transformation, Race, Community, Connection, Despair; Last Published: YouTube

Awkward Black Girl, 2011, Issa Rae; United States; Type; Web Series; Themes: Love, Passion, Individuality, Identity, Sexuality, Race, Connection, Community; Last Published: YouTube

Be Like Mike Nike Commercial, 1991, Spike Lee; United States; Type: Commercial; Themes: Passion, Desire, Sports, Pop Culture; Last Published: YouTube

Blondie's Rapture, 1980, Keith MacMillan; United States; Type: Music Video; Themes: Connection, Dance, Pop Culture; Last Published: YouTube

Blood Simple, 1984, Ethan and Joel Coen; United States; Type: Proof of Concept; Themes: Betrayal, Seduction, Retribution; Last Published: Film Ink and HBO Max

Celeste, 2018, Maddy Thorson and Maddy Makes Games; Canada; Type: Video Game; Themes: Discovery/Transformation, Despair, Hope; Last Published: Celeste Game

Childish Gambino's This is America, 2018, Hiro Murai; United States; Type: Music Video; Themes: Race, Identity, Justice, Passion, Death; Last Published: YouTube

Cipka (Pussy), 2016, Renata Gąsiorowska; Poland; Type: Animation; Themes: Passion, Sexuality, Renewal/Rebirth; Last Published: Vimeo

Cupid-19, 2021, Jono Freedrix; United States; Type: Quarantine Film; Themes: Non-Conformity, Discovery/Transformation; Last Published: Vimeo

Déjà Vu Chivas Regal, 2012, Wong Kar-Wai; Hong Kong; Type: Commercial; Themes: Passion, Connection, Love; Last Published: YouTube

Detour, 2017, Michel Gondry; France; Type: Camera Phone Film; Themes: Family, Loss, Love; Last Published: Vimeo

Disaster Panties, 2021, Alisha Bhowmik; United States; Type: Quarantine Film; Themes: Women's Health, Anxiety, Quarantine; Last Published: Vimeo

Do No Harm, 2017, Roseanne Liang; New Zealand; Type: Narrative; Themes: Retribution, Revenge, Justice; Last Published: Vimeo

Dreams, 1990, Akira Kurosawa; Japan; Type: Anthology Short; Themes: Adolescence, Discovery/Transformation, Nature; Last Published: Prime Video and DVD

Dr. Hugo, 1996, Kasi Lemmons; United States; Type: Proof of Concept; Themes: Relationships, Sexuality, Control, Women's Bodies; Last Published: DVD

Entre Mamushkas, 2020, Maribel Vásquez; Ecuador; Type: Narrative; Themes: Motherhood, Family Tradition; Last Published: FilmDoo

Every Frame A Painting, 2014-2017, Tony Zhou and Taylor Ramos; United States; Type: Web Series; Themes: Poetry, Youth, Womanhood, Discovery/Transformation; Last Published: YouTube

Fatboy Slim's Weapon of Choice, 2001, Spike Jonze; United States; Type: Music Video; Themes: Dance, Passion, Joy; Last Published: YouTube

Formation by Beyoncé, 2016, Melina Matsoukas; United States; Type: Music Video; Themes: Love, Renewal/Rebirth, Race, Community, Justice, Identity; Last Published: YouTube

Girls Section, 2019, Kathryn Everett; United States; Type: Documentary; Themes: Passion, Individuality, Hope, Community, Womanhood, Education, Overcoming; Last Published: Vimeo

Gracie's Corner, 2020, The Hollingsworth Family; United States; Type: Educational Short; Themes: Adolescence, Maturity, Individuality; Last Published: YouTube

Hair Love, 2019, Bruce Smith, Everett Downing, and Matthew Cherry; United States; Type: Animation; Themes: Family, Love, Race, Identity, Adolescence; Last Published: YouTube

Hair Wolf, 2018, Mariama Diallo; United States; Type: Narrative; Themes: Identity, Race, Cultural Appropriation; Last Published: Vimeo

Homemade, 2020, Netflix; Chile and Italy; Type: Anthology Short; Themes: Love, Family, Loss/Grief, Hope; Last Published: Netflix

How To Build a Fictional World, 2014, Kate Messner; United States; Type: Educational Film; Themes: Discovery/Transformation; Last Published: YouTube

IKEA Lamp, 2002, Spike Jonze; United States; Type: Commercial; Themes: Love, Passion, Renewal/Rebirth, Discovery/Transformation; Last Published: YouTube

ImMATURE, 2019, Sameer Saxena; India; Type: Web Series; Themes: Teen Life, Friendship, Love, Heartbreak; Last Published: Prime Video

Immoral Code, 2022, Matthew Harmer; United Kingdom; Type: Documentary; Themes: Identity, Retribution/Revenge, Discovery/Transformation, Nature; Last Published: Vimeo

LinkedIn, 2021, Nadia Hallgren; United States; Type: Commercial; Themes: Validation, Identity, Community; Last Published: Vimeo

LMFAO ft. Lauren Bennett, GoonRock—Party Rock Anthem, 2011, Mickey Finnegan; Type: Music Video; Themes: Connection, Individuality, Passion, Non-Conformity; Last Published: YouTube

Lockdown 28, 2020, Vesyee; Malaysia; Type: Quarantine Film; Themes: Discovery, Transformation; Last Published: Film Freeway

Love, Death, and Robots, 2019, Tim Miller and David Fincher; United States; Type: Anthology Short; Themes: Darkness, Discovery/Transformation, Individuality; Last Published: Netflix

Lucia, 2010, Niles Atallah, Joaquín Cociña, and Cristóbal León; Chile; Type: Animation; Themes: Darkness, Discovery/Transformation, Adolescence; Last Published: Vimeo

Luis Fonsi's Despacito, 2017, Carlos Perez; Puerto Rico; Type: Music Video; Themes: Sexuality, Connection, Passion, Loss/Grief, Despair; Last Published: YouTube

Mankind is No Island, 2008, Jason Van Genderen; Australia and United States; Type: Camera Phone Film; Themes: Connection, Love; Last Published: YouTube

Meet Me At the Stairs, 2021, Jesse Hunt; Canada; Type: Quarantine Film; Themes: Family, Loss, Grief, Love, Connection; Last Published: Vimeo

Meshes in the Afternoon, 1943, Maya Deren; United States; Type: Experimental; Themes: Identity, Sexuality; Last Published: Vimeo

Monster, 2005, Jennifer Kent; Australia; Type: Proof of Concept; Themes: Connection, Loss/Grief, Family; Last Published: Vimeo

Mound, 2011, Allison Schulnick; United States; Type: Experimental; Themes: Discovery/Transformation, Renewal/Rebirth, Nature, Death, Love; Last Published: Vimeo

My Josephine, 2003, Barry Jenkins; United States; Type: Experimental; Themes: Hope, Family, Connection, Loss/Grief; Last Published: Vimeo

Night Fishing, 2011, Park Chan-wook and Park Chan-kyong; South Korea; Type: Camera Phone Film; Themes: Death, Connection, Discovery/Transformation; Last Published: Vimeo

Nina and the Neurons, 2010, Katrina Bryan; United Kingdom; Type: Educational Short; Themes: Discovery/Transformation, Nature, Adolescence; Last Published: Pluto TV

Norco, 2022, Geography of Robots; United States; Type: Video Game; Themes: Connection, Love, Family, Loss, Discovery/Transformation; Last Published: Steam

Oats Studios, 2017-2020, Neill Blomkamp; Canada; Type: Anthology Short; Themes: Alternative World, Apocalypse, Politics, War, Science; Last Published: YouTube and Steam

Over and Out, 2019, Christiaan Van Vuuren and Adele Vuko; Australia; Type: Web Series; Themes: Family, Community, Loss/Grief, Love; Last Published: YouTube

Panda Express, 2021, Erica Eng; United States; Type: Commercial; Themes: Connection, Family, Hope, Love; Last Published: Vimeo

PSY's Gangnam Style, 2012, Cho Soo-hyun; South Korea; Type: Music Video; Themes: Non-Conformity, Pride, Dance; Last Published: YouTube

Quarantine Quarrels: Connecting in Quarantine, 2021, Sophia Stephens; United States; Type: Quarantine Film; Themes: Connection, Identity, Despair, Hope; Last Published: sophiastephens.com

Rebirth is Necessary, 2017, Jenn Nkiru; United Kingdom; Type: Experimental; Themes: Identity, Race, Connection, Community, Family, Love, Individuality; Last Published: YouTube

Reckless Eyeballing, 2004, Christopher Harris; United States; Type: Experimental; Themes: Sexual Desire, Racial Identity, Film History; Last Published: Criterion Channel

Schoolhouse Rock, 1973, David McCall; United States; Type: Educational Short; Themes: Discovery/Transformation, Nature, Adolescence; Last Published: Disney Plus

Seventh Grade, 2014, Stefani Saintonge; United States; Type: Narrative; Themes: Adolescence, Sexuality; Last Published: Vimeo

Sheilas, 2018, Hannah and Eliza Reilly; Australia; Type: Educational Short; Themes: Discovery, Identity, Individuality, Non-Conformity; Last Published: YouTube

Six Men Getting Sick, 1967, David Lynch; United States; Type: Experimental; Themes: Renewal/Rebirth, Despair, Non-Conformity; Last Published: Criterion Channel

Sojourner, 2008, Cauleen Smith; United States; Type: Experimental; Themes: Feminism, Afrofuturism, Community, Utopia; Last Published: YouTube

The Ancestor's Came, 2017, Cecile Emeke; United States; Type: Documentary; Themes: Growth, Love, Art, Connection; Last Published: YouTube

The Baby, 2014, Ali Asgari and Farnoosh Samadi; Iran; Type: Narrative; Themes: Family, Community, Motherhood; Last Published: Vimeo

The Customer is Always Right, 2004, Robert Rodriguez; United States; Type: Proof of Concept; Themes: Death, Darkness, Love, Passion, Retribution/Revenge; Last Published: YouTube

The Fourfold, 2020, Alisi Telengut; Canada; Type: Animation; Themes: Indigeneity, Animalism, Environment, Non-Human Materialities; Last Published: Vimeo

The Giverny Document, 2019, Ja'Tovia Gary; France and United States; Type: Documentary; Themes: Black Women, Safety, Integrity, Culture, History; Last Published: Vimeo

The Octonauts, 2010, Meomi: Vicki Wong and Michael C. Murphy; Ireland and United Kingdom; Type: Educational Short; Themes: Adolescence, Maturity, Family, Connection, Hope; Last Published: Netflix

The Painter of Jalouzi featuring Duval Pierre, 2015, David Darg and Bryn Mooser; Haiti and United States; Type: Camera Phone Film; Themes: Poverty, Art, Transformation, Community; Last Published: YouTube

The T, 2018, Bea Cordelia and Daniel Kyri; United States; Type: Web Series; Themes: Identity, Sexuality, Love, Community, Discover/Transformation; Last Published: Vimeo

The Unwritten Rules, 2012-2014, Kim Williams; United States; Type: Web Series; Themes: Race, Labor, Power Dynamics; Last Published: YouTube

Tin, 2013, Brandon Lake; United States; Type: Animation; Themes: Connection, Loss/Grief; Last Published: YouTube

Two Cars, One Night, 2003, Taika Waititi; New Zealand; Type: Narrative; Themes: Adolescence, Connection, Identity; Last Published: YouTube

Unsighted, 2021, Studio Pixel Punk; Brazil; Type: Video Game; Themes; Last Published: Connection, Adolescence, Love; Last Published: Steam

V/H/S 94, 2021, Jennifer Reeder, Chloe Okuno, Simon Barrett, Timo Tjahjanto, Ryan Prows; United States; Type: Anthology Short; Themes: Woman, Science, Cult, Politics; Last Published: Shudder

Virtual Human Interaction 1000 Cut Journey, 2018, Courtney Cogburn and Stanford University; Type: Video Game; Themes: Race, Adolescence, Coming-Of-Age; Last Published: YouTube

Walden, A Game, 2017, Tracy Fullerton and USC Game; United States; Type: Video Game; Themes: Dreams, Lifestyles, Connection; Last Published: Walden Game

Walmart The Box, 2018, Dee Rees; United States; Type: Commercial; Themes: Family, Connection, Adolescence; Last Published: YouTube

What Remains of Edith Finch, 2017, Giant Sparrow; United States; Type: Video Game; Themes: Home, Family, History, Discovery; Last Published: Steam

Women's Quarter, 1966, Kamran Shirdel; Iran; Type: Documentary; Themes: Loss/Grief, Adolescence, Sexuality, Despair; Last Published: YouTube

Notes on Directing:
The Directors' Tool

Re-Migration, 2011, Barry Jenkins; United States; Type: Narrative; Themes: Migration, Family; Last Published: Vimeo

Notes on Producing:
Guardians of the Cinematic Universe

And Nothing Happened, 2016, Naima Ramos Chapman; United States; Type: Experimental; Themes: Women, Everyday Life, Sexuality, Family; Last Published: Vimeo

Breathless, 2018, Oleksii Sobolev; Russia, United States, and Ukraine; Type: Narrative; Themes: Sport, Love, Competition; Last Published: Vimeo

Disaster Panties, 2021, Alisha Bhowmik; United States; Type: Quarantine Film; Themes: Women's Health, Anxiety, Quarantine; Last Published: Vimeo

Hoverboard, 2012, Sydney Freeland; United States; Type: Narrative; Themes: Adolescence, Girlhood, Invention, Imagination; Last Published: YouTube

The Ikea Lamp, 2002, Spike Jonze; United States; Type: Commercial; Themes: Love, Passion, Renewal/Rebirth, Discovery/Transformation; Last Published: YouTube

Lost World, 2018, Kalyanee Mam; Cambodia and Singapore; Type: Documentary; Themes: Environmentalism, Community, Creation, Destruction; Last Published: Vimeo

Pioneer, 2011, David Lowery; United States; Type: Narrative; Themes: Love, Connection, Family; Last Published: Vimeo

The Big Shave, 1967, Martin Scorsese; United States; Type: Experimental; Themes: Death, Identity; Last Published: Criterion Channel

EPILOGUE

I wrapped shooting one segment of my next project, *The Overextended*, while I was finalizing this book. *The Overextended* is a hybrid short film that serves as both a proof of concept and an anthology short for my larger feature project, *Shattered*, which aims to deconstruct black female stereotypes.

On this shoot, one of our new crew members asked myself and one of our producers what we loved about this process. I imagine that she was thinking about the countless hours we were both putting in, especially my producer, who had worked tirelessly from dawn till midnight making returns and balancing receipts to ensure the shoot was wrapped successfully.

My producer discussed an affection for equipment and cinematography. As for me, I mentioned that making a film always feels like forming a new family.

Making a film is not easy, and sometimes, it isn't fun. Yet, when I think about filmmaking, I consider it a wonderful introduction to the world. When I make a film, I see something I see less of in this day and age.

We engage with each other in a way that's not like a regular job, but it's not a party free-for-all either. It's a kind of concentrated connection in that it asks for our attention—to be between and interdependent on each other.

We step away from social media, our computers, and even our treasured books, and we live in the present. As I ponder making films, that's the one thing I see happen in ways that contrast with the everyday routine of going to work, paying bills, coming home to dinner, and starting again. It's probably not only about films either. I would wager that any collaborative art asks the same.

When we are present, we most fully experience what is happening in front of us. Not being elsewhere or even disappearing into our minds to hide out for a minute. It's terribly hard to be present these days in this demanding world of immediacy, where it feels like doing any one thing at a time doesn't feel acceptable. We often feel compelled to do everything all at once! We don't even think about doing nothing. Doing nothing gets eaten up with pretend nothings: sleeping late from exhaustion, high-intensity meditations, or the suspended state of avoiding our anxieties. In this era, being still, something a friend often speaks to me about, is something rare and intangible. It's almost unattainable, but it's so urgently important.

When we can be still, we can find this space of tranquil alertness. We can recognize the truth of things that are happening in front of us. We can find emotional grounding in our current reality. When we find this grounding, we can be the most ourselves and not whom others expect us to be.

What I love about short-film moviemaking is that a group of people come together into a special space, and they decide, for better or worse, that they are going to sacrifice to be in it with each other for this short amount of time for a small, but touching, gift at the end of the tunnel. It lets us be ourselves in these moments—even if the shoot could have been better, even if the shoot is a disaster.

The world is big, and the world's problems are even bigger, and that can be overwhelming during a time when our technology is both our friend and our foe. As AI looms over us, along with war, loss, conflicts, and the many injustices we face, it feels unimaginably daunting.

Yet, our humanity in these times is what I believe helps us make it through each day. There will always be obstacles, but there will always be courage, unexpected grace, and love. There will be hope too.

You can make short films to connect, discover, live in your time or others, but you can also make films to speculate and envision a better world. The movement of Afrofuturism is one speculative aesthetic based in Black culture that concentrates on themes of science fiction, and more specifically futurism. There are other futurisms: Indigenous, Asian, and others used by many filmmakers I mention here along with others you can meet online. Ytasha Womack, Ishmael Reed, Bill Gunn, Julie Dash, Asli Duncan, Ryan Coogler, Boots Riley, Nia DaCosta, Nikyatu Jusu, Nuotama Bodomo, Terence Nance, and Wanuri Kahiu envision what the world could be, what the world should be. What is the world that you envision?

EPILOGUE

Discovering your vision of the world is not an easy thing. You might ask, "How is my view any different from anyone else's?" It is. It is as distinct as you are. If you can't see it yet, it may be because you haven't seen enough other visions or perspectives to recognize how yours stands apart. That's why it's important to visit other people and places, to travel if you have the means, to read books and see works of art about other experiences, perspectives, and existences, and to contemplate them. That was my invitation to become a filmmaker.

Find your community, and if you can't find it, make it. Gather three or four like-minded film lovers. Start a writer's group, a collective, or a club. Meet, engage, exchange ideas and resources. Cultivate community, collaboration, or society. Take notes from those who have come before you, like the New Negress Film Society, SIFTMedia 215 Collective, Court 13 Arts, Echo Park Film Center Collective, or AgX Collective.

Finally, make short films to discover more about who you are. I've been surprised to find that I learn a little more about myself every time I make a short film! Remember how fascinating you are! Being present in the making of a film also brings an interesting awareness to you as a person, as an individual, and as a part of a community. There are parts you may or may not be proud of, but the process has uncovered a sense of freedom I have not found in any other space. It's where I've come to make choices about the kind of person that I *want* to be.

If you've never made a short film, make one today. And if you haven't made a short film in a while, take the steps to make one again. Never be afraid to try. Never be afraid to make a mistake. Never be afraid to take a risk. Always know there's still time! I suspect you'll find something you love about it.

ABOUT THE AUTHOR

Director Rae Shaw on the set of *Black Kung Fu Chick*
Photo Credit: Sascha Rice

Rae Shaw is an award-winning writer-director-producer of short-form media works. Her interests include exploring themes of diversity, connection, sexuality, and disparity. After working for industry veterans, Shaw turned to teaching and developing projects that uplift women and diverse perspectives. She is the recipient of numerous fellowships, including the Mellon Mays Undergraduate Fellowship, Leander Morris Memorial Music Scholarship, and Mass Cultural Council Artist Fellowship. Shaw received her BA from the University of Chicago and her MFA from the University of Miami. Currently, she teaches at San Francisco State University, where she splits her time between the east and west coasts.

MICHAEL WIESE PRODUCTIONS

IN A DARK TIME, a light bringer came along, leading the curious and the frustrated to clarity and empowerment. It took the well-guarded secrets out of the hands of the few and made them available to all. It spread a spirit of openness and creative freedom, and built a storehouse of knowledge dedicated to the betterment of the arts.

The essence of Michael Wiese Productions (MWP) is empowering people who have the burning desire to express themselves creatively. We help them realize their dreams by putting the tools in their hands. We demystify the sometimes secretive worlds of screenwriting, directing, acting, producing, film financing, and other media crafts.

By doing so, we hope to bring forth a realization of 'conscious media,' which we define as being positively charged, emphasizing hope, and affirming positive values like trust, cooperation, self-empowerment, freedom, and love. Grounded in the deep roots of myth, it aims to be healing both for those who make the art and those who encounter it. It hopes to be transformative for people, opening doors to new possibilities and pulling back veils to reveal hidden worlds.

MWP has built a storehouse of knowledge unequaled in the world, for no other publisher has so many titles on the media arts. Please visit www.mwp.com, where you will find many free resources and a 25% discount on our books. Sign up and become part of the wider creative community!

MICHAEL WIESE, Co-Publisher
GERALDINE OVERTON, Co-Publisher

**INDEPENDENT FILMMAKERS
SCREENWRITERS
MEDIA PROFESSIONALS**

**MICHAEL WIESE PRODUCTIONS
GIVES YOU
INSTANT ACCESS
TO THE BEST BOOKS
AND INSTRUCTORS
IN THE WORLD**

**FOR THE LATEST UPDATES
AND DISCOUNTS,
CONNECT WITH US ON**
WWW.MWP.COM

 JOIN US ON FACEBOOK

 FOLLOW US ON TWITTER

 VIEW US ON YOUTUBE

www.ingramcontent.com/pod-product-compliance
Lightning Source LLC
Chambersburg PA
CBHW050201240426
43671CB00013B/2201